A New Approach to Research Ethics

M000240135

A New Approach to Research Ethics is a clear, practical and useful guide to the ethical issues faced by researchers today. Examining the theories of ethical decision-making and applying these theories to a range of situations within a research career and process, this text offers a broader perspective on how ethics can be a positive force in strengthening the research community.

Drawing upon a strong selection of challenging case studies, this text offers a new approach to engage with ethical issues and provides the reader with:

- a broader view on research ethics in practice, capturing both different stages of research careers and multiple tasks within that career, including supervision and research assessments;
- thoughts on questions such as increasing globalisation, open science and intensified competition;
- an increased understanding of undertaking research in a world of new technologies;
- an extension of research ethics to a multidisciplinary and interdisciplinary approach; and
- an introduction to a 'guided dialogue' method, which helps to identify and engage with ethical issues individually and as a research community.

A New Approach to Research Ethics allows for self-reflection and provides guidance for professional development in an increasingly competitive area. Full of valuable guidance for the researcher and ethical decision-maker, this is an essential text for postgraduate students, senior academics and developers of training courses on ethics for researchers.

Henriikka Mustajoki has a career in professional ethics focusing on research ethics.

Arto Mustajoki has a long career as a professor and scientific administrator. He has been department head, dean and vice-rector of the University of Helsinki.

A New Approach to Research Ethics

Using Guided Dialogue to Strengthen Research Communities

Henriikka Mustajoki and
Arto Mustajoki

Routledge
Taylor & Francis Group
LONDON AND NEW YORK

First published 2017
by Routledge
2 Park Square, Milton Park, Abingdon, Oxon OX14 4RN

and by Routledge
711 Third Avenue, New York, NY 10017

Routledge is an imprint of the Taylor & Francis Group, an informa business

© 2017 H. Mustajoki and A. Mustajoki

British Library Cataloguing in Publication Data
A catalogue record for this book is available from the British Library

Library of Congress Cataloging in Publication Data
Names: Clarkeburn, Henriikka, author. | Mustajoki, Arto S. (Arto Samuel), 1948- author.
Title: A new approach to research ethics : using grounded dialogue to strengthen research communities / Henriikka Clarkeburn and Arto Mustajoki.
Description: Abingdon, Oxon ; New York, NY : Routledge, 2017.
Identifiers: LCCN 2016039038 (print) | LCCN 2016057482 (ebook) | ISBN 9781138682214 (hbk : alk. paper) | ISBN 9781138682221 (pbk : alk. paper) | ISBN 9781315545318 (ebk)
Subjects: LCSH: Research--Moral and ethical aspects. | Research--Planning.
Classification: LCC Q180.55.M67 C63 2017 (print) | LCC Q180.55.M67 (ebook) | DDC 174/.90014--dc23
LC record available at https://lccn.loc.gov/2016039038

ISBN: 978-1-138-68221-4 (hbk)
ISBN: 978-1-138-68222-1 (pbk)
ISBN: 978-1-315-54531-8 (ebk)

Typeset in Galliard
by Saxon Graphics Ltd, Derby

Contents

List of figures ix
List of tables xi
About the authors xiii
For the reader xv

Introduction: why research ethics is more important than
ever before 1

1 **Ethics by guided dialogue** 7
Why ethical choices do not always lead to ethical behaviour 11
Recognising ethical questions 14
Identifying stakeholders 15
Understanding rights and responsibilities 16
Defining options 17
Making ethical choices 22
Notes 31

2 **Doing research** 32
Identifying stakeholders 35
Understanding rights and responsibilities 37
Defining options 38
Selecting the topic 39
Misconduct 42
Methodology and material 44
Case study 1: motivation for selecting the research topic 57
Case study 2: where are the limits of 'sufficient'? 58
Case study 3: do the methods determine the value of research? 59
Case study 4: credibility of the research community 60
Notes 61

3   **Publishing**   63
    Identifying stakeholders 65
    Understanding rights and responsibilities 66
    Defining options 67
    Writing 68
    Forms of publication 73
    Authorship 78
    Peer review 80
    Case study 1: where to publish? 82
    Case study 2: limits of vague expressions 83
    Case study 3: who should be an author? 84
    Case study 4: an ideal conference 86
    Notes 87

4   **Supervising students**   88
    Identifying stakeholders 90
    Understanding rights and responsibilities 93
    Defining options 96
    Selecting students 98
    Conventions in supervision 103
    Process of graduating 105
    Case study 1: choice of doctoral student 108
    Case study 2: choice of supervisor 110
    Case study 3: rights and responsibilities in the supervisor relationship 111
    Case study 4: disagreement with supervisor 112
    Notes 112

5   **Recruiting academic staff**   113
    Identifying stakeholders 115
    Understanding rights and responsibilities 116
    Types of positions 118
    Selection criteria 120
    Phases of recruitment 123
    Case study 1: Capital University recruitment 126
    Case study 2: recruiting a professor of mockology 127
    Case study 3: potential as a criteria 128
    Case study 4: tenure track positions 128
    Note 129

6   **Funding research**   **130**
     Identifying stakeholders 131
     Understanding rights and responsibilities 133
     Forms of research funding 136
     Writing an application 140
     Making a funding decision 143
     Case study 1: should I apply or not? 149
     Case study 2: exploring the limits of honesty 150
     Case study 3: contract research case 151
     Case study 4: conflict of interest 152
     Notes 153

7   **Assessing research and researchers**   **154**
     Identifying stakeholders 156
     Understanding rights and responsibilities 157
     Defining options 158
     Methods 160
     Financing formulas and rankings 163
     Social impact 166
     Case study 1: proposals for enhancing research 171
     Case study 2: efficiency index of academic staff 172
     Case study 3: faculty assessment 174
     Case study 4: dealing with control 175
     Notes 176

8   **Interacting with society**   **178**
     Identifying stakeholders 181
     Understanding rights and responsibilities 182
     Defining options 186
     The media 187
     Citizens 191
     Public sector 193
     Case study 1: plenty of invitations 195
     Case study 2: which questions are scientifically significant enough? 196
     *Case study 3: limits between scientific knowledge and people's own
     experience? 196*
     Case study 4: science blog 198
     Case study 5: gaining public interest 198
     Notes 199

9   **Managing research careers**   **201**
    Identifying stakeholders 203
    Understanding rights and responsibilities 203
    Defining options 205
    Career 207
    Employment 208
    Case study 1: allocation of time 209
    Case study 2: allocation of tasks within a department 211
    Case study 3: big career decisions 211

10 **Conclusion**   **213**
    Egocentricity 217
    The power of personal experience 218
    Anchoring 219
    Understanding otherness 220
    Routines 221
    Conformism 222
    Frequently asked questions 224
    Notes 226

    Index   *228*

Figures

1.1   Why ethical choices do not always lead to ethical behaviour.   11
1.2   Recognising ethical questions.   14
1.3   Making ethical choices.   22
1.4   Consequentialist approaches.   23
1.5   Principled approaches.   27
7.1   Channels of researchers' influence on society.   167
7.2   Interrelations between research and welfare.   168
8.1   The media's filtering role.   188
9.1   Time allocation exercise.   210
10.1 Individual within circles of others.   216
10.2 Risks in guided ethical dialogue.   217
10.3 Guided dialogue feedback loop.   223

Tables

2.1	Differences in aims and traditions of different research fields	60
5.1	Qualifications of short-listed candidates	125
6.1	Share of funding sources in some fields in Theland	136
6.2	Research funding instruments in the State Research Council in Theland	139
6.3	Assessments of applications in a call of Theland's State Research Council	147
8.1	Differences between science and the media	189

About the authors

The authors of this book are a unique writing team. Henriikka completed her PhD at the University of Glasgow in bioethics and has taught research ethics at the University of Sydney, Australia as well as at several Finnish universities. She has published on various topics in research ethics under the name Clarkeburn. Arto has a very different background, and is a professor of Russian, soon to be emeritus, at the University of Helsinki, Finland. He has published on the causes of miscommunication, the cultural differences of people and the theory of linguistics. During his long career he has held and still holds various administrative positions, including vice-rector, dean, chair of the board of the Academy of Finland, member of the state Research and Innovation Council and President of the Finnish Learners' Society. He has gained international experience in global (International Association of Russian teachers), European (ESF and ESFRII) and Nordic European research organisations. Arto's and Henriikka's varying research backgrounds and diverse career paths complement each other and represent different generations and gender perspectives.

Henriikka's and Arto's book *Tutkijan arkipäivän etiikka* (Researcher's Everyday Ethics, 2007) has been successful in Finland. Its exceptional approach and content caused widespread interest and resulted in a particularly large number of citations, given the language area. More importantly, the new way of teaching research ethics has translated well into practice. Doctoral students have welcomed the opportunity to discuss *how* to do research and how then to publish it, and have been grateful for the practical tools, guided dialogue and avoidance of black-and-white thinking in ethics that this book provides.

In the summer of 2014 Henriikka and Arto held research ethics classes for doctoral students in a LERU (League of European Research Universities) summer school. The diverse audience was able to discuss a number of personal cases that had some local nuances but also common features. After receiving very positive feedback, Henriikka and Arto decided to compile a research ethics book for the international market. The basic idea of the guided dialogue approach was similar to the first book, but with an international context and updated regarding the current key ethical challenges in the research community.

The working pattern Henriikka and Arto developed in writing this book is unique. Henriikka has tried to keep ethical theories and vocabulary visible and alive, while Arto's role is to highlight and explain ethical challenges, which are frequent but often ignored in research communities. Despite this approach, they have internalised the whole concept of the book so deeply that in the final text you cannot identify which ideas and phrases come from each of the authors.

You may want to know whether Henriikka and Arto belong to the same family. They do. Arto is Henriikka's uncle, a rare combination of authors.

For the reader

Ethics is an inseparable part of doing research. Researchers have always wondered what is allowed and what is forbidden in research. By defining what is right and wrong within the scientific endeavour, the research community has also drawn boundaries around its activities within society. In recent years, ethics has gained increasing prominence within the research community. Society has also participated in this discussion, often with a focus on misconduct and other evidence of wrongdoing. The growing interest in research ethics is at least partially explained by increased competition and rapid growth in the volume of research work.

Research ethics has been codified in many countries. These rules and guidelines typically define scientific misconduct and offer procedures to manage any suspected cases of it. These form a common foundation for research practice, and many of these codes are now internationally recognised. This foundation is the base layer of research ethics. It captures the fundamentals and sets up the boundaries for policing and dealing with any wrongdoing. Understanding these rules is essential for everyone in research. This book, however, only starts with these rules and has its focus on collective ethical thinking and dialogue.

This second layer of research ethics looks at what should be done rather than what should not be done. Most ethical questions are not ones of right and wrong. They are considerations between options that are difficult to rank, rate or evaluate in terms of rightness or betterness. We can also approach ethical issues and choices collectively, which is fundamentally different to following rules. It is a way of looking at decisions and choices, identifying values that guide interactions, judgements and decisions, and seeking to find solutions both as individuals and as a community. This book will work through theories of making ethical choices and apply these theories to a broad range of situations and questions within a research career. Therefore, the focus of this book is not on what is wrong. The focus is a broader perspective on how ethics can be a positive force to strengthen the research community.

We have called this approach 'ethics by guided dialogue' to capture ethical questions before they become ethical problems. 'Guided' means that reasoning on research ethics it systematised by a toolbox of ethical skills. By applying such an approach, we arrive at choices that are transparent and grounded. As a result, the guidance we give is to help the reader and ethical decision-maker to ask a broad range of meaningful questions. These questions help to clarify the situation and create dialogue between stakeholders. As a result, the questions support more transparent and justifiable decisions. Answers to many of the questions proposed in this book reveal values, goals and the context of the decision-maker. We believe that this increased transparency and dialogue will lead not only to better individual decisions, but also to a stronger and more cohesive research community able to focus on what it does well.

We want to highlight the continuous nature of ethical thinking in research. Ethics cannot be done at the beginning or the end. It travels with the researcher through the entire research process from the original idea, through funding applications, into data collection, and finally into sharing results. Within the term 'ethics by guided dialogue' we also highlight the importance of collective ethical thinking and the value of transparency within the research community, to discuss ethical issues and to decide the best way to proceed.

We approach research ethics from a holistic perspective. In research, people actively interact with colleagues at different stages of their career – for example, senior professors work alongside students. Different ethical questions may take precedence at different parts of the research career, but all decisions influence the entire community. A PhD student will certainly read this book differently to a professor, but both will find it helpful in developing their research ethical thinking, asking ethical questions, as well as becoming more aware of how ethics shapes our research community and its practices.

According to a general view, ethics is an integral part of doing research and publishing research findings in scientific areas. In this book, however, we present a wider understanding of ethics in the researcher's life. Ethical questions travel not only through the research process, but also through the research career as a whole. The career perspective brings into focus questions that are not directly part of 'doing research' while they are an integral part of 'being a researcher' – supervision, academic reviews and evaluations, recruitment of people and interaction with the non-academic world are a few examples. Ethical questions concerning these aspects of the researcher's life will also be considered in this book.

This book is designed for everyone in the international research community. Most ethical questions are similar all over the world, and do not need localisation. However, for the sake of being more concrete, some examples and case studies are situated in a hypothetical country called 'Theland'. In Theland, research structures are funded only partially by the government; competition for positions, funding and publication is tight; research has rules and regulations; and the value of research is recognised by society.

The examples and case studies presented in the book sometimes demonstrate ethical questions in a certain research field or discipline. Researchers from other fields may see these sections as unnecessary. Nevertheless, we recommend the entire book to everyone. In fact, one of the general aims of the book is to widen readers' understanding of various ways of doing research, which is a necessary starting point for multidisciplinary research and engaging in meaningful dialogue on ethical questions in the research community. For those who are interested in the ethics of specific research methods or fields, there are fortunately many books available.

This book can be used both for self-reflection and teaching ethics. The 'ethics by guided dialogue' approach is also useful within research groups and within departments and faculties. It provides a shared language and starting point to making ethics first visible and second an integrated part of everyday decision-making. In other words, it provides tools for constructive dialogue. We have included a large number of case studies to guide the use of questions and to help practise ethical dialogue. All of the case studies are fictitious in terms of their context and characters. At the same time they are real; they are based around ethical questions faced by people like you – researchers in different stages of their careers. Through extensive experience in teaching research ethics, and working in different academic and management roles within the academic world, we have listened to a lot of stories. Ethical questions are often at the heart of situations where things have gone wrong. They are also present in stories where solutions have been found. We have captured the essence of these stories and shared them with you in the form of the case studies. These stories are also a key part of our motivation to write this book: to make this layer of academic life more visible and to be part of the progress towards a more transparent and ethically aware research community.

Introduction

Why research ethics is more important than ever before

This book was written as a response to ethical questions in the current research environment. Some of these questions are now asked more frequently or are more complex than before, while others are completely novel. For decades, the principles and nature of research have remained stable and unchanged. We can even talk about centuries of tradition. The research ideal of objectivity and honesty still form the foundation of research work. However, the last 10–20 years have brought into the research field many new phenomena that have significantly changed the parameters and conditions for research. These forces are equally at play for the research community and individual researchers, and create a new ethical landscape to navigate. Following is a short list of reasons why a fresh approach to research ethics is essential.

Increased number of researchers. The importance of research as one of the cornerstones of the modern knowledge-based society has been recognised by governments all around the world. The intensity of research is increasing in all of the traditional global research hubs in Western Europe, North America and Australia. Simultaneously, research investments have rapidly increased in countries keen to improve their economies and societies. This increase has in some cases been two- or three-fold over the past decade. This includes population-rich countries like China, Brazil, Indonesia, Iran and Turkey, as well as smaller countries like Singapore and South Africa. The USA still has the highest production of peer-reviewed articles, but China is quickly closing the gap if measured purely by the number of publications. Measured against population, Switzerland, Nordic countries, the Netherlands, Australia, New Zealand and Singapore are among the most productive in the world. When we look at research quality, measured by citations for example, the same countries appear at the top of the list.

As more and more young people engage in research, the research community grows more heterogeneous than ever before. The different traditions and sheer volume of players in the academic world makes it impossible to assume a shared set of traditions and beliefs. Therefore, it is essential to build, through explicit and transparent dialogue, a joint ethical foundation that makes research not only possible, but effective and exciting.

Increasing globalisation. Research has always had an international aspect. However, the mobility of researchers has notably increased in recent years. A global labour market has been the standard in research for longer than in most other sectors. However, individuals now move more frequently than ever in the search for the best possible research opportunity. Some countries and institutions try to attract the best research talent with salaries that can be many times higher than those offered in other countries. This mobility is aided by the relatively similar research practices and equipment across borders. This ease in mobility also has challenges, as traditions, aspirations and regulations vary significantly between countries and institutions. For this reason, academics need to be able to engage in ethical dialogue in the multicultural and diverse research world to make sure they are aware of their environment and to be part of the process of forming high standards of global research.

Intensified competition. More and more research is completed with applied funding. This translates to a very competitive environment to secure essential resources to carry out research. Funding opportunities are provided by governments or private sources within nation states, as well as by international funding bodies and corporations. In most instances, the number of applications greatly exceeds the amount of funding available. Competition increases also in the publishing sector, where being published in highly ranked journals is increasingly less likely. A growing number of applications are also received for academic positions as more and more early-career academics seek to consolidate their careers. The competitiveness is not only between individual academics, but also between universities, institutions, and research groups. It is not enough to do better research than others, it is also essential to get there first. Even nations compete in world research rankings. Countries often consider high-quality research to be one of the factors that make them appear more respectable and advanced in the competition for the best brains and biggest investments. The increased competition poses a clear risk to playing by the shared rules. These competitive pressures change the role of researchers and contrast other research ideals, including collaboration and transparency. To navigate this new competitive landscape requires new sets of rules, careful application of existing guidelines as well as strong motivation to create an ethically sound research environment.

More reviews. External funding is one of the forces that calls for accountability, which translates to an increasing need for academic reviews. Peer review has always been part of scientific practice. Senior researchers have for decades or centuries reviewed applicants for academic positions and ranked them according to their merits. Internal quality controls include review processes regarding doctoral dissertations, and senior academics have been the gatekeepers of research quality by peer reviewing research prior to publication. The new funding climate increases the demands beyond these traditional review structures. A significant part of this is pre-review work, which assesses funding applications against criteria with the hope of finding the best projects to be funded. In many instances the reviews are carried out by a review panel, which is formed from an international pool of distinguished academics. As a result, the senior academics spend an increasing proportion of their time and effort reviewing. The review process is always also a learning process for the reviewer, but this learning has a significant opportunity cost – time not spent on something else. Time pressures increase the risk of cutting corners somewhere, and the review process itself has considerable ethical challenges related to confidential information, appropriate criteria, sufficiency of information and the selection of appropriate reviewers. Guided dialogue can provide tools to manage this process.

The demands for post-review have also increased as entire research fields, research programmes, departments and universities are assessed. Besides the traditional peer review method, various bibliometric tools are increasingly used in these assessments. In fact, we have faced the birth of a new branch of industry that provides services to those who are interested in the effectiveness of research work. The use of numbers of publications and citations as an important indicator of quality of research has raised a lot of ethical debate. The method as such is explicit and transparent, but it is also potentially biased towards certain traditions in publishing and citation. Intensive use of bibliometric indicators also creates a push towards inappropriate publishing habits and manipulation of numbers of citations.

Social impact. Traditionally, research review has focused on quality – some research is good, some isn't. The reference point in such an approach is research done by other researchers. Citations tell us about the internal visibility and impact of research, about its influence on the scientific community. In recent years, research policies and funding structures have introduced a new, and increasingly more central, review aspect – 'social impact'. Social impact itself is not a new thing – research has always had a significant impact on society – but it is novel as an important component when governments and states assess the value of research and universities. Social impact relates to the connection between researchers and the non-academic world, including business, media, policy-makers and the general public. When people from different contexts come together, we are often faced with new ethical challenges. The importance of this interface between research and other social forces requires that researchers adopt a different role to the traditional focus on increasing knowledge and understanding. The need to quantify social impact is in itself challenging and an ethical question in its own right. Defining and prioritising concrete forms of social impact is a weighty question of the rights and responsibilities of different stakeholders. Many things are still open in this issue, and therefore it is especially important to decide who carries out the assessment and which indicators are used. There is, evidently, a lot of space for ethical dialogue.

Extending multi- and interdisciplinary research. Since the 1980s, those funding research have advocated a cross- and multidisciplinary approach to research.[1] The research community has taken its time to respond to this. Quite the contrary, scientific work has become more specialised than ever, with more focused and narrow research projects and subfields within which researchers identify themselves. Researchers commit to their research field and aspire to work and succeed within it. Communication challenges within multidisciplinary collaboration have also reduced the uptake. Different disciplines write differently, use concepts and methodologies, which are foreign to most others. For these reasons, multidisciplinary research requires extra effort and time, and the latter is most often in very short supply.

The push for more multidisciplinary research has further been intensified by the grand challenges facing humanity, including climate change, energy scarcity and social inequality. These wicked problems, as they are often called, cannot be solved by single disciplines or narrow research focus; collaboration of researchers using different approaches and methods is seen as part of the solution. The multidisciplinary nature of approaching these problems spans the entire research sector from technical subjects to humanities. The aim is often to create transdisciplinary knowledge. When researchers from different disciplines work together, they need the ability to discuss and agree on ethical issues relating to collaboration, funding and academic credit, as well as how the results will be communicated and published.

Formalised doctoral training. Educating the next generation of researchers has been one of the traditional tasks of universities. The last decades have seen a significant change in how this takes place. The change has had a different rhythm in different countries, but the direction is the same everywhere: doctoral training is increasingly systemic and controlled. The word *training* reflects the nature of the change well; it is done to someone by someone else in order to receive a certain and relatively standardised set of qualifications. This is in direct contrast to the more holistic approach of previous research generations, which grew and developed alongside their senior research colleagues. This doctoral training regularly includes imparting knowledge of research ethics as a compulsory element. These courses are often focused on the rules and guidelines of doing research to create an environment of accountability, where the individual can consider scientific misconduct as a conscious decision. Deeper and more fundamental ethical research thinking is more likely imparted tacitly when one is part of a research group. The ability to discuss difficult ethical dilemmas inherent in research is typically not formally developed. This forms a new challenge to managing ethical questions in research. Previously, academic traditions were passed to the next generation implicitly, without formal training, in a one-to-one mentoring relationship that is no longer a feasible model. As a community, we need to find new ways to create and support the development of learning to think deeply about research ethics, both individually and collectively.

New technology, new opportunities. Different equipment and technologies have been part of research for centuries. In many cases, development of equipment and technologies have not only changed how we do research, but also what we will study. Examples of these shifts include the development of a telescope in relation to the study of astronomy, particle generators in physics, PCR machines in genetics and large text corpuses in linguistics. Rapid progress in IT has changed research routines everywhere. We seek reference material, manage our data and produce results in ways we could not have imagined only a few decades ago. In some fields, progress has led to building very large infrastructures (e.g. CERN) or a race to secure ever more efficient (and expensive) equipment. One of the latest developments is large and digitised databases housing 'big data'.

All of this influences not only how we carry out research, but also how funding shapes the research opportunities and directions. Purchase and shared use of equipment requires planning, negotiations, and new ways to make shared decisions. Big data requires new methodologies to analyse data, assess their reliability and manage privacy and confidentiality. The fundamental question of what is worth studying remains pertinent.

Open science. During recent years, the openness of science has become a hot topic in research policy and various discussions on the development of research. The concept as such is rather vague, but different interpretations do not decrease the significance of the issue. By 'open science' we usually mean open access publishing and open data. The open access movement has its roots in the 1980s, but during recent years it has been transferred from an ideology of some enthusiasts to a general aim of many universities and research agencies. However, we are still far from real open scientific practice, which in itself forms an important ethical question. Open data, distribution of research evidence to the entire research community, corresponds very well with the basic principles of research. Nevertheless, the ideal world is not yet reached. One can see a further dimension of open science in crowdsourcing, which leads to a closer connection between researchers and the non-academic world. This may have positive consequences for science when people understand better what research is about.

Changes in researchers' lives. Comparing researchers' everyday activities to those of decades ago, we see several changes that have a common denominator – life has become much more complicated. Most of the changes are common phenomena in a modern society, such as demands to be active in social media, challenges to combine work with family life, uncertainty about the future and pressure to be more and more productive and effective. These things are a serious challenge for researchers, because innovative research work needs cognitive space and peaceful conditions. A contemporary researcher has to share her or his time between interacting with students, active networking with colleagues domestically and abroad, reading an increasing number of publications, doing experiments and other research work, writing articles and books, contacting non-academic people and, in most cases, also family. A further burden for researchers in universities is increasing administrative work. It has two origins: universities' efforts to save resources by reducing administrative staff, and new technological solutions which enable – in theory – easy handling of various administrative programmes without the help of supporting personnel. Due to the mess of mixed duties and tasks, researchers need skills in multitasking and time management more than ever.

***

All these changes in and around our research community raise new ethical questions. Some of the problems are familiar and now appear in a new environment, while some ethical questions are brand new. The entire research community needs to approach these questions, and communicate and share the process of searching for ethical solutions. Fast-paced change further emphasises the importance of dialogue within the research community.

This book looks into all of these questions and into many others from the perspective of guided ethical dialogue. The aim is to open a fresh way for those doing research or managing research to consider ethics as part of their research work. The examples used in this book are situated within everyday activities in research, and highlight the situations where it is not obvious what the most ethical decisions would look like. We are not offering ready answers, but the aim is to give tools that can be used in the research community to seek collective and personal answers to important ethical questions.

NOTE

1   The terms *interdisciplinary, multidisciplinary* and *transdisciplinary* are often used loosely, without a clear distinction between them. A starting point in the discussion on different approaches is the idea of two modes of research (see, e.g. Michael Gibbons, Camille Limoges, Helga Nowotny, Simon Schwartzman, Peter Scott and Martin Trow (1994), *The New Production of Knowledge*, London: Sage). Mode 1 is the traditional *monodisciplinary* approach aimed at revealing 'pure knowledge'. Mode 2 represents application-oriented knowledge which by its nature is interdisciplinary. Short definitions of Mode 2 approaches based on the paper of Marily Stember ((1991), Interdisciplinary approach to knowledge, *Social Science Journal*, 28: 1) are given by Alexander Refsum Jensenius (www.arj.no/2012/03/12/disciplinarities-2):

   - *Crossdisciplinary:* viewing one discipline from the perspective of another.
   - *Multidisciplinary:* people from different disciplines working together, each drawing on their disciplinary knowledge.
   - *Interdisciplinary:* integrating knowledge and methods from different disciplines, using a real synthesis of approaches.
   - *Transdisciplinary:* creating a unity of intellectual frameworks beyond the disciplinary perspectives.

Chapter 1

Ethics by guided dialogue

The main ethical themes and values in using guided dialogue are:

1   All choices and decisions reflect our values, and guided dialogue creates an opportunity to consciously align values with actions.
2   The research community has a clear set of values that guide its work, and their meaning in reality can be explored using guided dialogue.
3   Shared values and tools to participate in guided dialogue assist researchers to make ethical choices that strengthen the community.
4   Guided dialogue incorporates personal values and contextual reflection, which allows for a holistic approach to choices and decisions in research ethics

Approaching ethics by guided dialogue typically requires researchers and research communities to consider the following key ethical questions:

•   What are ethical questions in research? How do they differ from research questions?
•   How do we make ethical choices and decisions? Are there better or worse ways to make them?
•   Can ethical decision-making be taught and learned?
•   Who should we consider when we consider ethical questions in research?
•   What are our rights and responsibilities as researchers?
•   How can we use ethical reasoning to understand ethical choices?
•   How can my personal values be incorporated into my research work?

The starting point for this book is to see ethics as a set of skills that support both an individual researcher and the research community in making ethical choices. When we see ethics in this way, it takes shape through questions and concerns arising from common, everyday situations. We call this approach 'ethics by guided dialogue'. Responding to ethical concerns and making choices benefits greatly from a structured and systematic approach. The guided dialogue approach to making ethical choices incorporates both analytical and decision-making tools in an interactive and collective process. Ethics by guided dialogue provides a structure to make choices, which can be justified by sharing the process and values. This transparency aligns with the call for open science and research. The ethics by guided dialogue approach is described briefly in this chapter.

Before we look at the ethical skills within the dialogue approach, it is important to define what is meant by ethical questions/challenges/dilemmas/problems. We can start with certain common characteristics:

- Ethical choices are present in all aspects of research work and private lives.
- Most ethical questions do not have clear and unambiguous answers.
- It can be difficult to recognise an ethical question nested within scientific or social questions.
- Ethical questions cannot be answered using scientific methodologies of observation, testing or measuring.
- Typically at the heart of the problem is an inability to follow different values/ beliefs simultaneously.
- Ethical questions are often tacit and not recognised by those who have to make ethical choices.

The last point leads to one of the central ideas of this book. We can engage in dialogue on ethical questions only when we are aware of them. Conscious and transparent reasoning regarding ethical questions forms the foundation for fruitful dialogue on ethically important issues within the research community. This makes more solid and well-guided decision-making possible. When we see ethics as a skill, we learn to recognise ethical processes. Through this recognition, we can apply our values in practice.

Dialogue requires an ability to both contribute and listen. Listening requires an open mind, a willingness and ability to understand the values, goals and the thought processes of others participating in the dialogue. The ability to contribute requires us to adopt willingness to understand our own values, goals and thought processes, and a willingness to share that with others. Often we listen with a very specific intention to find evidence of either agreement or disagreement. In ethical dialogue, like in most dialogue, it is vitally important to try to listen openly. In many situations, we agree more than we disagree. Finding some common ground, something we have in common, is a great place to start building guided ethical dialogue.

The terms *ethical* and *moral* are used in multiple different ways by different authors and thought traditions. Sometimes they are used interchangeably; at other times they are distinctly different. In this book we do not draw strong distinctions between the terms. However, we refer to *ethical* as something we can collectively recognise and analyse, to issues and questions we can approach using both our values and ethical skills. The term *moral* refers more to personal values and considerations on what is right or wrong. Morality is by nature normative and personal, while ethics carries a more collective and neutral tone.

The following examples are used to highlight the often elusive nature of ethical questions.

Trap selection process. As an example of a layered scientific and ethical question we can examine a research team considering how to capture rodents in the wild as part of their population study. The team has identified two trap options. In their decision-making, the team considers which trap will be less painful for the captured rodents. This appears ethical from both the perspective of the process and the outcome. However, the use of pain as a criterion has distinct scientific elements and the ethical question is hidden from view. This approach is scientific because it is possible to design an experiment to determine which trap does indeed cause less pain. The result may not have absolute accuracy as measuring pain is complex and not completely understood, but it is most likely that a reasonably objective result can be produced. Therefore, the decision can be made using scientific results and thinking.

The ethical question lies within choosing the decision-making criteria, and the team may not be conscious of having made an ethical choice. Using pain as criteria is a choice, even if it may appear as the most obvious or ethical one. The team could have used multiple different criteria as well, including economic (cost of each trap), performance (maximising yield of rodents during study period) or logistics (ease of acquiring and transporting the traps). The team is able to look at each of these options individually and find an answer to which trap is most economical, has the best performance or is the easiest to transport. Now they have to make a choice regarding the appropriate criteria to use. The challenge is that the same trap is rarely the cheapest, the most effective, the easiest to transport and causes the least pain. Therefore the team needs to consider which criteria should be prioritised, revealing their values of what is fundamentally important in choosing a trap. This ethical question is often tacit and not discussed or even recognised. If there is a conflict in choosing the trap, it is very likely that the conflict stems from different unspoken decision-making criteria.

Case of plagiarism. Is plagiarism acceptable? The scientific community gives a clear and unanimous answer: *no.* This categorical answer may, however, give a misleading picture of the simplicity of ethical concerns relating to plagiarism. In addition to the 'cut-and-paste-without-a-reference' plagiarism, there is a significant grey area where it is more difficult to determine whether the action is indeed plagiarism and thus unacceptable. For example, a more challenging ethical question is how extensively is it acceptable to borrow from one's own previous work before it is considered self-/auto-plagiarism, or when a research idea or plan can be considered as the property of an individual/team, or how to reference 'general' knowledge that can be found on Wikipedia?

Case of authorship. Who can demand to be included as an author in an article? The formal answer is an academic who has participated in the writing of the article or the experiments/investigations upon which the article is written. There are international guidelines and conventions to clarify these criteria.[1] Those who have experience in writing with others are usually aware of borderline cases where the obvious can transform into a challenge. For this decision there is a rather simple principle: the colleague who has participated in the research sufficiently will be included as an author. But what does 'sufficiently' mean? Mostly this decision reflects both the local traditions and conventions within the field of study. There are, for example, differences in the appropriate way to include supervisors or other senior academics as authors. Determining authorship is a good example of a common academic decision, which typically has more than one ethically acceptable solution.

Managing students. Teaching is an integral part of academic life. Many ethical issues are present when making decisions on time and effort devoted to teaching and preparation in relation to research and administrative tasks. What is the right balance and how does it reflect a good academic life? Teaching opens up a different relationship level as well – there is an obvious power imbalance, and fair treatment of students both in marking and in support can raise significant ethical challenges.

When we approach ethical choices through guided dialogue, the responsibility to make conscious and well-justified ethical choices rests on the shoulders of everyone doing research. All academics make ethical choices throughout every working day. The 'ethical fitness' of a research community is based on these daily decisions. Understanding ethics as a skill fits well with Western tradition valuing rationality and individual responsibility. Seeing ethics as a dialogue expands the individual realm to seeing ethical choices in their natural collective space. Many research ethics questions, as we will expand on in later chapters, are impossible to resolve by individuals. They are amorphous and complex, and require the community to engage with them and make choices towards the best possible ethical outcome. The guided dialogue approach also makes teaching and learning ethics possible in multicultural and multidimensional universities. The skill based components and structures can be taught and the structure itself can be effectively used in the classrooms and staff meetings to create a space for learning and collective decision-making.

WHY ETHICAL CHOICES DO NOT ALWAYS LEAD TO ETHICAL BEHAVIOUR

Ethics by guided dialogue does not automatically lead to sound and solid ethical behaviour. To avoid any confusion and false promises that this approach could somehow transform our ethical landscape by making us all better people, we wish to briefly explain at least one reason for the discrepancy between ethically justified choices and potentially less sound behaviour. To understand this discrepancy, it is helpful to break up the process of an ethical (or unethical) action into four interlinked steps (Figure 1.1).[2]

Step 1 – recognising an ethical question. There appears to be significant differences between individuals' natural ability to identify the presence of an ethical concern.[3] For some of us, the world is full of ethical issues and most actions are ethically multi-layered processes. For others, the same situation appears as a set of routine actions that can be approached without any further ethical consideration or analysis.

We can look at postgraduate training as an example. Senior researchers can approach supervision with experience and a level of routine. They may have effective or inefficient habits and processes. Supervision may be more or less successful when measured by completed PhDs. However, these characteristics do not reflect the solution of concrete ethical questions in PhD supervision. For example, is the recruitment of PhD candidates fair for the applicants? What would gender-neutral and fair supervision look like in practice? Should we even consider gender as an aspect in supervision? Who is responsible for guaranteeing that the

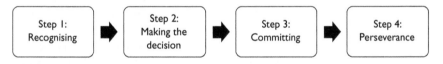

Figure 1.1 Why ethical choices do not always lead to ethical behaviour.

PhD topic is meaningful and advantageous for the student? Should the PhD training include elements that assist in finding employment outside universities? This first step involves the ability to recognise these ethical questions.

The ability to see the ethical layer in everyday research work is an essential skill. If the questions are not recognised, it is impossible to seek solutions to them. Because this ability can improve through training and education, it makes sense to call it a skill rather than a characteristic or personality trait. Research also suggests that seeing the ethical layer is not something people naturally develop alongside their research work or as they grow older.[4] Therefore, increasing ethical sensitivity is an essential part of the ethical skills toolkit and the precursor for engaging in guided ethical dialogue.

Even though ethical and scientific questions are distinctly different in nature, there is a clear analogy in this process of recognition. If no one had paid attention to the potential link between hygiene and allergies, or violence on screen and violent behaviour, it would have been impossible to start investigating the nature of these links. In the same way, it is necessary for ethical questions to be recognised, made visible and accepted into shared dialogue before they can be answered.

Step 2 – making the ethical decision. This step requires a conscious choice to seek a solution to an ethical issue. In practice, it is often marked by asking questions about the situation as a way of making sense of it. Typical questions could be: Should we do this or that? If I do this, is too much weight placed on that? On the other hand, with this option...? Is this a fair way to deal with this situation? Do we have a right to do this? Choosing a course of action or forming a judgement is a core aspect of an ethical challenge.

Every ethical question produces options – at least the option to do something or to do nothing. The process of making a conscious ethical choice will also equip the decision-makers to describe and justify why they have chosen this over that. Not everyone necessarily agrees with the decision, but the ability to describe a process will help others to understand the decision and the values behind it. Awareness of the ethical decision-making methods, which we examine more closely later in this chapter, helps the decision-maker to approach decisions more systematically and from a broader perspective. Ethical dialogue opens up the decision-making process and invites participants to both share their own thinking process and to take part in forming a process for making a collective decision. Sometimes collective dialogue is preceded by extensive inner dialogue by participants.

Step 3 – committing to an ethical choice. At this point we have arrived at an ethically justifiable solution. The next step is to commit to that choice. It is often a question of priorities. The ethically right decision may contradict other important considerations, and we have to evaluate what is most important to us. These competing values and desires may include a desire to be liked, financial gain, desire to help others, hedonistic desires or career opportunities.

Step 4 – perseverance under pressure. At this step we have made a commitment to the ethical choice, but face pressures to change it. This commonly happens when the pressures at work or home position the researcher in a situation where it is increasingly difficult to maintain multiple values. In the current research environment, these strains include increasing pressures on time (i.e. internal or external needs to use time for something 'more important'), lack of resources, ambitions of the group or other external pressures. These pressures can originate from various hierarchical sources: above (supervisors, institutional strategies, funding bodies or societal demands), parallel (colleagues, research community) or below (research students, support staff). The pressures are enhanced by different material and social rewards and believed or real punishments associated with failing to meet expectations or targets. At this point we have to look at the price of committing to an ethical choice. What are the opportunity costs associated with following this path, or are there direct costs that force re-consideration of the commitment? No one makes decisions in isolation, and all choices are acted out within a multidimensional research and work community, as well as society at large.

Let us consider a situation in which a researcher acts as a reviewer for a funding body. This reviewer looks at the proposal and considers it broadly and according to given guidelines in terms of, for example, innovation, feasibility and international significance. The reviewer gives the proposal a score of four out of five. Then the reviewer recalls another research team that has applied for the same funding. The reviewer has a friend as the group leader and they have plans for future collaboration. To boost his friend's chances of being funded (and thus increasing the chances of collaboration) the reviewer changes the score to three out of five. Therefore the original process of following an appropriate and ethically transparent path of reviewing the proposal using the given and known criteria is abandoned and an additional hidden criteria is included as part of the process. Therefore the correct path of action is known, but something else is considered more important than adhering to the ethically appropriate course of action. The reviewer may be able to justify his actions by revisiting the original report and re-writing some aspects to allow the score to be lowered and remain consistent with the review.

This book focuses on the first two steps of ethical actions – recognition and making a choice. They are part of an ethical skillset and contain an opportunity for learning and dialogue. In other words, we can learn skills to improve our ability to recognise ethical questions within our research practice and to find well-considered solutions to them. The last two steps focus more closely on the character of the decision-makers and reflect their individual values. These aspects can also evolve and change, but it would seem inappropriate to consider one book or course in ethics to have a significant impact on them. In addition, there would be noteworthy ethical concerns with any programme aiming to change the character and values of others. At the same time, we believe that discussing ethical issues and improving our ethical skills is likely to encourage academic decision-makers to reflect on their values and ability to commit to doing the 'right thing'. This is the foundation for development and growth.

The next two sections of this chapter provide the basis for understanding and developing ethical skills for guided dialogue. The first section looks at the process of recognising and analysing ethical questions. The second section focuses on understanding different approaches to making ethical decisions. Most people make most of their ethical choices using a holistic approach and the decision-maker may or may not be conscious of the steps or the values informing the process. For ethical skills to be used successfully in dialogue with others (or with oneself) or taught to others, it is essential to make them visible and describe them as a process with distinct parts. The process and steps described in this chapter are not a description of actual decision-making, but tools and structures to give this process shape and form so that it becomes useful and applicable in everyday situations. We use these theories, steps and processes in analysing and investigating the case studies throughout this book.

RECOGNISING ETHICAL QUESTIONS

Now we turn to the first step of ethical reasoning: recognition of ethical questions. The analysis typically follows three steps, which create a comprehensive picture of the ethical question in hand (Figure 1.2).

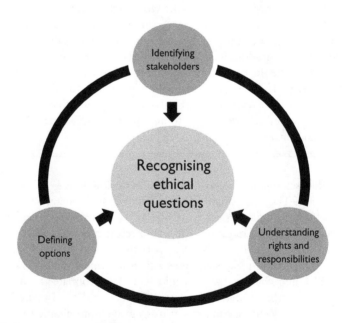

Figure 1.2 Recognising ethical questions.

The importance of ethical analysis is based on the understanding that any decision or choice is always assisted by understanding the actual question as deeply as possible. It also grounds all dialogue in shared understanding of the focus.

Ethical questions are typically complex and multidimensional, and the analytical process is non-linear. Different aspects of the question are usually revisited and re-shaped as the analysis progresses. Often, the analytical process produces a number of potential ethical questions. The process then requires a prioritisation of these questions to allow an appropriate focus on core ethical concerns. We differentiate three steps in the process: identifying stakeholders; understanding rights and responsibilities; and defining options.

We will explore the analytical process using the following case study:

As part of her PhD research, Kate produces an interesting result: a carefully controlled diet appears to have a significant impact on the management of a relatively rare genetic disease. Her results suggest that completely avoiding certain commonly used preservatives is the key for better disease management. Kate's research is funded by the food industry and she understands that drawing attention to these results is not in the financial interest of her funding bodies. At the same time, Kate has a strong motivation to make these results known to the people living with the disease in order to enable them to improve their quality of life. Kate finds the situation problematic as she recognises her inability to serve the patient community, her funding body, and her own research interests with one solution. Simple solutions are not available as stakeholders have contradictory definitions of a good outcome. Kate sees her dilemma as choosing whose interests she should protect if she is unable to find a solution to protect them all simultaneously. In addition, she contemplates the question of when is her evidence 'strong enough' to be used as a new guidelines in disease management?

Identifying stakeholders

Everyone influencing the choice or affected by it can be considered as a *stakeholder*. Stakeholders are typically people, but also animals, communities, ecosystems or even artefacts can be considered as stakeholders. It may also appear appropriate to consider future generations as stakeholders. Some stakeholders can be individually identified – we know exactly who they are – while others represent a group or a collective having common interests. Giving something or someone stakeholder status also indicates they have intrinsic importance in the process. Identification as a stakeholder also highlights a commitment to considering their interests in the decision-making process. Therefore, identifying stakeholders is one of the key steps that reveal and shape the values we bring to the dialogue. In addition, the choice of stakeholders significantly shapes the decision-making process and thus there is great benefit to identifying them explicitly.

Not all stakeholders are necessarily equal, and they can be given different weight in the decision-making process based, for example, on whether the decision will directly or indirectly affect them. Consistent treatment of similar stakeholders is a requirement for good ethical thinking. For example, if animals, who are capable of experiencing pain, are considered stakeholders, it is not consistent to exclude rats from the stakeholder group because they are ugly and to include bunnies because they are cute. If ugliness is used as an exclusion criterion, then it is important to make the criteria transparent and explicit, though this criterion may be difficult to logically defend or apply.

An ability to explain and justify the chosen criteria is often necessary, because in many situations multiple different criteria can be justifiably proposed. The selection of stakeholders typically reflects our values of what and who are important to us. The stakeholder identification is often a multistep process, as we find the need to revisit our stakeholder group boundaries as the guided dialogue progresses and new aspects of the ethical issue appear. Often, some stakeholder groups have been omitted in the original identification; at other times the group is later considered as too inclusive and the key stakeholders need to be more specifically re-identified.

When revisiting Kate's ethical challenge, it appears that the stakeholders in her situation include herself, her research group, the academic department, the patient community, and her funding body. The larger scientific community could also be considered as a stakeholder. An even broader definition of stakeholders would bring in a larger social group of consumers and focus would include general social responsibilities to produce healthy and safe food items. As part of her decision-making, Kate will need to consider: how broadly situated her ethical question is; whether all her stakeholders are given equal consideration; and how she is going to compare very different stakeholder groups. The stakeholder groups are not only different; Kate knows some stakeholders as individuals, whereas other stakeholders are anonymous members of a collective.

Understanding rights and responsibilities

Typically, stakeholders are protected by some legal, contractual or moral rights and may have responsibilities also codified in law, guidelines or recognised as moral expectations. Understanding rights and responsibilities often provides boundaries that differentiate between socially and legally acceptable and unacceptable options to respond to the ethical question. This understanding deepens our perception of stakeholders and their relationships. It is also quite common that the definition of rights and responsibilities become the key ethical issues we are trying resolve through our dialogue.

In Kate's case, she may have legal responsibilities towards her funding bodies; these are commonly written in an official contract between the financer and the researcher. There may also be some implicit responsibilities she feels regarding the financer. On the other hand, Kate is a member of the scientific community and this may include such values as openness and transparency in relation to scientific findings. These responsibilities are typically fulfilled through appropriate publications. Kate may also consider that she has a social and/or moral responsibility towards the patient community to provide them with the latest information regarding best management of their condition. Kate may also be considered to have a right to make her own decisions regarding where, when and how she reports her scientific findings. On the other hand, she has certain responsibilities towards her department to make sure she graduates. In the same way, it may be beneficial to consider rights and responsibilities of all key stakeholders to gain a full understanding of the boundaries. This analysis may change the nature of the actual ethical question by including an inquiry about the nature of moral and ethical rights/responsibilities of different stakeholders.

Defining options

Every situation offers us options, even if it is an option between doing something or doing nothing. In complex collective ethical issues, most typically none of the options is automatically or unanimously considered as the only 'right' answer. This requires us to consider options and to predict what would happen if each option was chosen. An ideal outcome would be a 'win–win' situation, where all the key interests of all the stakeholders could be upheld without concurrently violating any rights or failing to fulfil any responsibilities. In reality, these situations are rare. Striving to find options that would be as close as possible to this ideal is often part of the ethical motivation described earlier in this chapter. This step in the ethical analysis is also about openness and persistence in terms of seeking solutions through dialogue beyond the immediate and most obvious ones and to commit to determining options broadly before a decision is made.

Kate has numerous options she can consider when choosing the best way to manage her results. She can publish immediately in a journal, though the actual publishing of results will take some time; she can share her results informally with healthcare providers or within the patient community; she could publish in a non-scientific journal; or she could continue her research and consider publication at a later stage. With each option, Kate will benefit from contemplating how the option would affect each stakeholder and how they would fit within her previous study of rights and responsibilities.

A few cases are the best way to illuminate how to define and develop our understanding of ethical issues. The first case relates to selecting a PhD student and the second one to making decisions around a research plan.

PhD student selection

Arjun is a senior professor and has received an application to commence a PhD in his group. Arjun has ten PhD students already and he struggles to find time to supervise them as he has numerous managerial roles within his university and international collaborations. Camila has completed her Master's degree by research with a distinction and has sent her application to Professor Arjun. Her Master's research is similar to the focus of Arjun's group and she is aware that Arjun is a liked and thorough supervisor. Arjun appears to have a yes-or-no decision – either he accepts or rejects Camila's application. Based on the application, Arjun considers Camila a high-calibre candidate, but is concerned about his own ability to provide adequate supervision.

The core ethical challenge has its roots in the common dilemma of not having enough time. Arjun cannot achieve all he aspires to and what he feels is his responsibility. He is faced with a need to prioritise. The conflict is born of the incompatibility of Arjun's pre-existing work commitments and Camila's desires and aspiration. Arjun's ethical question could therefore be identified as: how should a senior professor divide his work time? Or, how much time should a supervisor have for his students? Or, in broader terms, what does a good professor do? How should a PhD student be selected (e.g. merit, opportunities, fit in the research team)? One could also consider what is in the best interests of the research group, department or university?

Identifying stakeholders

In addition to Arjun and Camila, the department/faculty could be collectively considered as another stakeholder. There may be pressures associated with funding resulting from other PhD students and there may be guidelines on the appropriate number of students a professor should have. The existing PhD students and the research group are typically stakeholders as the decision affects them and should reflect fairness in the selection of PhD students. Arjun's other colleagues and collaborators may also be stakeholders as the decision has an impact on Arjun's available time for different work tasks. Arjun's family is a further stakeholder as his decision may have a knock-on effect on his home life as well.

Understanding rights and responsibilities

In this case, rights and responsibilities are more moral and social in nature, and typically not codified in formal guidelines or contracts. The university may have guidelines on who is entitled to apply for a PhD position, but it is unlikely to have a process that guarantees a place in a doctorate programme for all qualifying to apply. Typically, as a supervisor Arjun has a right to decide who to accept as a student, though this decision is morally bound by demands of equal and fair treatment of applications and students. Camila, on the other hand, possesses rights to have her application treated fairly and even be selected based on merit, as long as new students are accepted. This type of examination of rights often requires re-visiting the original ethical question: are the definitions of rights and responsibilities in the end at the heart of this issue?

Defining options

The options for Arjun are simple on the outset: he either accepts Camila or he does not. However, defining options also requires the decision-maker to consider the impact and outcomes of these options in some detail. The potential impact of this decision on Camila may be life-changing – with her abandoning research aspirations – or benign – as she has applied to numerous other research groups as well. The decision to accept Camila may also have a positive or negative impact on Arjun: Camila may require a lot of attention, which can significantly restrict his other options or leave Camila poorly supervised; or Camila may turn out to be a student who inspires others and creates a great collective among PhD students and thus reduces the supervision burden Arjun already has. While these outcomes are hypothetical, it can help Arjun to understand the impact of his decision to consider best- and worst-case scenarios and estimate how likely they may be. Arjun may also consider the situation more broadly – could someone else become a second supervisor for Camila perhaps, or could he recommend Camila for a colleague with fewer students?

Recognising the ethical question

Arjun has an option to view the decision as balancing benefit and harm for all stakeholders, or he could as easily justify viewing it as a task to identify boundaries of desirable behaviour for a professor. He may also choose to look at the question from both perspectives. He could identify that an ideal professor for him is someone who seeks to maximise benefit – for example, either in relation to his students or for the research community as a whole. The choice of the question will focus the decision-maker on capturing certain details of the situation and seeking a way to form a decision that will be supported by them. Alternative ethical questions are also possible and justifiable. Often, if multiple questions are considered and they all indicate the same choice as the most justifiable, it is safer to assume that the choice is ethically robust.

Making a funding decision

Maryam is a member of a national research council. In the final round, two applications remain in consideration. On a scale of one to five (five being the best), application A has received evaluations of four and four from both expert academic evaluators, and application B has evaluations of five and one. Mathematically it appears that application A should be selected for funding due to its higher average evaluation score. Application A represents mainstream research and is excellent in that category. However, application B appears more innovative. It is interdisciplinary and applies a new methodological approach. Based on the written review, Maryam suspects that one of the experts has disliked the approach and thus given the application such a low score. Maryam knows it would be easy and straightforward to present application A to be funded based on the evaluations. However, the funding body has a new strategy of funding innovative research projects, creating new methodologies and connections across disciplines. Maryam wonders whether choosing application B is ignoring the appropriate role of the expert evaluators and taking on their role? Or is this what she is actually asked to do as a council member?

Maryam's position in the research council is, by its nature, an ethical one. There is no scientific or other type of formula to determine the best research plan; therefore, a decision will always include an element of judgement involving values, preferences and/or beliefs, which often take the form of goals, aims or criteria. What we aim for is informed by what we value; and the criteria we use reveals how we value different aspects. Maryam's task is to combine different selection criteria and prepare a recommendation to the council. Maryam's ethical question could therefore relate to aims and criteria: how to interpret the research council's policies and which application is the best match to them. She can also consider her own role and query what rights has she to make decisions, particularly without unanimous support from the academic expert evaluations.

Identifying stakeholders

Stakeholders include Maryam herself, the applicants and the research council, which makes collective decisions. The academic experts are also included as they have a key role in the selection process. Secondary stakeholders could include future applicants as the decision may influence their application process – who braves applying with an innovative research plan if one has never previously been successful? The decision also has an indirect impact on scientific policy and the research field in general.

Understanding rights and responsibilities

Applicants have a right to a fair and transparent application process. They may or may not have a right to appeal the council's decision. Maryam and the research council are bound by the policies of the council to promote innovative research projects. They also have a right (and responsibility?) to interpret the selection criteria and council policies in the light of their own scientific expertise and experience.

Defining options

There are two clear options, funding either application A or B (assuming the council has a policy against partial funding of projects, which would open a host of other options). The outcome of the decision is that one project will be completed and the other will possibly remain unfunded. It is not easy to estimate the likelihood and impact of the decision from the perspective of the unsuccessful application because there are multiple other funding options and structures to complete the project. The council can also consider what the funding decisions 'look like' from the outside; what do they tell applicants and other research stakeholders about the council, its policies and procedures? Funding application B could be perceived as incomprehensible because not everyone is likely to perceive or agree on the innovative elements. On the other hand, the decision could be identified as a brave one, which encourages applications that open new research directions, even when they may not all be successful. It is also possible to consider the impact of the decision from the perspective of the academic experts. Diverting significantly from their evaluations in the decision-making may have a demoralising impact on them and thus may reduce their willingness to participate in future funding rounds. The decision may also influence Maryam's motivation to be part of the council: is the council just a mechanical entity confirming expert opinions or a dynamic decision-making body with its own will?

Recognising the ethical question

After considering the stakeholders, rights and responsibilities, and options, it is possible to see the ethical issues more clearly. For Maryam the ethical challenge is to identify the option that will maximise the benefit. This is challenging because of the diversity in the stakeholders as well as limited information on the outcome of each option. When decision-making is complex, we have to apply many assumptions, which typically align directly with what we believe about people, what we know about our context, as well as the position we represent. Therefore Maryam's ethical question is largely about whose interests she is going to adopt as a priority.

MAKING ETHICAL CHOICES

The previous section looked at the process of recognising ethical issues. The focus was on the ways we can structure the process and thus improve our understanding of the ethical question in dialogue. Once the ethical issue has been identified, it is essential to find a reasoned response to it. Multiple different approaches can be used in the search for a solution. Three broad approaches are described in this section: *consequentialist*, *principled*, and *virtue* approaches (Figure 1.3).

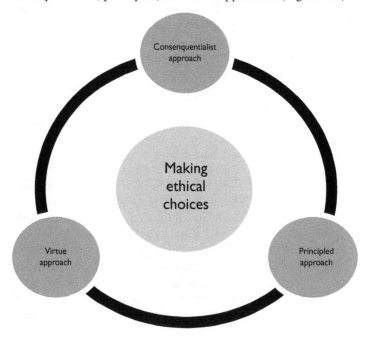

Figure 1.3 Making ethical choices.

They all have their roots in long philosophical traditions, mainly within Western philosophy. They are all founded within certain values and worldviews describing how to arrive at a judgement of what is valuable, good and worthwhile. One is not superior to another, and often an essential part of reasoned ethical decision-making involves a process of choosing a decision-making approach itself. A transparent ethical process includes the explanation of why and how an ethical approach has been used.

Consequentialist approaches

Consequentialist approaches are focused on the outcomes of an ethical choice. In very simple terms, if the outcome is the best possible one, the decision is ethically justified. The process of delivering an outcome itself does not influence the ethical evaluation of the decision. In these approaches it is common to talk about maximising net utility, that is the best possible positive balance between benefit and harm (hence the commonly used term *utilitarian*, according to one philosophical tradition), meaning the best ethical choice is the one that maximises the intended benefit in relation to unintended harm (Figure 1.4). One of the guiding thoughts in the consequentialist approach is the value placed on the ability to gain the best possible outcome and not foregoing an opportunity to achieve what is considered as ideal.

Determining the following parameters is an essential part of using a consequentialist approach. These can be used in guided dialogue as key questions in creating both an understanding and shared foundation for making decisions.

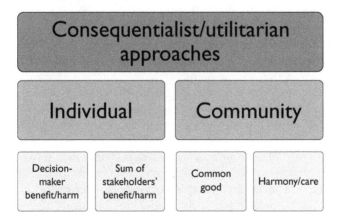

Figure 1.4 Consequentialist approaches.

Whose benefit and harm are included?

One of the fundamental aspects of consequentialist approaches is its rationality and sense of equality. The decision-maker is removed and the decision-making process is distanced to make space to look at the outcome as objectively as possible. Consequentialism has a number of philosophical traditions and while they share these basic principles, they often differ significantly in the way they include and define stakeholders in the process of measuring benefit and harm.

On one side, the approach can be based on individual stakeholders whose benefit and harm can be either known or estimated. The decision-making process is then principally to sum up the accumulated benefit and harm for each stakeholder and the ethical decision is the one maximising benefit for the largest number of stakeholders. Identification of stakeholders in understanding the ethical question has the most direct impact on this ethical decision-making approach.

Another sub-group of the individualistic approach is the assumption that we have only one stakeholder, whose interests have ethical validity for the decision. Typically, the one stakeholder is also the decision-maker. This approach is often related to the economic concept of an 'invisible hand', where seeking individual benefit also creates public good.[5] It can also be a purely hedonistic concept, suggesting that each person has ethical responsibility only to himself or herself and egoistic decision-making can have deep ethical acceptability.

A third consequentialist approach considers collectives as stakeholders, allowing consideration of stakeholders like universities, research fields or research communities to have ethically valid benefit and harm, which cannot be reduced to the sum of the benefit and harm defined by the individuals who are part of these collectives. Defining collectives as stakeholders has the challenge of many collectives being nested and overlapping, while having different definitions of benefit and harm. For example, an interdisciplinary research team is nested within a university but also overlapping with the different research fields it combines and with its international collaborators. Therefore, it can be difficult to determine benefit and harm for collectives and communities. However, this approach allows a broader view to consider benefit and harm from a non-individual, and often hedonistic, perspective. In the philosophical tradition, this approach is typically known as communitarianism, which highlights the importance of tradition and social context in ethical reasoning. This importance is founded within the understanding of social nature of individuals and the value of communities as themselves.[6]

The fourth way of looking at stakeholders is to focus on relationships and placing the connection between individuals as the key stakeholder in ethical decision-making. The decision-maker is always seen as interdependent and within a context. This approach has a foundation in the value of harmony and collaboration and the harm and benefit are understood through the impact of a decision on the well-being of relationships. This ethic-of-care approach adds a contextual perspective, which allows the study of ethical decisions without taking an objective and distant standpoint. The human relationships and affections are thus considered as valid ethical considerations.[7]

Determining definitions for consequences (benefit/harm)

In the utilitarian tradition, the original definition for benefit and harm was happiness/unhappiness.[8] In most Western countries at least, liberal economic theory has simple principles in which the benefit and harm are reduced to a single monetary measure with profits/income as benefits and losses/costs as harm. In ethical decision-making these simplistic definitions are rarely the most appropriate. Benefits are typically related to things, actions, outcomes and feelings that stakeholders seek and want to obtain; harm is the opposite collection to be avoided. In this perspective, benefit and harm embody what the stakeholders value in life. In research, benefits could be described as meaningful results or applications following from the results, successful funding applications, accepted publications, awards, collaborative opportunities or the pure joy of doing research. One of the challenges in this approach is to compare different types of benefit or harm together, which are rarely quantifiable in single measures. For example, wasted research funds could be considered as harm if a longitudinal study does not produce clear answers, while at the same time the project has given many early-career academics a great opportunity to learn within a funded project, which could be counted as a benefit. Research on animals also results in harm for the animal subjects, but possible benefit through results improving health.[9] Therefore, skilled use of consequentialist methods requires explicit dialogue on the definitions of benefit and harm before it is possible to understand the decision-making process.

Measuring consequences

Comparing benefit and harm is essential for the consequentialist approaches. Maximising net benefit is the key to determining the most ethical decision. In practice, this rational and structured principle turns out to be very complicated, because the measurements of harm and benefit are vague and often lacking in any true quantifiability. For example, while social impact is an essential criterion for many research funding decisions, there is no systemic measurement for it even within a discipline, let alone across disciplines. We can try to use virtual scales to compare the social impact, but there is no way to calibrate the process. In our everyday conversation it is equally difficult to make sense of statements like 'Ren is five times happier than Airi' and possibly even more challenging to comprehend comparisons like 'Ren experiences three times more happiness than Airi experiences safety.' Similar challenges are apparent when comparing research results from a fast-moving technological field to a longitudinal study in social sciences. In reality, comparisons between incompatible benefit and harm are an unavoidable part of complex decision-making. This is one of the reasons why ethical questions rarely have simple and straightforward answers. For some, this aspect of ethical decision-making is a source of great frustration and for others it appears as a great challenge and intrigue, which opens an opportunity for deeper thinking and collective dialogue.

Timeframe for benefit and harm

The comparisons between benefit and harm can significantly change when we alter the timeframe within which they are considered. For example, large genetic studies may have very limited benefits within the first 3–5 years, but possibly significant benefits in the 10–20-year perspective. If research indicates a new and more effective way to teach, adoption of the new approach may originally yield only harm (economic cost, confusion, time cost, etc.), but may yield significant benefits after a few decades. In the current economic climate society is increasingly adopting a short-term approach to measuring benefit and harm, sometimes down to quarterly reporting cycles. In contrast, it may be ethically appropriate to consider future generations as the appropriate framing of benefit and harm, as is commonly suggested for decisions related to ecology and natural resources. From an ethical perspective, it is important to consider and question the timeframe for analysing benefit and harm and prepare reasons for choosing any given framework.

As a summary of the consequentialist approaches, it is important to understand the complexity of defining benefit and harm in a system that on the surface looks attractively simple and rational to use to make ethical decisions. It would appear ideal to have empirical facts supporting the identification of harm and benefit to different stakeholders and thus be able to give a reliable estimate of the net benefit with each considered option. In reality, the decision-maker has to settle for often contradictory and insufficient evidence to evaluate benefit and harm, further complicated by the incompatibility of them and the challenges of identifying stakeholders clearly and distinctly. If the aim is to maximise benefit and the information we have is limited, it is necessary to use other variables in the decision-making process. Values, psychological patterns, the importance placed on aims and goals and previous experiences all influence the analysis of harm and benefit and how they are weighted against each other.

Despite these challenges, the consequentialist approaches provide the decision-maker with great tools for accessing ethical questions. For both individuals and collectives making decisions, the consequentialist approach offers ways to structure the ethical question into sub-questions, which may in turn re-focus the decision-making. The aspiration to understand benefit and harm in relation to different stakeholders and timeframes gives the ethical challenge shape and depth. It is not a formula into which values can be entered to result in the ethical decision, but it makes the ethical decision-making process more visible and transparent. It also supports collective dialogue, where values and aspirations can be given a name and focus, and it is possible to identify points of agreement and disagreement more accurately and thus open the door to finding a shared solution.

Principled approaches

This cluster of approach changes the focus to the decision-making *process* rather than the *outcome* as was described above. The foundation is the principles and/or rules that have been identified prior to and independently of the decision-making process; the decision-making process is bound by these principles and/or rules. From an ethical perspective, it is more important to follow the rule than to produce a particular type of outcome. Therefore, the most significant difference between these approaches is the definition of what makes a decision ethical – the outcome or the process.

The principled approach (Figure 1.5) has its foundation in the understanding of independently identifiable rules that should be applied to all decision-making situations (rule of universality[10]). The key is the understanding of these rules prior to making an ethical decision and thus the key to good decision-making is both the understanding of ethical rules and the commitment to adhering to them. Typically these rules have only limited flexibility within their contextual application. The decision-maker cannot choose to uphold a rule in one instance and then choose to ignore it in another if the outcome of following the rule no longer feels desirable or the rule becomes difficult to follow. Similarly, if the research group has a rule to offer a PhD position to all applicants with a successful completion of a particular earlier degree, they could not refuse it to a candidate even if they seemed difficult to work with.

The origin of rules divides principled approaches into two main types. In one approach, the rules are considered to exist independently of the decision-makers as some kind of divine and/or natural law. These laws have a permanent and inflexible nature. The task of the decision-maker is to study and learn to recognise these rules and make sense of them within their life. Depending on the origin

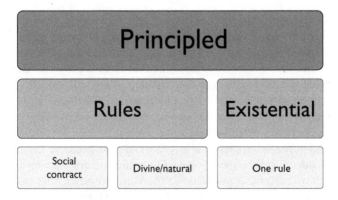

Figure 1.5 Principled approaches.

of rules, this task requires either logical and rational thinking or spiritual contemplation. Examples of this type of rule include 'do not kill' or 'do not lie'.[11]

Alternatively, rules can be viewed as binding agreements born of negotiations between stakeholders and designed for the benefit of the society and its individuals. This 'rule utilitarian' approach takes two steps. First, to understand the dynamics and complexity within a society or community and to define its key benefits. From this understanding is born a set of rules that allow that community to flourish. These rules are applied in a single decision-making situation as rigid rules, but they are open to negotiation in the broader context. Typically, these rules define boundaries and rights to freedom, safety and property. The legislative process follows the same logic as can be applied in ethical decision-making.

The research community at large has sets of rules and guidelines that are considered universal and binding. These rules give research work a foundation within which collaboration, trust in research results and individual credit are made possible. These general principles typically include at least the following:[12]

1 **Scientific honesty:** forbids fabrication and falsification of results and biased presentation of others' work.
2 **Carefulness:** aim is to do research of the highest standard and with the greatest accuracy.
3 **Transparency:** in relation to results, used methods, theories and equipment, which allow critical assessment of all research work.
4 **Recognising achievements of others:** not adopting work of others as one's own and appropriately referring to the work of others.
5 **Ethically sustainable methodologies:** in reference to data collection and research design in respect of human, animal and inanimate research subjects.
6 **Academic freedom:** researchers should be able to interpret their results and follow research avenues based on their academic understanding.
7 **Social responsibility:** make results available when they have an impact on well-being and have adequate scientific validity.

In this approach, even though rules have an inflexible nature, their application is rarely simple or unproblematic. Carefulness, for example, is already in its nature a concept with a sliding scale, which is used to calibrate an acceptable space between disregard to detail and level of detail focus that forbids progress. Defining and exploring rules and guidelines is an essential step in guided dialogue. It is safe to assume that people understand them differently and dialogue is necessary for creating a shared understanding. Often what is understood by rules or guidelines turns out to be the key ethical choice to be made.

The second principled approach is here labelled existentialism. In this approach the only considered rule relates to protecting individual freedom to follow one's own life path and ethical consideration. There are no other rules than to make sure one's decisions do not limit the freedom of others. Beyond this, the ethically appropriate decision is based solely on the reflections of the individual on what is good in life. The task of every individual is to give meaning to their own life, which cannot be formed through others or given by community or traditions. This often resonates with modern liberal economic theory, with the focus on choice and individualism and the respect of individual freedom.[13]

Virtue ethics

Virtue ethics is the third and last ethical approach to be considered here. This changes the focus to the individual or collective making the decision, in contrast to the consequentialist approaches focusing on the outcome and principled approaches focusing on rules guiding the process. In virtue ethics the decision-maker is fundamentally reflecting the decision in relation to the type of person he or she is and desires to be. If, for example, the ethical question relates to telling the truth, a consequentialist approach would lead one to consider whether truth telling will lead to the best possible outcome; principled thinking would suggest that telling a lie is wrong; while a virtue approach reflects on whether one is/ wants to be an honest person. Having a virtue is more than doing actions that align with a particular value, it is a multidimensional attitude in life which in relation to honesty, for example, would suggest that the person will seek to spend time with honest people, bring up his or her children to be honest and despise even stories of dishonesty. Virtue has its roots in Ancient Greek philosophy and has recently been given more modern interpretations.[14]

In ethical decision-making this approach can help the decision-maker by asking whether each option reflects the virtues and values the decision-maker holds important and aspires to have. For the cases above, it is possible for Arjun to consider this decision in relation to being a good professor; what does it mean and how well does he accomplish this aim? Maryam could similarly consider the virtues embodied within a research council member and how well making each decision would reflect those virtues. In guided dialogue it may be helpful to use virtue in a less personal way. For example, we can ask what we think an ideal university teacher would be like or what are the virtues in research or academic administration.

It is possible to consider the previous approaches within the virtue approach; for example, considering which consequentialist aims would be virtuous or how a virtuous person would act in relation to certain rules. Virtue ethics is not, however, a different way to dress the previous approaches. It provides a different approach by focusing on the deeper sense a decision-maker has about the impact of decisions on their personhood. From this perspective, it is significant if a certain outcome has been achieved as part of a deliberate action rather than an accidental outcome of different intentions. For example, if Arjun accepts Camila as a student because he believes it would be a positive and rewarding collaboration for both of them, it would be significantly different to Arjun making the decision based on Camila's great looks. Similarly, if Camila had observed inappropriate behaviour between Arjun and other female students, her decision to speak with a desire to cause trouble has a different ethical merit than a decision made based on her understanding of fairness and equality between supervisor and student. Intentions are often included in principled decision-making as well, but the virtue approach highlights the ethical weight of intention.

When reflecting on virtues, a simple night-/daytime test can reveal the potential challenges of a decision in relation to virtues. If one would be happy to tell everyone about the decision and its motives, it would have passed the daytime test; on the other hand, if the decision keeps on affecting the decision-maker's sleep, it has failed the night-time test. Virtue is about consistency within the decision-maker and making decisions that truly reflect the values and virtues the decision-maker believes in.

***

Every ethical decision-making approach provides a valuable way to look at an ethical problem. The decision-making process is often cyclical rather than linear, and different approaches and steps in ethical analysis are applied in order to arrive at both an understanding of the ethical problem as well as the reasoned solution to it. How the decision-maker defines the question or identifies stakeholders will most likely change during the decision-making process. For this reason, the process typically requires revisiting previous steps and re-applying different approaches. Similarly, it is not possible to define at the outset which approach is the most appropriate in each situation. The interest and challenge in ethical decision-making is born from this very ability to reason and justify different ways to arrive at an ethical decision. The core of the process is increased transparency in the definitions used and approaches applied. These are key steps in developing guided dialogue

Using different approaches in sequence is often a fruitful way to arrive at an answer. For example, using a principled approach first could allow ruling out options that violate moral or legislated rules. The next stage could apply a consequential approach and consider which of the remaining options would best produce a desired outcome. The virtue approach could be used as a way of checking the match of the choice with the sense of self to allow the decision-maker a sense on consistency and coherence. People typically have a decision-making approach they use most regularly and sometimes it can be beneficial to try out a less favoured method to see how thinking can be expanded and fine-tuned.

The awareness of the ethical decision-making cycle and the approaches will also assist in understanding how others make ethical decisions. The ability to make reasoned decisions will also assist in raising shared ethical problems to be considered constructively together and create an understanding of why a common solution may be difficult to find. For example, in the ethical debate involving the use of laboratory animals in research, those supporting this methodology typically provide consequentialist reasons regarding the positive balance of benefit and harm, while those opposing the use of animals provide principled reasons for giving animals a set of rights. It is difficult to find a common language between these two approaches when one uses the arguments relating to outcomes and the other refers to principles. The ability to understand how the opposing argument is structured does provide a possibility of understanding, and if a common solution is beyond reach at least more amicable disagreement can be achieved and space is created for ongoing dialogue.

NOTES

1 For example, see the Vancouver guidelines at: www.icmje.org/recommendations.
2 See, for example, J. Rest (1986), *Moral Development. Advances in Research and Theory*, New York: Praeger.
3 See, for example, H.M. Clarkeburn, J. Roger Downie and R.G.S. Matthew (2003), Measuring ethical development in life sciences students: A study using Perry's developmental model, *Studies in Higher Education* 28:4, 443–456.
4 On the ability to recognise ethical questions and the development of that ability, see H. Clarkeburn (2002), A test for ethical sensitivity in science, *Journal of Moral Education* 31:4, 439–453.
5 The invisible hand theory is attributed to the Scottish economist Adam Smith. The original text can be found in his 1776 book *An Inquiry into the Nature and Causes of the Wealth of Nations*.
6 Philosophers promoting communitarian thinking and analysis include Alasdair MacIntyre, Michael Sandel, Charles Taylor and Michael Walzer.
7 Ethics of care is often associated with feminist philosophy. Philosophers best known for developing the theory include Carol Gilligan and Nel Noddings.
8 See, for example, John Stuart Mill's 1863 *Utilitarianism*, or the writing of Jeremy Bentham, e.g. Introduction to the Principles of Morals and Legislation (1780), who famously defined the 'fundamental axiom': 'the greatest happiness of the greatest number that is the measure of right and wrong'.
9 Most animal research ethics committees apply a consequentialist approach to quantifying the acceptability of the use of animals contrasted with the potential benefits of the research results.
10 See, for example, Kant's writing on maxims to be willed as universal laws: http://plato.stanford.edu/entries/kant-moral.
11 On the side of rationality, Immanuel Kant's theory of categorical imperative is a good place to start. Christian philosophers Saint Augustine, Duns Scotus and Thomas Aquinas have written extensively on the divine source of ethical rules.
12 Collected from a number of sources, including the European Code of Conduct for Research Integrity (2011). For many national codes, start with D.B. Resnik, L.M. Rasmussen and G.E. Kissling (2015), An international study of research misconduct policies, *Accountability in Research* 22:5, 249–266 (www.ncbi.nlm.nih.gov/pmc/articles/PMC4449617/pdf/nihms691915.pdf.)
13 Sartre, Nietzsche and Kierkegaard are often considered the key existential philosophers. The theory is typically not considered as a normative ethical theory stating what is good in life, but due to its resonance with modern economic theory it is included here as a potential approach to making ethical decisions.
14 For more in-depth study of virtue ethics, start with Aristotle's *Nichomachian Ethics*, as well as writings by Elizabeth Anscombe, Alasdair MacIntyre and Bernard Williams.

Chapter 2

Doing research

The main ethical themes and values in doing research are:

1   The researcher is a member of a research community and has to follow
     common guidelines and rules, but has also individual goals and aims.
2   The safest way of doing research is to follow mainstream thinking and
     settings, while one of the basic values of research is to be able to
     challenge previous research and transcend boundaries.
3   There is always a certain time pressure in doing research, which may
     lead to slipping in principles.

Approaching ethics by using guided dialogue typically requires researchers
and research communities to consider the following key ethical issues when
doing research:

• Are all research questions equal from an ethical point of view?
• Which ethical issues are connected with selecting methodology
  and approach?
• How does the research community discuss the balance between harm
  (e.g. for research objects) and cost (e.g. expensive research infrastructure), on one side, and on the other, the possibilities to do
  ambitious and ground-breaking research?
• What does responsibility of a researcher towards his or her employer
  mean in the research context?
• Which kind of decisions and choices are researchers obliged to make as
  members of a research community?
• How do individual researchers and the research community as a whole
  handle the grey areas surrounding strict ethical rules?

The research ethics guidelines and rules compiled in many countries during the last 25 years concern mostly the process of doing research.[1] The striking faults and shortcomings discussed in public are usually violations of these strict principles.[2] The agreements and understanding that has led to these rules has been a major step towards a new, more ethically conscious, culture within research communities. However, in the real discussion on research ethics questions, these violations of ethical guidelines comprise only the tip of the iceberg. They raise the question about the reasons why a researcher has violated ethical guidelines of research. This question is often psychological, organisational and/or educational rather than ethical. While pondering on the reasons for violations is interesting, the community has an even more important task in engaging with everyday ethical questions in doing research and working in academia. In the process of creating an ethically conscious research community we have to speak of the iceberg under the water, where we find a lot of complicated and unclear situations. While the tip of the iceberg may be clear and simple, everyday ethical questions are typically situated in the vast grey area, commonly hidden from view. This chapter aims to provide tools to discuss these often obscured issues using guided dialogue.

Ethical questions follow researchers in all phases of research: in the selection of the topic; when the methods are determined; when the group agrees on the distribution of labour; when deciding whether the results are reliable enough; and when the study is ready to be published. Recognising and providing reasoned solutions to these types of ethical questions is a core professional skill in research.

For example, one of the guidelines of research is the strict prohibition of any kind of falsification or fabrication of results. However, in reality a researcher meets complicated situations where guidelines do not give a clear answer. Let us suppose that the results of an experiment do not unequivocally support any suggested hypothesis or theory. However, if only a few of the results were excluded, the situation would be quite different. It is quite clear that a researcher cannot just remove some results in order to reach a desired conclusion. On the other hand, sometimes it is correct to brush aside odd results that are caused by an evident mistake or based on a standard practice for 'noise reduction' in a particular field. Often, it is not clear whether the outlying results fall into a category that allows them to be reasonably and appropriately omitted from the analysis and subsequent conclusions. An ethically solid, and also wise, option in this situation would be to repeat the experiment and collect more evidence. However, this is not always possible due to, for example, time or funding pressures. Another option is to openly discuss the decision to omit results in the following publications. The researcher may think that this will decrease the possibility of the paper being published and thus faces an ethical question requiring the decision.

How and when outlier data can be removed is an example of an ongoing need for dialogue within a research community. This dialogue focuses on both methodology and ethics, which is typical as ethical questions are in most cases embedded within the research questions themselves. A researcher is able to take part in this dialogue only after comprehension of wider contexts of research. This requires awareness that individual decisions all reflect concerns beyond the researcher her- or himself and the methods/materials. Almost everything is part of a larger whole in which individual research belongs to the global network of researchers closely engaged with society as a whole. Ethical validity of research methods and outcomes is an important element of ethical dialogue between the research community and society.

This chapter focuses on the actual process of doing research. A stereotypical understanding of research is based on the assumption that researchers publish the results of their own studies in scientific publications. Indeed, this is often the case: science progresses on the basis of new materials and data collected by individual researchers or research groups. These may be results of laboratory experiments in which certain materials or physical laws are tested or test persons are set into strict planned situations or they have answers to a set of questions. Data can be collected also by interviewing people or observing their behaviour.

However, not all research is based on results reached by the researchers themselves. One can develop new statistical analyses or qualitative findings by using a data/material commonly available, e.g. statistical data on the weather, people's personal data or opinions, texts produced by people or data based on longitude time series. Much of this material can be collated without any intention for it to be used in research.

Publishing new analysis based on concrete data is not the only way researchers develop science. Science is also progressed by creating theories, methods or models which help us to do better research and understand the essence of phenomena more deeply. In some fields the researcher's role is to bring out fresh interpretations of well-known texts, such as the Bible, Shakespeare's *Hamlet*, or Wittgenstein's *Tractatus Logico-philosophicus*. New interpretations may be based on a better contextualisation of these works or a new point of view that has gone unnoticed by previous researchers.

Results in the common language are often interpreted only to mean the first type of results stemming from actual investigation and collection of data. However, when we speak of research results in this book, we explicitly refer to all possible outcomes and findings made by a researcher, not only concrete results of experiments made by the researcher his- or herself. This broader understanding of 'results' allows us to capture research endeavours more completely and to show how ethical issues are present regardless of how we do research.

This chapter applies the guided dialogue process to understanding the everyday ethical issues in doing research. Guided dialogue helps to make visible everyday small ethical questions and allows communities to approach them collectively. When discussing concrete ethical challenges, we will often put them in this larger collective, and sometimes global, context. As guided dialogue is a systematic way of understanding an issue rather the producing simple answers, this chapter, like all those that follow, is filled with questions to support the process of decision-making in practice.

Our discussion begins with three important elements of ethical reasoning, as described in Chapter 1: identification of stakeholders; rights and responsibilities; and defining options in the context of doing research work. We will then explore the decision-making process through cases and examples. The three ethical approaches are coded: [CONSEQUENTIALIST], [PRINCIPLED] and [VIRTUE].

Identifying stakeholders

An important phase in ethical thinking is the identification of stakeholders. The **researcher** him- or herself is an evident stakeholder when discussing ethical issues in the process of doing research. She or he may approach the ethical question as an individual or as a member of a **research team**. The forms of cooperation vary. In biosciences and medicine a research team comprises half a dozen to ten researchers. It is possible for hundreds of researchers to take part in large projects like accelerator experiments in physics, where each of them has a very specific role in the group. On the other hand, in sociology scholars may still write books alone, but in the foreword they may thank 20 colleagues who have been somehow involved in the process. Independent of the scale and cohesiveness of the team, the researcher has a certain influence on close **colleagues**. In many cases, the research group comprises also **laboratory assistants**, **IT-specialists** and other **supporting personnel**. They may not be mentioned as a co-author in publications, but they are inescapably also stakeholders who must be taken into consideration in ethical thinking.

The **research community** is a definite stakeholder. In most fields, there are always several competing research groups. Every move taken by one of them influences the others – for example, in the grant application processes they all participate in. Research by its very nature is a global endeavour and that is why the global research community is a stakeholder as well. Although the influence is often invisible and very small, the general idea of research is that every researcher is building the joint worldwide stock of knowledge, which is then globally available for other researchers. Thus, it is possible and reasonable for an individual researcher to consider ethical issues from a global perspective. This is especially relevant in the selection of a research theme/question.

Enablers of research, the organisation (faculty/university/research centre) that provides a physical environment for research and various funding bodies and agencies (national/regional/global), comprise an important group of stake-holders. Among financers of research there are different actors: state-owned funders of basic research and innovation (research councils, agencies, ministries, etc.), private non-for-profit foundations as well as commercial and for-profit sources of funding. They set their own rules for spending money and may demand results that are in accord with their own goals and principles. They are enablers of research in the proper sense of the word, because a substantial part of research would not be conducted without their support. We return to the ethical questions connected to funding research in Chapter 7.

We already mentioned one group of **users** of results of research, namely colleagues forming the research community. A further important group of users located outside the academic world include commercial enterprises, not-for-profit organisations and the public sector. Benefits transfer also to the level of individuals. Schoolchildren, patients in hospitals, consumers and citizens in their everyday lives may gain from the new knowledge produced by researchers. The benefit coming from research is always possible, but never certain. Individuals and other beneficiaries are only potential stakeholders of research to a differing degree, depending on the applicability of the research and mechanisms of transferring research into practice. However, this potentiality does not mean they may be forgotten in considering the harm and benefit of research.

The **research subjects** are evident stakeholders whenever research uses individuals or material from and by them in any way as part of the research. If we are dealing with surveys, the number of stakeholders may easily exceed thousands. When a researcher observes wild animals in nature, their role is naturally quite different from that of experimental animals, but nevertheless they must be taken into consideration. In addition, it may be necessary for a researcher to think of whether the research inquiry influences different types of stakeholders or stakeholder groups, like a lake ecosystem, a historically important object, or a school class. In most cases, one can see an immediate effect: changes in water, the object wears out in the researcher's hands or for the school class the visit of the researcher is an important event. Therefore, the subjects of research are important stakeholders that must be taken into account in all research design.

In guided dialogue it is essential to explore and explicitly identify stakeholders within the context of the actual choice to be made. Stakeholders cannot be assumed as the context is essential in understanding who they are.

CONSEQUENTIALIST

Stakeholder identification is crucially important for all considerations of consequences. Without knowing stakeholders, definitions and comparisons of utility are at the very least weak, if not pointless. When considering harm and benefit estimates and comparisons, the stakeholders are often considered in the light of research goals and costs in both time and resources. In addition, stakeholders may need to be prioritised against each other – for example, should we give more value to objects of art than new information about that particular era, or to animals rather than the potential for new medical knowledge?

PRINCIPLED

Identifying stakeholders has a direct link in considering their rights and responsibilities. This embodies an important ethical consideration, where we are asked to define whether it is even reasonable to speak about rights in relation to fruit flies or historical objects. Alternatively, the defining of stakeholders invites us to explore whether there are inherent rights or responsibilities that can never be lost.

Understanding rights and responsibilities

In this section we focus on the researcher perspective. In reference to responsibilities, the researcher has at least three different kinds of responsibilities to consider. There are legal responsibilities set typically by national legislation, including privacy, treatment of research animals or use of genetic material. In addition to these, there are research guidelines set by national committees, regional (e.g. EU) agreements and international collectives (e.g. the Singapore Statement) describing responsibilities, particularly towards colleagues and enablers of research as well as towards core research principles like honesty, diligence, accuracy and giving credit to others. Unwritten and silent responsibilities formed by the research group, field and/or institution are the third source of responsibilities to consider. All of these responsibilities define boundaries within which research must take place if the researcher desires to continue working within the research community. One of the key challenges appears when different responsibilities become contradictory and upholding them simultaneously appears difficult if not impossible.

These responsibilities produce certain corresponding rights as well. Researchers have a right to be recognised for the work they have done. They also have a right to trust the work of other researchers and to build on their work. A considerably more complex question is to define a right to academic freedom, which is often formally noted as a right in itself. If we operate within the boundaries given by responsibilities, are we completely free to study whatever we are interested in? Or is there an unwritten limitation to this freedom to study something 'useful'? This question is an enduring one and has become increasingly more significant in the current era of external funding. For this reason we will visit this question several times in this book.

Another interesting issue to consider is researchers' responsibilities towards the enablers of research – in other words, the funders and the institutional context. Are all responsibilities fulfilled when the research is done with the greatest care and adherence to research principles? On the other hand, is there a reasonable duty for the researcher to include or accept suggestions for methodology or choice of topic? At the same time, we can ask whether the researcher has responsibilities towards the research community to conduct certain types of research or at least conduct their research in a particular way. Or is it rather a responsibility to remain independent to avoid excessive compliance pressures, traditions and expectations imposed by the research community in exchange for belonging?

Defining rights and responsibilities is an ongoing process. It reflects changes within the research community and society as a whole. Advances in technology, changes in knowledge or shifts within the social and natural environment often initiate these changes. It is vital for the research community to engage in this dialogue at all levels to create the best conditions for research and researchers to flourish.

Defining options

There are typically multiple options when responding to any ethical issue. Each option often supports a particular set of values, advances only some of the goals or reflect only partially values held by each stakeholder. A true ethical dilemma appears when all options require us to give up on an essential value or goal. On the other hand, we have a real winning option when we feel it aligns with all key values and goals held by key stakeholders. Guided dialogue can be used to explore options, evaluate them and seek further options where an ethical dilemma appears.

At the early stage of any research project the researchers are faced with a plethora of realistic and possible options. For example, there is an endless variety of possible themes to be studied. Of course, availability of equipment, research material and other external circumstances limit the reasonable alternatives for selecting the topic, but still the buffet of choices remains extensive.

When reasoning around options, different ethical approaches may be used to create questions and considerations within the dialogue that will clarify the options and how they align with values and goals:

- What is beneficial/harmful for the individual/
  research group/university/society?   [CONSEQUENTIALIST]
- What aligns best with the general principles
  of research?   [PRINCIPLED]
- How does an ideal researcher make this decision?   [VIRTUE]

In another example, when ethical issues appear in research collaborations, there are usually a vast number of options as a response. The challenge may be in the very number of options with uncertain outcomes or in the varied ways different stakeholders understand the options and the values they attach to them. Asking specific and guided questions will help to reveal true values and assist in managing uncertainty.

- How do I define the harm and benefit of each
  option to each stakeholder before I even start to
  evaluate the balance of harm and benefit?   [CONSEQUENTIALIST]
- Are there binding agreements that affect what
  can be done to resolve the problem?   [PRINCIPLED]
- How do I wish to appear in the research
  community and which options align with my
  vision for myself?   [VIRTUE]

When ethical issues appear during the research process there are always at least two options: to continue the research according to current process/plan/ methodology or to refrain from doing it. As the research develops, the latter option becomes increasingly problematic as different stakeholders have made commitments to achieving the identified research goals. To stop the project and to return the funding is usually too radical of an outcome for all parties. Typically, further options are available. These allow for negotiating alterations in one or more critical aspects of the process.

In the rest of the chapter we utilise these steps of defining stakeholders, rights and responsibilities as well as options, and explore key ethical issues in doing research. This is done to show how the guided dialogue approach can work in different phases of research. In the life of a researcher, research builds a chain whereby new topics grow upon the current work. This is why it is not easy to differentiate phases of research. However, from the point of view of ethical discussion, it is helpful to split research into smaller and more concrete phases which each typically generate their own ethical issues. At the same time, we see ethical reasoning as having a cyclical nature where previous decisions influence the new questions posed and many questions require several iterations before the conclusion of the research question or project.

In this chapter we will follow a typical and natural research cycle from the selection of the topic to the collection of material and application of research methodologies. The ethical issues arising from sharing research results will be the focus of Chapter 3.

SELECTING THE TOPIC

Research work commences with the selection of a research topic. This often self-evident step incorporates multiple ethical choices. The research topic may be selected in various different ways. Most common ones are a topic given by a supervisor, a research request from a client and a topic chosen by the researcher independently. As the last option represents the greatest level of freedom and thus ethical options, we will focus on it.

The researcher may pause to consider whether the topic is worth the time and effort. In other words, is the topic worthy of being investigated? It is possible to seek answers to this question from many perspectives. Within academic freedom the researcher is theoretically free to choose. However, the researcher is bound to consider at least some of the following, which are issues to be included in guided dialogue:

• **Compatibility.** How does this topic suit the research profile of my employer (university, department, research institute)? We can ask to what extent the employer should dictate research directions of individual researchers. Some level of coherence is typically justifiable from a utility perspective as it produces collective and accumulating benefits. Coherent research directions improve the quality of research in the given collective and allow better utilisation of resources. On the other hand, the search for new directions is a core part of research and a strong requirement for coherence may not be justifiable ethically if we hold as a principle the right to academic freedom. It may also be problematic as a very narrow research focus may lead to a dead end for the whole group. Finding a balance is partly an ethical negotiation requiring decisions on defining benefit and harm and the appropriate timelines to consider them in association with core rights and responsibilities.

- **Facilities.** Is it possible to follow the chosen research direction in the current facilities (equipment, supporting personnel and other required resources)? Because resources are always finite, it is reasonable to consider how they are best utilised. The answer to this is directly dependent on the overall research goals the collective has identified. Sharing resources requires continuous balancing between research goals and individual needs and rights.

- **Publication potential.** Are there appropriate and desirable forums to publish the research results? Publishing results is not only the most important measure of academic worth, but also a key principle around transparency and openness in research. It is easier to publish on well-established topics following familiar research traditions rather than finding a way to publish interdisciplinary research or work concluded with novel methodology. How far should we let the potential for publications direct our choice of research is another broad and fundamental ethical question around the core goals of research enterprise as a whole and to every individual directly.

- **Impact.** How do results influence the surrounding society? Is the research topic important for people outside the academic world? This leads us to consider stakeholders, particularly identifying whose harm and benefit we should focus on and how we choose our timescale. Impact-related considerations bring to the forefront traditional ethical debates on the possible value-based difference between applied and fundamental research. Researchers' personal attitudes to this question vary. We will return to ethical considerations around impact in Chapter 7.

- **Boundaries.** Do I step into someone else's research domain that may lead to social and personal challenges? Can anyone consider owning a research question? Owning a research topic may seem far-fetched, but every collective has its set of boundaries, personal chemistry, traditions and power plays. In a research community it is most often possible to function in a way that will not limit the freedom of others directly. However, it is still common for researchers to consider how many sacrifices and changes to their research plan they are ready to make in order to manage their social research environment. Again, we approach the questions on values held by the collective, individuals and choices between them.

- **Background knowledge.** Does the research team or I have enough existing background knowledge to complete the planned research? There are hardly any topics to be studied where no previous knowledge exists. All research requires knowing the already discovered. But, because time is limited and the amount of information is exponentially growing, it is justifiable to ask how much the researcher should know before they are appropriately prepared to research the topic or participate in a discussion on it. In some fields the existing knowledge pool is so large that a requirement for everyone to know it all would essentially lead to very limited time to do new research. So we have to draw a line somewhere and we cannot define that line in advance or from the outside.

- **Reputation.** How does the research topic influence our reputation? Research reputation is made out of different parts – research publications, participation in research activities (conferences, committees, seminars, etc.), and interaction with colleagues, students and administrators. The choice of a new research topic may threaten the existing reputation if it diverts from the known research path, particularly if this involves crossing boundaries described above. New directions could lead to dead ends and consume all the time available for the researcher. Similarly, an early career researcher may consider how to choose a research topic for maximum reputational gain – is it through a novel research topic or excellence in a known field? Would it be more advantageous to study the exotic wolf rather than the mundane fly? Would the study of a rare and serious disease be more influential than a study on the common cold? Behind these questions there are values around reputation, its definition and importance. These values guide our research goals.

All of the above questions are important, but most commonly the trump card is held by a different question – the availability of funding. All researchers, whether tenured or not, are expected to increase their research budget from an external source. At the same time there is considerably less funding available than the amount applied for. Therefore funding decisions directly influence the selection of research topics. Every researcher feels this pressure to choose research topics with the maximum funding potential.

This leads us to discuss the ethical questions around selection of research topic from a broader perspective. As funding directs the selection of research topics and directions, we need to explore possible values attached to the selection process. In this chapter we will look at the funding process from an individual researcher perspective; in Chapter 6 we will focus on collectively held values.

Due to funding structures, the trendiness of a research topic becomes a point of consideration in comparison to choosing a topic that has very little momentum. Trendy topics are likely to attract more funding than other topics. But if we always choose trendy topics, are we participating in a process where research becomes mainstreamed and locked into patterns that no longer serve the ultimate research purpose of discovery and novelty? Chasing trends encourages us to choose topics with known methodologies, quick and measurable outcomes and clear social application. It is reasonable to ask whether these considerations are appropriate ones for individual researchers. Maybe they should be the responsibility of collective decision-makers defining funding criteria and selecting successful projects. Ethical responsibility is often defined by an opportunity to choose differently. When funding pressures increase, it appears that the room for an individual researcher to choose risky topics with new untested methodologies may be diminished.

We may also consider topic selection from the perspective of global fairness. Can we justify that privileged and often Western researchers study only topics concerning themselves? Is it acceptable that research topics can be selected based on the national and individual ability to pay? This type of questioning will lead our dialogue to consider appropriate stakeholders of research and evaluate the impact of research results. At the same time it raises a question of rights and responsibilities. If we define stakeholders globally and impact in terms other than immediate ability to make financial profit, we open a completely new discussion on the purpose of research. We can illuminate this perspective by contrasting research topics of high blood pressure vs malaria; impact of global marketing vs start-up businesses in Africa; or variations in modern English vs study of Mpur, a completely unstudied language spoken by 7,000 people in West-Guinea.[3]

When completing a PhD, the topic selection is further limited by different criteria. The supervisor must approve of the topic and typically it has to be formally accepted by the faculty/department as well. In many research fields the student is accepted into a research group, where the topic must closely align with the work of the group. In some other fields the PhD work is much more independent and thus allows for broader selection of the topic. We will explore PhD topic selection more closely in Chapter 4.

Above we have touched upon the most common ethical questions that are inescapably part of research topic selection. We have offered very few answers along the way. These questions are designed to provide guideposts for guided dialogue. In addition, it is impossible to give answers. Topic selection is very context-specific and rich with values held by individual and collective stakeholders. The most important aspect is the ability to raise these questions, as questions can only be answered once they have been asked.

Next we move on to explore ethical issues and questions in the actual doing of research, the nitty-gritty of collecting samples/material/data, analysis and drawing conclusions.

MISCONDUCT

Research ethics literature has given great attention to forms of research misconduct typical at this stage of the research project – fabrication and falsification.

Fabrication refers to making up research data and falsification refers to altering the data in order to give a wrongful and distorted message about the research methodology and/or results. Both of these are considered completely at odds with the core research values of honesty, accuracy and transparency, as well as contradicting research goals of discovery and improvement. All research guidelines clearly and strongly forbid these activities as part of research. Most often fabrication and falsification are easy to see as dishonest and undesirable activities. We will focus on illuminating situations where the definitions are not so clear and we are asked to define what counts as fabrication or falsification in a particular field of study.

Scientific misconduct is intentional deception. Both words are important. Being **intentional** indicates that the person is aware of the fact that what is being done is against the rules and they choose to do what they are doing. **Deception** indicates that what is presented is not what should be truthfully presented. The audience, be it other researchers, the public or the funding body, is asked to believe something that is not a true account. The dishonesty can relate to the people involved, the methodologies used and/or the results presented. The audience is deceived essentially with a story that does not tell what has actually happened.

The reasons for scientific misconduct are various. You can probably recognise many of these as factors in your own research as they influence us all:

- time pressures, juggling multiple tasks and looming deadlines – the pressure to publish quickly is familiar to most researchers;
- the pressure to take steps to advance your career;
- the increasing pressures for funding research work e.g. with short-term funding cycles the expectations for significant results can be very high;
- pressures of other aspects of life, the desire for pleasure, other pursuits and family commitments affect most researchers;
- there might be internal or external pressure to become famous either within the research community or in society at large.

Research practice forms a continuum. At one end we have misconduct and at the other end we have good research practice. The ethical challenges are formed in the grey area in the middle when we are not sure if this is acceptable or not. Every research field has its own grey area. On the edges of this area we find the most fruitful questions for advancing guided dialogue.

The grey area around misconduct is important to recognise in your own field as every research field has its own unique patterns for misconduct. The ambiguity can be born from the use of statistics in a way that distorts the real findings: dealing with large data sets where with careful selection almost anything could be proven to be true; rich qualitative data that would allow your subjective interpretation to influence analysis greatly; or managing research conditions in a way that allows you to get the results you want while claiming to have had a different set-up or methodology.

It is everyone's responsibility to know what constitutes misconduct and to make choices to avoid it. Explicitly exploring the risks and potential will strengthen both the ability to avoid misconduct as well as increase the motivation to avoid it.

METHODOLOGY AND MATERIAL

Methodologies vary greatly between research fields, as well as within a field. This variety allows researchers to make choices in most cases. There are, however, research fields where the methodologies are established to a degree that new research is equivalent to turning the same mill with new grains.

Even when the choice of methodology is easy, its application will always carry ethical considerations. Many of the ethical questions have universal appeal, while others only relate to very specific methodologies. In this chapter we will touch upon key ethical considerations across some major methodologies. We suggest that understanding the basics of key methodologies in all research areas is a skill every researcher should have. It paves the way for interdisciplinary collaboration and dialogue.

The ethical questions around methodology have been given detailed attention in research ethics literature previously. For this reason we will explore them in general terms and from the perspective of the research community and guided dialogue. Researchers are usually interested only in very concrete ethical questions concerning their own research. In practice, researchers may think that it is enough to be able to write a description of research procedures to an ethical committee and get a green light for one's research. An aim of this chapter is to give a wider understanding of ethical reasoning as a basis for guided dialogue to take place within the research community. This all-round comprehension of at least some of the ethical issues helps researchers to communicate with their colleagues from other fields and to take part in the general discussion on guidelines of research ethics.

We will explore the following themes:

1 experimental use of animals
2 gene technology
3 humans as research subjects
4 study of material and objects produced by humans
5 intervention research
6 questionnaire studies and representative samples
7 study of human-made environments
8 study of natural environments
9 use of research equipment and infrastructure
10 big data

I Experimental use of animals

Experimental use of animals brings up some of the core research ethics questions. They are also questions that most people even outside research are aware of and often hold strong opinions on. Use of experimental animals is one of the starting points for the entire field of research ethics and the need to form shared and acceptable guidelines on how research is carried out.

Experimental use of animals is typically discussed using two polarised ethical approaches based on either utility or principle. These often lead to two opposing judgements on the appropriateness of animal use in experiments. Let us start with the consequentialist approach.

CONSEQUENTIALIST

The experimental use of animals from the consequentialist perspective focuses on the balance between the harm experienced by the animal (e.g. pain, life in captivity) in comparison to potential benefits of the research (new/more effective health care solutions, improved farming outcomes, etc.). Ethical justifiability is based on the positive balance of less harm than benefit. This can be achieved by both reducing harm and increasing benefit.

It is common to approach this harm minimisation by adopting 3R principles.[4]

- **Replace** the use of experimental animals with other methodologies whenever scientifically possible.
- **Reduce** the number of experimental animals to a minimum within the scope of the research.
- **Refine** the procedures used on experimental animals to minimise any pain, suffering, distress or harm.

The adoption of 3R principles does not remove the need for ethical consideration. The definition and meaning of pain and suffering are, for example, always deeply ethical considerations. These considerations are further expanded by considering timing of research – should you wait for a later time, when less invasive methodologies might be available, for example? Funding adds another dimension – how to justify spending research funding in the development of less painful/ harmful methodologies? Or what if the more humane methodologies are considerably more expensive? Is there an ethical limit on how these costs can be justified?

The number of animals used is typically suggested by scientific reasoning and funding restrictions. However, if funding would allow only the use of an absolute minimum number of animals, which may or may not allow for conclusions to be drawn at the end, should you even begin the research project?

In the case of experimental animals, the utility approach is deeply complicated by the comparison of very different types of harms and benefits. There are no standardised measures of (animal) pain and there is even less agreement on how this pain could be quantified against the benefits of their use in terms of products for people or other animals. Personal and collective values around animals, research, health, environment and farming are inescapably part of all consequentialist reasoning.[5]

PRINCIPLED

The principled approach is an alternative to the consequentialist argument, which typically leads to allowing, at least on a theoretical level, some use of experimental animals. The principled approach typically focuses on animal rights. These rights are considered to require our respect and are not subject to utility considerations. The rights may include right to freedom, opportunity to lead a natural life, and to be pain free. Typically, these rights are similar to those assigned to humans. We reject the idea of using humans for harmful experimental purposes even if great and significant research gains could be made. So why should we subject animals to them? Assigning strong rights to animals is typically based on the concept of experiencing pain and the difficulty of differentiating between all humans and all animals in any logical way.[6]

In addition to the discussions on the general ethical acceptability of using experimental animals, we are also faced with a value judgement between the types of animals used. The animal experimentation discussion typically refers to vertebrates about the size of a mouse. References to pain make sense with these types of animals. However, where do we draw the line in our consideration of pain as we go further down the list of animals? Are we worried about pain in invertebrates, including insects, for example? If their ability to sense pain is less than with vertebrates, does that translate into a different ethical acceptability in their use as experimental animals? Do we extend the same animal rights to them?

It is difficult to find consensus between the consequential and principled approaches in relation to the use of experimental animals. As use of animals in research is tightly legislated, society has made collective ethical decisions around these issues. National and international legislation typically gives ethical consideration to a defined group of animals (for example, non-human vertebrates and cephalopods (type of molluscs)), defines appropriate use and methods of killing, and usually makes reference to 3R as a core principle.[7] This type of legislation attempts to incorporate both utility and principled thinking by granting animals some rights, though not the same rights as humans, and considering the positive balance between harm and benefit.

Everyone has to form their own opinion on the use of experimental animals. This involves identifying rights associated with different types of animals, the definitions of potential harm and benefit in relation to a given research plan and finding an acceptable balance between these considerations. These need to be contrasted and compared with legislation and the available research methodologies. In addition, it is important to keep an eye on the coherence of the argument – animal rights should not be different between rabbits and rats just because one animal is more appealing than the other. Similarly, if one arrives at a conclusion that animal rights should forbid their use in experiments, how does this compare with the use of animals for farming and other human purposes? It is easy to see that this is not a simple or easy set of questions.

2 Gene technology[8]

Another much-discussed research area is gene technology. By gene technology we refer to a wide range of methodologies that explore gene expression, seeking to take advantage of natural genetic variation and make efforts to modify genes and transfer genes to new hosts.

PRINCIPLED

We can approach it from a principled perspective by asking whether genetic modification, cloning or use of stem cells violates core principles or rights associated with living creatures, or just humans.

CONSEQUENTIALIST

Alternatively, we can consider the consequences of gene technology. Are the benefits of these new technologies comparable with the resources required for the research, possible negative social impact of their use or the risk embodied in the unknown? For example, genetically modified crops for arid areas would improve food safety in many regions of the world, they would change the methods for purchasing seeds and there would be a risk of unexpected environmental impact by the new monoculture crops. How would the balance of harm and benefit fall between different stakeholders considering different possible time spans?

Both approaches lead us into complicated considerations. The core value questions invoked by the principled approach ask us to explore our deepest religious and existential values related to humanity, how it evolves and the way things should be. Similarly, the consequential considerations are often extremely complex, with a very large and diverse group of stakeholders and a great amount of outcome uncertainty. Virtue ethics brings us to consider motivations of different stakeholders in the complex social change brought forward by new gene technology.

A different set of questions with similar roots is raised when considering the use of stem cells, for example. Stem cell research data appear to provide great health care benefits, at least in the short term. The cost of stem cell research as well as the cost of providing stem cell-based care are prohibiting factors in the utilisation of these results. Guided dialogue asks, for example, if it makes sense to develop health care methodologies that wildly exceed current health care resources and would only be available to a lucky minority with significant personal ability to pay. This is an example of a core research question on what we wish to achieve and what are suitable ways to achieve these goals. Associated with this is a question on whose responsibility is it to direct and manage research to address these ethical concerns. In other words, when, if ever, is it your personal business as a researcher to make choices with these considerations in mind?

The use of gene technology with human cells has a second layer of ethical questions associated with privacy, confidentiality and rights. Who owns what when we study genetic material, and how can information be shared when we deal with cells that have great potential and hold detailed information about the donating individual? As gene technology develops, these questions morph into new forms and require ongoing attention from the research community in collaboration with society. Guided dialogue becomes useful as ignoring these considerations in research work can have seriously detrimental impacts on the usability of the results. Both nationally and internationally these questions are debated, and this dialogue is necessary for research to remain ethically robust and to be able to contribute to society.[9]

Gene technology is one of the research areas where international agreements on ethical guidelines are necessary. It is not fair from the perspective of equal opportunities for researchers if research in one country is less strictly regulated than in other countries. It is not favourable if researchers travel around the world seeking the environment that offers the most permissive ethical rules.

3 Humans as research subjects

There is a long history to consider in the ethical use of humans as research subjects.[10] The main focus is to protect test subjects' autonomy to make decisions for themselves as well as their privacy in relation to personal information. Together with debates about the use of animals in research, these questions are part of the foundation and momentum to discuss research ethics at all.

Autonomy is a foundational value in Western societies. Autonomy allows every rational person the right to make decisions regarding their life. These include decisions on how they want information about themselves to be shared and used. Typically, these core values translate into requirements of **informed consent** to becoming a research subject.

Both parts of this concept are important. While consent refers to giving permission and thus exercising autonomy, informed refers to conditions within which exercising autonomy is made possible. A rational decision can only follow from knowing enough about the situation. In the case of consenting to becoming a research subject, the following aspects are typically necessary for informed consent to be possible:

- aims and duration of the research;
- experimental design and possibly associated risks;
- how to leave the study if you no longer wish to participate;
- any responsibilities or benefits associated with being part of a study (compensation, additional care, travel);
- possible benefits of research both to the subject and society at large;
- how the results will be analysed and stored;
- who has a right to access results or data;

- how, where and when the results will be published;
- where to find out more about the research.

Typically, an agreement is formed between the research team and consenting subjects. Forms of valid agreements are often described in national legislation or guidelines.

Despite the extensive literature on gaining informed consent, researchers need to make considerable decisions on how the rules, regulations and guidelines translate into practice in each given research project. Typical questions we need to ask include:

- What is enough information about the project?
- How do we share this information to make sure the subjects understand it?
- How do we check that the consenting participants are in fact informed?
- How much time am I expected to devote to educating the subjects about the research?
- How broad can the consent be, considering all possible uses of the material collected?

Additional challenges appear when the researcher and subject represent different linguistic, cultural, social or education groups. In these situations it may be very difficult to confirm whether given consent is based on adequate information.

A further challenge arises with research subjects who are unable to give consent to research. These include children, people with intellectual disabilities or seriously ill individuals. Typically, a proxy decision-maker gives consent. It is ethically important to confirm who has a right to give proxy consent – do we think a family member or someone with formal authority is suitable, for example?

Anonymity is often considered the gold standard for any study involving human subjects. This could be challenged, however, when doing interviews as an ethnographic method. Let us consider two areas which raise general questions. First, anonymisation needs special methodological skills, but an ethical dilemma rises if an interviewee is against it. She or he may think the researcher is exploiting her or him for scientific purposes and is refusing to even give credit by mentioning the subject's correct name. Guided dialogue can be used to explore the concepts around this request and seek options to find a way to maintain key values for all stakeholders.

Second, when doing pioneering research among indigenous peoples a researcher bears great responsibility for labelling a certain human group in a specific way. Consider a situation in which a researcher is examining the sexual behaviour of a small ethnic group living in the jungles of New Guinea. Ten men are interviewed, but women refused to take part in the study. All the men said they have sex with female partners only by standing against a wall. The researcher reports about these findings in an ethnographic journal. The readers of the journal understand the limitations of this type of research. Nevertheless, the article gets a lot of citations and publicity. Finally, the facts arrive in textbooks and on Wikipedia. After 40 years, another researcher visiting the same ethnic group finds out that the interviewees of the previous study had lied. Their answers reflected old religious traditions according to which they should behave, but in reality no one had followed it for a long time. The example demonstrates well the tentative character of scientific findings and truths, but at the same time it illustrates the responsibility of researchers in distributing the results of their studies.

A good case for reasoning is the situation with refugees in many countries. It is of paramount importance to study their needs, expectations and future plans, but refugees make a very challenging group of interviewees and test-persons because of their linguistic, cultural and educational variety.

4 Study of material and objects produced by humans

Research may not involve an individual directly, but their objects and materials (e.g. personal belongings, written material or bio-samples). This type of research engages similar ethical considerations as the direct use of human subjects described above. In addition, new ethical issues may arise when it is no longer possible to ask for informed consent to include objects or material in research or to use the material for which the researcher does have consent in a different way to what has been agreed.

When seeking consent to use materials and objects, it is helpful to spend time forming the consent procedure to cover all potential longitudinal research requirements. If this is not done, it may be possible to use some of the collected material in an anonymised form for further research or archiving, but it is considerably more complicated, both ethically and technically.

There are interesting national differences around the use of material in research other than its original purpose. The EU has a principled decision to encourage archiving and multiple/longitudinal use of research material, while some countries have strict rules for destruction of research material in the name of privacy and confidentiality. This may be seen as different ways of balancing potential benefits via ongoing research use and reduced cost of collecting material against the potential harm to individuals from either real or perceived violations of privacy and confidentiality.

5 Intervention research

Intervention in this context refers to influencing the course of events. In the research context, this means the research setup deliberately alters the conditions to study the impact of these changes on behaviour, motivation or health in workplaces or on interactions of humans or animals, for example. This type of research may be considered for studying new care approaches, educational innovations or management styles.

Many of the above-mentioned ethical considerations apply to intervention research as well. In addition, intervention research is typically longitudinal, with the research spanning weeks if not years before the impact of intervention can be observed and verified. This requires significant commitment from both the researcher and the research subject. In intervention studies, the subject typically has an active role and the cyclical engagement between the research setting and the subject adds a new layer of influence. As multiple variables influence the research subjects during the research, validity of the results is always difficult to prove. On the other hand, interventions are often the only way to explore important research questions. So, in order to widen the scope of objects of research, we have to give up the strictest demands for objectivity, being one of the cornerstones of scientific research. This is a big ethical dilemma to be discussed. There are other interesting things to consider in harm–benefit comparison. The length of the study can often be seen as a harm, while the opportunity to gain extra tuition, care or facilities can benefit the research subjects themselves rather than unknown future individuals. A possible benefit is a more positive attitude to research among persons involved in the study. They feel that research is not something abstract and far from their real lives, but something that helps people to solve their everyday problems.

6 Questionnaire studies and representative samples

Research is also interested in the opinions and knowledge people hold. An essential ethical question is found in the decision on subject selection – who are they and how many are included in order to be able to draw the desired conclusions from the study? The research term **representative sample** incorporates these ethical concerns as well, though we are not often aware of the ethical dimension of it. Many fields of study have their own traditions around appropriate sample sizes, but there are no generic rules on how many subjects are necessary to be able to state that they adequately represent the studied population. It is often a balancing act between time and resources available to do the study and the ability to draw significant conclusions.

The choice of research subject evokes considerations of scientific procedure as well as ethical considerations for justice. The appropriate choice of subject is often suggested to include an element of randomness, which distributes both the burdens of participating as well as possible benefits in a fair manner.

Results, particularly from qualitative studies, are rarely simple or straightforward to interpret. As researchers, it is our responsibility to interpret results, as presenting raw data is rarely an appropriate option. We can often rely on research conventions of significance ($p \le 0.05$) and conventions on how to remove outlier data. While these conventions are helpful for the research community, we are still often faced with questions and decisions around defining significance, and the accuracy we use to measure/present our results.

Typically, we have a choice around whether we attempt to publish our results or not. Funding and career pressures will always add weight toward publishing, even when results lack significance or strong demonstrative power.

7 Study of human-made environments

Challenges in the study of human-made environments are often born from contradictory needs between researchers and society. For example, if historically important artefacts are found on a site prepared for a major construction, whose interests are prioritised? It can be assumed that more valuable artefacts are present in the area and that for the interest of research an opportunity for archaeological excavations would be paramount. On the other hand, the construction company has financial interests and the community may be relying on the building being finished for housing or to provide essential services like childcare or healthcare.

We have different options to approach this conflict of interest:

- allow construction to proceed as planned;
- delay construction until further research has been completed;
- place an indefinite ban on construction in the area;
- place a temporary ban on construction in this and surrounding real estate until research has been completed;
- allow for destruction of existing structures to allow for study in adjacent blocks of land.

PRINCIPLED

There may be rules that give rights or responsibilities to different stakeholders. These rights and responsibilities may be clear enough to negate any need to consider harm or benefit. However, even then, the rules typically include value-rich terminology such as 'scientifically significant', 'considerable importance to the community' or 'great financial burden'. All of these invite a value judgement that defines 'significant', 'considerable' and 'great'.

CONSEQUENTIALIST

Each of these options treats the stakeholders in different ways. If rules and guidelines do not provide simple solutions, the decision will inevitably define priorities between stakeholders. What is more valuable – the research or the building? Timelines become an important factor in evaluating options – how long are we ready to wait to find a solution that would eventually meet everyone's needs? The decision-makers' values will translate into a decision on whose interests are given the greatest consideration.

Research on human-made environments may also require us to explore how much harm research can cause to people in their everyday lives. Many decisions in society carry the same ethical concern of acceptability – when can essential services be reduced or cancelled, generate noise or block traffic if these are balanced by social or research benefits?

Consequentialist approaches allow for balancing harm and benefit between different stakeholders at different timeframes. The balancing becomes challenging if the harm is assigned to a different group than the benefit, for example. When can we accept such an imbalance?

Often some established rules and guidelines assist in this decision-making. These reveal values held by the community. A city council can give permission to close a section of a road for a racing event but refuse permission for a research group that wants to perform aerosol testing on a much smaller section of road. Behind these decisions there may be some rules made by the city council regarding the conditions for granting road closures. However, if one considers the ethical background of these rules, it is easy to see some value-based harm and benefit reasoning. The car-racing event creates pollution, increases noise levels and blocks a big area of the city for hours, but the benefits are more important: entertainment for a huge amount of people, and a boost for the economy and reputation of the city. For the work of the research group, the harm is much smaller but the benefits are much more abstract and future-oriented, especially if we take the perspective of the inhabitants of the city.

From a different perspective, we can also consider research on objects that will be damaged to some degree in the research process. Research may require scratching a surface, for example, to identify the origin, process, or maker of the object. Would this be acceptable? It may be difficult to speak of rights assigned to an object. We may, though, consider rights of future generations to have access to historical objects in their current/original condition. If such a right exists, it is often contrary to rights held by researchers to study and explore objects.

8 Study of natural environments

Questions relating to the use of experimental animals have led to discussion on most research ethics questions. We have considered ethical questions related to humans and human-made environments and now return to considering research in the natural environment. What can we do in and to the environment in the name of research?

Would it be acceptable to destroy to any extent the natural environment for the purposes of research by bringing in heavy equipment, taking samples, capturing wildlife or restricting natural growth and development? If it is, then how do we balance the harm we do in the name of research and advancement of science? These questions increase in importance when we deal with vulnerable or endangered environments or animals – the values of protection or research may become contradictory and we are forced to weigh the value of knowledge against preservation, even when knowledge may assist with further preservation efforts.

These questions align with questions around harm caused in any effort to achieve good. How much harm are we ready to accept in order to achieve our desired outcome and how do we treat stakeholders in the decision-making process and deal with imbalance between the recipients of harm or benefit? This utility-based thinking is at the core of most social decision-making where finite resources are paired with multiple definitions of good translated into varied goals and desires.

9 Research use of equipment and infrastructure

Research equipment is used for measuring, observing, recording and generating research data. The ethical issues with the use of equipment typically concentrate around acquisition decisions and utilisation of the existing equipment.

Acquisition is closely related to research questions and the suitability of the equipment for the intended purpose. From an ethical perspective, the acquisition decision is about defining an acceptable level of utilisation to justify the purchase. We can describe this as the added value the equipment produces for the research. When the equipment is very expensive, the justification has an increased importance at times of reduced research funding and tight competition for it. Good questions to ask include:

- Is the utilisation rate high enough to justify the acquisition?
- Could sharing the equipment or using equipment already in possession of other research groups increase utilisation?
- How does the equipment increase the research potential and effectiveness now and in the future?
- What are the other possible uses of these research funds? In other words the opportunity cost of the equipment acquisition in terms of personnel, travel, collaboration, etc.?

If the equipment acquisition is associated with choosing a new research topic, we can also ask at least the following questions:

- Is the research topic itself such that this investment will support the department/university/national research profile?
- Is the research topic itself important and beneficial enough to justify expensive equipment, i.e. comparing opportunity costs across different research topics?
- How do we define the benefits? Is it suitable and acceptable to refer to applicability, international reputation or interests of researchers?

The stakeholder group is typically our own research group or department. From an ethical perspective, this narrow focus may not be easy to justify. It is an ethically stronger position to consider a broader group of stakeholders. These could include other research groups, research directions and universities. Considering benefit and harm from this broader perspective can lead to a very different conclusion on what is worth doing.

Once the equipment has been acquired, another set of ethical questions appears:

- How do we define priorities for use if it is not possible to allow everyone the level of use they would prefer? What are the criteria to have a higher priority – seniority, research topic, stage of research or experience with the equipment?
- If the use of equipment requires training, how do we choose those to be trained to use it? Is it a privilege, duty, burden or opportunity to be trained in this way?
- If the equipment generates occupational health and safety risks (e.g. radiation or chemical exposure), how are the risks divided between users? Would it be justifiable to treat young female researchers differently to other groups?
- Who decides acceptability of risks and how they are managed?
- If the equipment is shared, how do we share costs of maintenance, use and training? Can the group who purchased the equipment, possibly with public funding, profit from the equipment?

Libraries create an important part of the academic infrastructure. The purchase cost of electronic material has become so high that it can be compared with any other significant equipment purchase. Access to electronic databases is no longer an assumption, as even larger universities have to make decisions on which databases they subscribe to. This generates many ethical issues partly related to academic publishing, discussed in more detail in Chapter 3:

- Who decides what material is purchased and what are acceptable selection criteria?
- Can different access criteria be assigned to different members of the academic staff and students?

10 Big data

The rapid development of computer technology has also opened up new opportunities for research. Three things are behind the boost: availability of very large collections of data; continuous growth of computational capacity of computers; and development of programmes and techniques for combining data from different sources. Due to this progress we are nowadays able to collate huge databases of information in many research areas, including meteorology, environmental research, genomics, complex physical simulations, as well as various fields of social sciences and humanities. 'Big data' is often used as a common label for these unprecedented data collections.

While this ability to collect vast data sets has a possibility to increase objectivity and reliability of research, at the same time, it entails several risks with an ethical component.

A large amount of data may give an illusion that it automatically leads to more reliable results. If data are one-sided, the size does not increase our understanding of the phenomenon under scrutiny. If we collect more and more data about air pollution (aerosols and particles) in one location, this does not directly tell us about conditions in other locations with different conditions. The ethical question is to define what provides an acceptable definition of significance to draw conclusions and possibly suggest application and change in behaviour, when the amount of data do not automatically provide that. This question applies to all research and needs to be revisited especially when new methodologies emerge, like now with big data.

Traditional statistical tools have limited applications with big data. With limitless data combinations, traditional tools can be used to prove almost any connection within these vast data sets. This increases the need for transparency of methodology and shared discourse on the conclusive power of any results drawn from big data.

Big data allows for impressive visualisation options. One picture can summarise complex information or provide an impressive way to mislead the reader to interpret the data in various ways.

The collection and analysis of big data raises also the question of cost-effectiveness of research. Expensive 'big data machines' can provide so much raw material that nobody can use it in a reasonable way. Another question is the balance of resources distributed to research where different methods are used.

The utilisation of big data is a typical case of a trendy method. However, what is popular and frequently used at this very moment is not necessary the only feasible way of doing good research. Machine translation is an area where methods have been re-shaped along with technological development. This methodology is based on a structural analysis of two chosen languages. The methodology is partly compensated by statistical methods based on a large amount of linguistic data. The development of the methods themselves definitely leads to scientific progress and it also opens new avenues for practical applications. On the other hand, concentrating on development of statistical methods leads to neglecting the development of other means of machine translation. These approaches do not treat everyone equally. We have large text corpora for only a few languages in the world. Harm is therefore experienced by the speakers of languages that lack a large text corpora.

***

In this chapter we have explored the research process from an ethical perspective both chronologically as well as thematically. The chapter has presented far more questions than even attempts to find answers to them. The structure of exploring stakeholders, rights and responsibilities and defining options are suggested as ways to start guided dialogue on many of these issues. The questions themselves are signposts for the types of issues most likely present when we stop to consider the actual doing of research. Each piece of research is both deeply contextual and simultaneously shares core elements with all other research. In other words, the questions even have global relevance, while the answers are often meaningful only in their local context.

Case study 1: motivation for selecting the research topic

In this chapter we have discussed different factors influencing the choice of the topic of research. Contemplate to what extent the following issues have affected the selection of **your** research topic:

1 availability of funding;
2 priorities/traditions within your research group/department/faculty/ university;
3 availability of equipment/laboratory/material/test persons;
4 your supervisor/colleague/friend/fellow student has given you a hint or advice for that;
5 the topic is trendy in your research field;
6 the topic gives an opportunity to make a breakthrough in research;
7 your previous research career gives good skills to do this kind of research without extra training;
8 the topic is rather narrow and that is why you are able to publish on it in a reasonable time;
9 you are enthusiastic about the topic;
10 the results of the study can be utilised somehow – in developing new products or service concepts, in legislation, in helping people to live a better life, in widening people's worldview or addressing an imbalance in studying third-world problems.

Consider, in a similar way, the choice of another researcher you know well.

After answering the question, think of the ethical approaches you have followed. Have you paid attention to the benefits of research (consequentialist approach)? If so, have you thought about whose benefit you have put into the foreground – your own, that of the department/university or something else? Or have you weighed the questions from the point of view of an ideal researcher (virtue approach)?

How do you think research topics should be selected in an ideal situation? Do you think the current situation is satisfactory, particularly considering how research addresses current world problems? Who is responsible for guiding the selection of research topics – the researcher, research group, financing bodies or policy-makers?

Case study 2: where are the limits of 'sufficient'?

Previously we discussed the issue of 'what is sufficient?'. This is a very practical question. In most cases, the thing to be weighed is the juxtaposition of spending more time in order to fulfil the research standards more rigorously and publishing as quickly as possible. In this issue, the consequential approach may lead to tactical considerations rather than to ethical ones, when a researcher estimates the risks of being caught for unethical behaviour. This is the wrong way to solve the problem. The principled and the virtue approaches give a more fruitful tool for discussing these cases. Consider various aspects of this important question by using the following example as a starting point:

1   **Extent of previous research.** A general idea of research is that it is based on results achieved by other researchers. The aim of research is to bring something new to the worldwide stock of knowledge. This way of thinking leads to the demand to be acquainted with all possible publications where the topic in hand has been touched upon. However, you may think that some of them may be skipped because (a) they were published in another country and/or language; (b) they represent another scientific approach, school or method; (c) they are old-fashioned and no longer relevant.

2   **Added value.** Does the research contribute sufficiently to the current knowledge, appreciating that research fields develop differently? If we are studying phenomena X (e.g. chest cancer or causes of misunderstandings in verbal communication) and we currently assume we understand approximately 50 per cent of the phenomena, and after our article would understand 50.2 per cent, would that be sufficient added value? Or how much more should we know? Alternatively we can ask how much 'new' material there should be in an article, book or PhD thesis.

3   **The scale of material.** In most research fields there is a certain consensus about the number of test persons, experiments or examples which are needed to fulfil the criteria of 'good research'. However, there may be certain practical reasons that hinder the researcher from reaching the satisfactory limit of cases (e.g. time pressure or costs). Are there circumstances where fewer is enough?

4   **Representativeness of test persons.** Test persons for psychological experiments and interviews are often collected on a voluntary basis. The easiest way to find them is to turn to students and pay them a cinema ticket. In the publication based on the experiment, the researcher naturally explains restrictions and possible biases in results

to the readers. In doing so, the researcher leaves the interpretation of results to them. Is this a satisfactory situation from an ethical point of view?

5   **Information given to test persons and interviewees.** According to general ethical guidelines, people involved in research have to be informed about the relevant features of research. However, in practice it is not always clear how to guarantee they have understood everything correctly. Some groups (children, elderly people, mentally or otherwise ill people) are a special challenge here. What is the role of relatives in these cases? How much time should the researcher spend in order to fulfil all the requirements needed?

6   **Degree of reliability.** Repetition of experiments (in cases when it is possible) is a general requirement for research. Every iteration makes the results more reliable. On the other hand, with each iteration the improvements in reliability are less and less. The costs of experiments and the time they need certainly influence the number of reasonable repetitions. Are there other factors regulating the number of needed repetitions?

Case study 3: do the methods determine the value of research?

Some methods seem to be 'more scientific' than others because they reflect more precisely the general principles of research, such as objectivity and quantification. The ideal of science is to achieve univocal and unambiguous results, which can be proven by other researchers repeating the study in a similar way. One may argue that this makes the crucial difference between scientifically proven facts and opinions of people, which are just based on indefinable and vague observations and arguments. The archetype of favourable research is a double-blind arrangement where test persons get real drugs or placebos and the researcher her-/himself, when analysing the results, does not know the distribution of the two test groups. However, if we take the double-blind test as the only acceptable method in medical and health research, we are not able to study such effective cures as psychiatry, physiotherapy and physical exercise. Thus, the principled approach to research methods brings another answer than the consequentialist approach. Similar discussion arises when we compare case or intervention methods with quantitative methods in social sciences and humanities, sometimes valued differently among researchers. One may also speak 'hard' and 'soft' methods in this area.

There are also other differences in aims and traditions of different research fields. What is your opinion about As and Bs in Table 2.1? How about your colleagues or the majority of researchers? Are there scientific principles which make A the better option compared to B, or maybe the contrary is true? Which kind of values are behind such reasoning? Can one use these characteristic for defining what science is about?

Table 2.1 Differences in aims and traditions of different research fields

	Column A	Column B
1	Double-blind method is the only way to reach reliable results on phenomena we are interested in.	Other methods are as important because there are many phenomena that cannot be studied by using the double-blind method.
2	In research we should always strive for quantitative methods because otherwise we fall into the trap of subjectivity.	There are topics that cannot be approached by using only quantitative methods. Sometimes exact figures give a false illusion of objectivity.
3	Only results are important.	The process of doing research is also important because it is a learning opportunity for all taking part.
4	Proven widely used methods are a hallmark of research and researchers should be content with them.	Seeking new, more effective methods is a part of the research process.
5	Research is primary: when there are conflicts between the needs of research and principles widely accepted in society, we should give priority to research because in the long run this benefits society.	Research is secondary: when there are conflicts between the needs of research and principles widely accepted in society, we should follow the same principles as society.
6	Researchers should be given the infrastructure they need in order to compete in the international arena.	Procuring research infrastructure should be seen as an opportunity cost balanced with other needs of researchers.

Case study 4: credibility of the research community

Collaboration between different parts of society is based on trust. Research is no exception. Those utilising research results, be it the research community itself or someone else, assume that the research is done honestly and diligently. In other words, it can be trusted. Trust is the foundation for the division of labour within a research group as well: everyone does their part, which together make up the whole. Research subjects and those answering questionnaires trust that they have been given correct information regarding the research. When research is sent for review, both the editorial team and the authors trust that the reviewers will do their job with fairness and care.

Exposure of research misconduct may be considered to erode this trust, particularly when the cases of misconduct receive extensive negative media attention. Public and open discussion on research ethics, and particularly violations of codes of conduct, can be considered dangerous and unadvisable. Consider this issue from the perspective of the two polar-opposite opinions below. Which of them presents the most convincing argument? What values and assumptions support each argument? How do you think we should act when misconduct is discovered?

1   It is sufficient that we have the codes and guidelines given by authorities on research misconduct defining fabrication, falsification, plagiarism and misappropriation. Each researcher can reflect on how these codes and guidelines apply to their own research. Open discussion and emphasis of these issues within the research community and especially in the media will only reduce credibility of research work. Any actual misconduct cases should be dealt with quietly within the research community and wrongdoers reprimanded appropriately, without any undue publicity.

2   Open and explicit ethical considerations are necessary as research is filled with questions and grey areas where the codes and guidelines must be applied or where their guidance is only very limited. Only open dialogue can develop the true ethical strength of the research community and shape its identity in society. The research community will lose its credibility if it shows an inability to openly deal with difficult issues like misconduct. Actual cases of misconduct should be dealt with as transparently as possible and people from outside the research community should be invited to explore the issues together with the research community.

NOTES

1   D.B. Resnik, L.M. Rasmussen and G.E. Kissling (2015), An international study of research misconduct policies, *Accountability in Research* 22:5, 249–266 (www.ncbi. nlm.nih.gov/pmc/articles/PMC4449617/pdf/nihms691915.pdf).

2   To learn more about the prevalence of research misconduct, you could start with the following: D. Faneli (2009), How many scientists fabricate and falsify research? A systematic review and meta-analysis of survey data, *PLoS ONE* 4:5, e5738 (http://journals.plos.org/plosone/article?id=10.1371/journal.pone.0005738); L.K. John, G. Loewenstein and

D. Prelec (2012), Measuring the prevalence of questionable research practices with incentives for truth telling, *Psychological Science* 23:5, 524–532 (http://citeseerx.ist.psu. edu/viewdoc/download?doi=10.1.1.727.5139&rep=rep1&type=pdf); C. Gross (2016), Scientific misconduct. *Annual Review of Psychology* 67, 693–711 (www.annualreviews. org/doi/full/10.1146/annurev-psych-122414-033437).

3   Mpur has approximately 7,000 native speakers. The language also has other names: *Amberbaken, Dekwambre, Ekware* and *Kebar*. It is classified as 'isolated' – that is, not having any relative languages. As a matter of fact, we know more about Mpur than about hundreds of other languages spoken in West Guinea, thanks to fieldwork done by C. Ode (2002), A sketch of Mpur, *Languages of the Eastern Bird's Head*, ed. G.P. Resink, Canberra: Australian National University, 45–107.

4   See: W.M.S. Russell and R.L. Burch (1959), *The Principles of Humane Experimental Technique*, London: Methuen (http://altweb.jhsph.edu/pubs/books/humane_ exp/het-toc); and The Interagency Coordinating Committee on the Validation of Alternative Methods (US) (https://ntp.niehs.nih.gov/pubhealth/evalatm/iccvam/ index.html).

5   See P. Singer (1975), *Animal Liberation: A New Ethics for Our Treatment of Animals*, New York: Avon.

6   See T. Regan (1986), *The Case for Animal Rights*, Berkeley, Ca: University of California Press.

7   See for example:European Directive on Use of Experimental Animals: Directive 2010/63/EU (http://eur-lex.europa.eu/LexUriServ/LexUriServ.do?uri=OJ:L: 2010:276:0033:0079:en:PDF); US Government Principles of Use of Laboratory Animals (http://grants.nih.gov/grants/olaw/references/phspol.htm#USGovPrinciples); and Australian Acts and Regulations (www.animalethics.org.au/legislation).

8   See: R.M. Berry (2007), *The Ethics of Genetic Engineering*, New York: Routledge; R.W. Kolb (ed.) (2007), *The Ethics of Genetic Commerce*, Malden, MA: Blackwell.

9   Examples of public bodies regulating gene technology are: Australian Gene Technology Regulator (www.ogtr.gov.au/internet/ogtr/publishing.nsf/Content/ section-about); European Society on Human Genetics (www.eshg.org/home.0.html); and the National Institute of Health, Stem Cell (http://stemcells.nih.gov/Pages/ Default.aspx).

10 Examples of agreements and codes around the use of humans as research subjects: Nuremberg Code (1947) (http://ohsr.od.nih.gov/guidelines/nuremberg.html); World Medical Association, Declaration of Helsinki (1964) (www.wma.net/e/policy/ b3.htm); CIOMS International Ethical Guidelines for Biomedical Research Involving Human Subjects (www.cioms.ch/frame_guidelines_nov_2002.htm); Council of Europe, Recommendation No. R(90)3 Concerning Medical Research on Human Beings (1990) (www.coe.int/T/E/Social_Cohesion/Health/Recommendations/ Rec(1990)03.asp); and the EU Convention for the Protection of Human Rights and Dignity of the Human Being with Regard to the Application of Biology and Medicine: Convention on Human Rights and Biomedicine, European Treaty Series No. 164 (http://conventions.coe.int).

Chapter 3

Publishing

The main ethical challenges in scientific publishing are:

1. Research is an ongoing process and it is not always clear when the results and findings are sufficient to be published.
2. Publishing is a sort of competition where the researchers want to be the best and the first. This increases the risk of misconduct.
3. The referee practice (peer review) is the cornerstone of scientific publishing; therefore it is important to conduct it in an ethically sustainable way.

Ethics by guided dialogue typically requires researchers and research communities to consider the following key ethical questions in publishing:

- What does it mean to be exact in referring other researchers' work?
- Where is the line between acceptable quoting and plagiarism?
- Is the author or the reader responsible when a detail or the whole idea presented in a paper is understood incorrectly?
- When is dividing (splitting) research outcomes into more than one publication acceptable?
- Are there circumstances where double publishing is justifiable?
- Who has the right to authorship?
- Whose benefits (researcher, research group, department, university, grant provider) must be given the greatest weight in selecting the forum for publication?
- What is the ethical codification the editor and the referees of scientific journals should follow?

Research is meaningful only after it has been published. Doing research in secrecy does not bear the hallmarks of scientific research. Therefore, it appears reasonable that research merit is also assessed through publications. This influences all decisions for positions, funding and collaborative projects. Therefore, publishing is an essential activity in the research community. Publishing also has another important dimension: peer recognition of scientific findings and statements is one of the ways to determine what the truth is in science.[1]

We publish for multiple reasons. If you brainstorm with your colleagues, you could easily come up with 20 reasons why you wish to or should publish your results. Typically these answers can be grouped in the following categories:

- the core purpose of research is to share results;
- to collaborate with research colleagues;
- to gain funding;
- helping to make the world a better place;
- personal benefit and interest.

Some of the ethical issues within publishing are born out of conflict between these reasons. Our awareness of ethical issues is increased when we understand (1) why people publish; (2) how they define their harm and benefit, as well as their goals in publishing; and (3) what type of research community they wish to build. Asking these questions can be a starting place towards building a stronger and more robust research community through guided dialogue.

Research ethics frequently concerns the publishing process. A substantial part of research fraud relates to publications. The general principles are unequivocal: do not publish in your name anything that is not yours; and publish honestly what you have discovered in your investigation. As is discussed in this chapter, the line between right and wrong, even in these apparently simple guidelines, is often fuzzy.

Science is a very competitive activity: you have to publish new findings before other researchers. This is especially important in research fields, where it is possible to have breakthroughs that are a significant step forward. It is not enough to be competent and capable; you have to be quick as well. There are no prizes for the runner-up. Competition is so obvious that it often comes up as a strong motive in a researcher's life. The importance of timing and the drive to be the first can be shown by the following thought experiment. Let us suppose there are two research groups, one from Spain and the other from China. They are trying to identify the genetic code for dog allergy. The Chinese group manages to publish their findings three months before the Spanish group has their results ready. Are the Spaniards happy with this or are they disappointed? If the main motive of researchers was to produce knowledge for the benefit of humankind, they should take pleasure in this success because this important piece of information has been presented to its users earlier. If their main motive is personal credit for being the first to discover this, they are disappointed. You may guess which of these reactions is more common among researchers.

The main target group in the distribution of new scientific knowledge is the research community of that particular discipline or field. Quite another question is knowledge transmission to its users; this important issue is discussed in Chapters 8 and 9. The main channels in revealing scientific findings to colleagues are oral presentations and peer-reviewed publications. Oral presentations raise some interesting ethical questions, e.g. the possible use of preliminary results or hypotheses conveyed by colleagues. However, in this chapter we concentrate on ethical questions that relate to publishing typically in a peer-reviewed forum.

Apart from the writing process, we discuss phenomena connected with the act of publishing itself. People responsible for the selection of publications, editors and referees are often called the gatekeepers of science. They look after the quality of the publications, and they decide what kind of research will get publicity and when. In doing so, they regulate development of science and influence the ethical directions research takes.

Identifying stakeholders

The first obvious stakeholders are the **authors**. Behind the group of authors there is typically a larger group of people supporting the research, but not achieving author status – these include **technical assistants** and **other supportive personnel**, as well as **supervisory and mentoring colleagues**. In many prefaces of PhD theses, **family and friends** are recognised for their support and indirect role in making the research possible. They do not have a direct role in the writing process, but through their indirect support they are also secondary stakeholders.

The research community is an important stakeholder as it is the main audience of published research. Depending on the nature of the publication, the size of this audience varies. Regardless of the size of the readership, all publishing shares the collective aim to increase the knowledge base of the research community. In this way, the research community owns and utilises research knowledge. This relationship is conditional, because published research does not necessarily have an impact on the research community. It is likely that most research has no or only minimal impact on the direction of future research.

Even in sole-author publications, the **colleagues** of the author form a secondary stakeholder group. Colleagues may give ad-hoc advice or discuss the research topic in seminars or the departmental social room. Sometimes the draft paper is given to a large group of colleagues to read prior to submission. As the department or research group typically shares funding and research quality assessments, all published research has the potential to affect the entire collective.

As mentioned above, the **journal editors** and **reviewers** are also important stakeholders. If the research has received external funding, the **funding bodies** become stakeholders as well through possible expectations or confirmation of successful use of funds. We can also consider **all those whose lives may be influenced** by the new knowledge as stakeholders – for example, students taught using a new pedagogical approach, patients receiving new treatments, policy-makers changing policy or social groups changing their image of themselves.

The author's role is primary, but while the other stakeholders do not share the same primary status, they also cannot be ignored. The whole idea of publishing is to communicate with others; without the others there is no meaning in publishing results. The ethical concept relies on the presence of all stakeholder groups. Guided dialogue is often beneficial for identifying stakeholders and considering whether any of the ethical issues are born from the potential conflict of interest between stakeholders.

Understanding rights and responsibilities

As researchers/authors we have both rights and responsibilities when it comes to publishing. We have a right to choose our publication forum. We have a right to present our results in a manner we see as most appropriate. We have a right to our manuscript during the writing process and possibly post-corrections as well. Simultaneously there are multiple responsibilities. We have to comply with principles of honesty, diligence, transparency and giving credit to others via references and citations. We also have a joint responsibility for possible mistakes in any manuscript where we are listed as authors.

If we are part of a research group, we also have a responsibility to work towards the shared goals. Our colleagues have a right to expect our full commitment to the work. Our colleagues also have a right to understand how authors are selected and ordered in any article we write. Particularly those not included as authors deserve to know the reasons for this.

The publisher's responsibility is to guarantee fair and just treatment of all authors. The time taken to review and assess whether to publish a manuscript must be reasonable. The publisher has a right not to publish a submitted manuscript – this right is connected with a responsibility to justify a decision for the rejection.

An expert reviewer has a right to refuse to give a review without having to justify their decision. If the expert accepts the role of reviewer, it is essential to do the review with diligence and within a given timeframe. We can ask whether a researcher has a right to systematically refuse to do reviews and concentrate on her or his own research. If everyone made the same decision, the foundations of the research system would collapse. Would this translate to a responsibility to take part in the review process in some way, at least as a member of the research community? The reviewers also have a right and responsibility to reject the reviewed manuscript based on scientific reasons and their professional judgement.

The research community has a right to trust the truthfulness of published research and that all meaningful research is published in recognised and available fora. When published research is later referred to, everyone has a responsibility to appropriately and accurately cite the original source. Ethically, it is interesting to discuss what kind of responsibility the readers have in making an effort to understand the material correctly and draw appropriate conclusions from it.

Defining options

The academic writing process is often long and requires stakeholders to choose between different options. The timelines of these decisions overlap and link with each other, and we will here group them somewhat artificially into three sequential steps of options. All of these steps contain multiple ethical issues and choices to be considered. Guided dialogue can be used to understand these choices and to make justifiable decisions.

An important moment in the publishing process is the decision that there is enough material to be published. A person who has no experience of research may think this is an easy thing to decide: when experiments and analysis of material have been done, they will be published. In practice, research consists of a continuum where new findings are based on old ones and different phases of research overlap. Therefore it is not obvious when a researcher has a sufficient amount of new findings upon which to base new meaningful conclusions, and when the reliability of results has been confirmed in a sufficient way. It is necessary to decide whether the time is right to publish or not to publish.

A decision must be made on authorship and the order in which authors are listed on the manuscript. Typically this is linked with the decision of when to publish. This characteristically provides multiple options. Authorship is often linked with the long process of writing the manuscript with the required wording and skilful argumentation. It is possible to improve any scientific text again and again. At some point the author(s) must make a decision that the manuscript is complete.

Related to the decisions above, another decision relates to how to publish. Researchers may think, for tactical reasons, that it is wise to split their findings into two or more publications. There may be personal motives (more items in the list of publications) for this reasoning, or pressure from above ('points' for the department or university). Another question may arise: could it be possible to publish the same results from different perspectives? If we are dealing with a multidisciplinary study, publishing in journals of different research fields could give the work more visibility. In such a case, the same results may give grounds to write substantially different articles. Splitting up a publication and duplicate publication generate serious ethical questions; we will return to them later in this chapter.[2]

The decision of where to publish is also of considerable concern for researchers. In every research field there is a certain hierarchy of journals and publishers. This hierarchy is codified in multiple different journal rankings based on different definitions of impact. The choice of journal is mostly a tactical decision through which the researcher or research group tries to optimise the prestige of the journal, the risk of being turned down and the time until the publication is complete. However, the choice of publishing forum may require ethical reasoning if the opinions of the major stakeholders (researcher, research group, department, university) differ: one may prefer an open access journal, another a journal with a high impact factor, and the third whichever is the fastest option. Who is entitled to make the decision?

Journals and publishers evaluate manuscripts they have received and decide which of them is good enough to be published. They have five options: to reject the manuscript, to accept it without revision, to accept with minor revisions or to accept with major improvements of the text, or with demands to conduct some further investigation. The editor and the referees may have slightly different views of the selection criteria, and the process can vary significantly between journals.

In examining the steps in more detail, we will use the tools described in Chapter 1: the *consequentialist*, *principled* and *virtue* approaches.

WRITING

Individual researchers face most ethical questions as part of the writing process. Writing a manuscript is a multifaceted process. The relationship between writing and research varies. Years of research can be written up in a couple of weeks, or the writing process can take months as it is closely connected to the research process in a cyclical pattern of writing and further research work. Sometimes the writing is a way to arrive at conclusions. Despite these myriad patterns, similar ethical problems appear in most writing processes.

Most publishers have tight and clear guidelines on the technical aspects of a manuscript; following these is unlikely to cause any ethical challenges. On the other hand, the content and choice of wording can be an ethical minefield. We will look into three different aspects: explaining the research context, referring to previous research and accuracy of wording.

I Explaining the research context

The general research principle is to transparently explain all factors influencing the presented results. These could be internal or external factors. Internal factors include experimental set-up; research subjects/informants; and the data/material, equipment and methodologies used. All of these can have a significant impact on the research results and thus they must be accurately described to allow both reproducibility of results as well as assessment of generalisation potential. Space restrictions make it impossible to explain all aspects in detail, but it is essential to include all elements that may have influenced the results. Ability to identify these factors can be improved through guided dialogue.

The definition of **potential significant impact** can be explored with the following example. Let us assume that participants in a psychological experiment were more likely to be left-handed than the general population. Would this be a relevant factor with potentially significant impact on the results? This could be the case if the equipment used included a right-handed mouse, for example. Or it could be relevant if the experiment measured brain response to verbal stimulus. On the other hand, it is unlikely to have had potentially significant impact if the study focused on descriptions that participants gave of pictures they were shown.

Another example relates to the time at which the experiment was performed. If the study focused on acceptability of particular syntax in a given context, the time may not be an important factor. On the other hand, if the study was on associations between concepts or frequency of use, the time of day or year may have a significant impact on the results and should be mentioned.

External factors refer to non-research activities of the researcher, personal relationships, funding and possibly dominant political or research contexts. Their impact on research is often unrecognised and their discovery requires a conscious process by the researcher. Subjectivity statements can be utilised to explore these aspects further. In addition to personal circumstances, certain key biased structures affect everyone's thinking. These are sometimes called cognitive traps:

- **Anchoring and belief perseverance.** This is a tendency to hold onto existing beliefs even when evidence suggests otherwise. Part of belief perseverance is a biased subconscious selection of evidence for consideration in the first place. Anchoring refers to choosing a 'true' piece of data or knowledge around which all future knowledge and data are compared and judged as correct or incorrect.
- **Epistemic conformity/cognitive inertia.** The desire to be part of a group strengthens the potential for belief perseverance. A variation of this is the desire to think differently regardless of what others are thinking. In addition, a reluctance to review perceptions and existing knowledge makes this tendency even more powerful.
- **Power of repetition.** Things that happen often come to be viewed as truths. For example, if a particular statement is titled as a fact, it becomes a fact in the minds of those that hear it, independently of its true nature.
- **Vivid/pallid dimension.** The closer things happen, the more weight they are given in any decision-making. Closeness can refer to time or place.
- **Wishful thinking.** A desire to believe that things will turn out the way we want. This could be an optimistic or pessimistic wish, and behaviour is adjusted in accordance with these assumptions based on a viewpoint.
- **Choice supportive bias.** We seek evidence to support the choices we are about to make or the ones we have already made. In marketing this is called post-purchase reinforcement. We want to feel good about ourselves and the decisions we make.

These natural biases can be most clearly visible when a researcher presents evidence contradicting the standard scientific view. This can create a real challenge for reviewers and the whole research community. Experienced researchers do not necessarily welcome a young (or old) colleague who tries to prove that all others are wrong. Recognising these biases and minimising their impact on research work is part of good research practice.

These biases are also present very clearly when research knowledge is transferred and shared with the rest of society. Public debate is often biased and out of balance, which is further complicated by strong personification of knowledge with a few identified researchers, where the focus is transferred from what is said to who has said it. We return to this question in Chapter 8.

2 Referring to previous work

As a research community, we require proof that the presented results are really novel and original. The assumption is that the author(s) provide the readers with an extensive and complete description of the previous results without leaving anything out. This has become increasingly more difficult for multiple reasons:

1   How do you know that you have access to all relevant previous research? Not all research is published in international journals and very few people have access to all the possible journals. In some research fields you have to be aware of other types of publications as well, e.g. scientific journals in languages other than English, or certain non-academic publications.

2   How far back in history do you have to go? Is it enough for us to provide a snapshot of the current knowledge, or should we provide some timelines of how the knowledge has developed and where some of the key thoughts and research questions have originated?

3   How much should you read and reference? The volumes of scientific publications are growing all the time and the amount of information out there to read and refer to is becoming unmanageable. If we wanted to know all that is done, even in some specific fields, there would be time for nothing other than reading new publications. This challenge is particularly problematic in interdisciplinary research, where we would need to reference multiple fields.

4   Many journals restrict the number of references, which requires explicit and conscious culling of the reference list; we are asked to reference only the key papers, not all the papers that relate to our research. The freedom and responsibility that go with this process are meaningful and important also from the perspective of the whole research community, where impact factors and citations count.

We have to decide how to apply distinct rules in each situation. Principles of referring to previous work are simple: do not present as your own the work, ideas or pictures of others. If you do that, you commit scientific misconduct (plagiarism) and are likely to be identified and reprimanded for your actions. References must accurately describe the original source and all quotes must be in their original format. There is no rule against extensive quoting or referring to the work of others as long as it is done transparently and according to agreed rules. It may not be great scientific practice to do so, but it is not misconduct either.

Rules around referring to the works of others are based on a clear set of research values. First, the value of fairness and justice. We have a right to be known for the work we have done. In the research world this has added significance because publications and references are almost solely used to evaluate research ability and career progression.

Plagiarism is often compared with stealing: the work belongs to someone and it cannot be claimed by others as their own. A second value refers to transparency as an important guarantee for research quality. It would be very hard for the research community to function if we could not know who has done what, when and how. If we lose sight of where knowledge comes from, the knowledge also loses credibility. Plagiarism thus harms individual researchers and the research community as a whole.

Even though the basic principles of plagiarism are simple, there are numerous borderline cases where it is difficult to decide what to do. Let us look into some of these cases.

Universal facts. The main principle is that you do not need to cite universal facts. Thus, a citation is not needed if we state where Theland is located and that its capital is Capcity, because all this information is mentioned in every encyclopaedia and on Wikipedia. The situation is different if we say that Thelanders are sympathetic to various medical experiments and their attitudes to their neighbouring countries are negative. It is not clear whether we need to name the source of these pieces of information. You may not find them in encyclopaedias but, on the other hand, they have been a topic of general discussion for a long time. This interpretation goes for non-scientific publications, but is it valid for scientific publications? If it is impossible to find a certain study that could be referred to, is it possible to say that 'a generally admitted fact is' or 'a widespread fact is'? What is classified as a universal fact will change between fields – in specific journals certain facts are assumed, but in more generic publications they would need to be cited.

Accuracy of citations and quotes. It is difficult to read text with lots of direct quotes. On the other hand, accuracy with paraphrasing can be challenging as much plagiarism detection software treats strings of ten words as the unit of analysis and comparison. Just changing a few words or the sentence structure is not enough for appropriate paraphrasing.

Every time we refer to a previous text in our own words, we take a risk of misrepresenting the original source. Let us assume that an author cites and paraphrases in the following way:

Georg Birke (2007) based on his research findings states that communication between cells does not only happen when there is an external threat, but that cells also send 'all is good' messages. Similar research results can be also found from Berjozov & Osinina (2006), Björkman & Asplund (2006) and Koivisto-Haapala (2006).

Let us first look at the statement in the second sentence. It looks clear and uncomplicated, but what exactly is meant by 'similar'? Does it mean that the referenced research has noted cell communication based on external but not threatening situations? Does it mean they also have found that cell communication does not require any external stimulus? From the perspective of cell communication, the distinction is important.

For the main statement, what has Birke said exactly? There could be three options:

1   Threats are not the only reason cells communicate. It is not possible to show a cause for this communication. It could be a need to maintain an open channel, or it could mean that cells also send positive messages.
2   Threats are not the only reason cells communicate. Measurements in the receiving cells indicate that the messages could be sent for the purpose of spreading positive states between cells. The matter requires further research to be confirmed.
3   Threats are not the only reason cells communicate. The result is surprising as the communication has no known purpose. One possible explanation is that cells have a need to express their existence. The message content is 'no threats' or 'everything is OK'.

The statement made by the authors in the quote appears inaccurate regardless of whether Birke actually meant option 1, 2 or 3. The statement in the quote is more categorical than any of the possible options of Birke's meaning. There are a number of different reasons that can lead to this type of inaccuracy:

• Simple lack of attention to the original text.
• Due to different background knowledge or different interests, the text is understood differently to what the author originally intended.
• It could be intentional, though minor, inaccuracy to support other statements in the text.
• It is possible that the author has a systematic habit of making inaccurate interpretations.

It is likely that the intentional or unintentional mild manipulation of previous works has a more significant impact on research than does plagiarism.

3 Accuracy of wording

While scientific language is perceived to be structured and accurate, it typically still contains inaccurate and ambiguous wordings and statements. Here is an example:

Unemployment/genetic mutation/racism is clearly more common in the Northern part of Theland than the rest of the country.

The terms *unemployment*, *genetic mutation* and *racism* in themselves carry multiple interpretations. In addition, there are at least three potential inaccuracies in this short statement:

1   Geographical location: what is meant by the Northern part of Theland?
2   The statement *clearly more common* could have multiple potential interpretations. Similar words are 'significantly', 'substantially', 'considerably' or 'largely', for example. There is no way of knowing how much more common or even how it is measured.
3   Timeframe: the sentence is written in present tense, but when was the research done and the data gathered?

There is a spectrum of reasons from acceptable to fraudulent that can lead to the use of potentially inaccurate or ambiguous language:

• A text filled with numbers and definitions is very difficult to read, and the main message is easily lost as details draw much of the attention.
• There may be no more accurate information available and the accuracy may not be essential for the interpretation of current results.
• The author may have been negligent in a situation where an accurate statement was called for and the information was available.
• The author may have intentionally used an inaccurate statement to manipulate the way results are viewed.

Intentionality is a significant factor in evaluating inaccuracies. While misconduct/ fraud requires intentionality, it can be argued that negligence in use of accurate language is not acceptable in research based on the core values of honesty, accuracy and diligence.

The aim is to write text in which the author and the reader understand the content in the same way. As we always bring an element of subjectivity to reading any text, this remains an ideal we strive for in research communication.

To assist in accuracy, most fields develop their own discourse with specific terminologies. On the other hand, the more specific the terminology and discourse, the fewer people can actually understand the meaning of the articles. The balance in writing accurately and keeping the text accessible is a challenge in most fields. Use of specific discourse can have the unspoken intention of creating an inner circle with exclusive access to new knowledge.

FORMS OF PUBLICATION

The results of research are usually published as a whole. Preliminary data can be presented in oral presentations and as part of university courses. Here, we concentrate on scientific publications written for a research community, which as a rule consists of researchers working in the same field.

As researchers we are given the freedom to choose how and where we publish our results. The use of this freedom is guided by internal rules in the research community and guidelines for ethical decisions. The core idea is that every publication should offer the research community something new. Therefore it is not acceptable to re-package results for different publication fora. These would be called duplicate publications. You may be able to justify publishing the same results more than once, for example, when publishing interdisciplinary research in each field of the study to allow each field access to the results. From a principled perspective, this may be problematic due to potential copyright infringements. Further, while publications are the key measurement of academic ability and excellence, artificially inflating publication lists in this way would be unacceptable. The consequentialist perspective leads us to consider the potential impact that publishing the same research more than once has on the opportunity for other novel research to be published. Also, duplicating research results could inappropriately affect literature reviews and thus mislead the review process.

Another aspect is divided publications. Each publication should present the complete results from an experiment, observation or analysis. Therefore it would be inappropriate to publish an article on the impact on women and another on the impact on men if these two were variables in the same experiment.[3] Divided publications are ethically problematic for the same reasons as duplicated publications. In addition, they mislead readers on the research questions and results as the methodology and questions are artificially separated into pieces without context. Knowing what a complete result is may be difficult in the continuous scientific work, where experiments are interlinked and overlapping. It is then essential to consider and discuss how to define the suggested 'completeness'.

- The target audience often defines the publishing language. If the researcher aims to tell the domestic research community something, it is reasonable to do it in their language. However, in most cases the aim is to take part in the global scientific discussion and to gain international visibility. This means publishing in a widely understood language, which is currently English. There are some exceptions to this principle. For example, in research on Portuguese language and culture the researcher may expect that researchers outside Portugal are also able to read Portuguese. In English-speaking countries (the USA, Great Britain, Australia, etc.) the language question is not relevant, but similar reasoning may take place in selecting the publishing forum: some may be more domestic-oriented while other ones are purely international.   [PRINCIPLED]

Understanding the research community as a target audience and a stakeholder provides an interesting angle on the language of doctoral theses and other publications in the humanities and social sciences.

- We may weigh the benefit and harm for the research community if one publishes in the local language on Wittgenstein's language game theory or changes in Chinese society in the 1560s.   [CONSEQUENTIALIST]

By doing so, the author minimises the size of the audience. There are, for example, only 5–10 researchers who are interested in these questions and are able to comprehend the language used in the paper. This does not sound rational and one could say that one general idea of science is neglected, namely the reaction and control by researchers of the same discipline.

The language issue can be considered also from the point of view of principles. Researchers may fear that English totally overtakes Thelandish in scientific publishing and there is a duty to protect other languages and their use in scientific work. The conflict can be decided by the 'two-front policy': if a researcher wants to reach a global audience, the article must be written in English; if the audience is purely local, writing in the local language is justifiable. In acting so, the researcher is conscious of being a member of the international research community but at the same time understands his or her responsibilities to take part in the discussion in Theland. When we have two separate audiences, duplicate publishing may be justified. After publishing something in international fora we can share the same research results with domestic readers.

The 'two-front policy' invites some further ethical questions.

- According to a definition of a good researcher, the international research community must be addressed. Homeland visibility is usually seen as an additional merit rather than as a main goal of scientific activity.   [VIRTUE]
- However, what is beneficial for a young researcher aiming at high scientific merit, may be less important for a senior researcher with significant homeland expert responsibilities. The university or department may put further pressure on publishing only in specific types of scientific journals. In these instances different stakeholders have different definitions of harm and benefit, and finding the option that benefits all stakeholders can be difficult, if not impossible.   [CONSEQUENTIALIST]

Let us imagine the following situation of multiple stakeholders. An established professor makes a decision to no longer chase international publications, but to concentrate on supervising junior researchers and on creating societal networks around the research topic. Simultaneously, the department badly needs 'scientific points' in the form of publications. This dilemma can be approached by using all three ethical tools:

- Whose benefit has the most weight? [CONSEQUENTIALIST]
- Which principles determine the professor's working profile? [PRINCIPLED]
- How does an ideal professor choose? [VIRTUE]

Publication fora vary between research fields. While peer-reviewed articles have a dominant role, in some fields monographs still play an important part in the scientific discussion. This is sometimes justified by arguing that the format of an article does not fit for handling large complicated research questions. Similarly, conference proceedings can carry great significance in some fields, especially in technical and computational sciences. Journals typically have their own hierarchy in each field. Most researchers aim to publish in the best possible journals based on rankings measured by different impact factors or ones generated by universities or ministries as priority journals.

A special type of publication is the review article, which provides an overview of the state of the art in a given research area. As a rule, the authorship of such an article is given to an experienced and prominent researcher. The compilation of a review article includes much more subjectivity than a normal article, which reports on results of a certain study. The author of a review article determines which research questions and researchers are significant and worth mentioning. We see a similar approach in meta-analyses, which are especially popular in medicine. They are statistical generalisations of a large number of publications dealing with the same problem. Due to the significant influence of these analyses, researchers taking part in them bear great responsibility for their choices of the selected publications and the methods used in the statistical calculations. The impact of meta-analyses becomes greater through the fact that the media are also interested in them because they give a generalised picture of a certain phenomenon made by a specialist instead of having separate publications concentrating only on a limited aspect of the phenomenon.

An important new dimension in the scientific world is open access publishing.[4] Nowadays it is one of the hottest discussion topics in the research community. It is a rare phenomenon in the research world that includes as many ethical questions as this.

The idea of open access publishing started from two fairness questions:

1   Is it right that researchers do twice as much work
    – first they write scientific papers and other
    researchers act as referees of them, for free – and
    then a commercial enterprise take from this the
    profits by selling the publications back to the
    researchers? The researchers seldom pay for
    journals and books directly, but their universities
    or research institutes use their financial resources
    to pay for them and so have less to spend
    supporting research. Protests against publishers
    intensified when the prices of journals rose quickly.   [PRINCIPLED]

2   An increasing number of universities have been
    unable to provide their researchers access to all key
    journals. The situation is particularly difficult at
    universities located in developing countries. This
    begs the question: is such unfairness something we
    should fight against or is it an inevitable feature of
    international competitive research that we have to
    contend with?   [PRINCIPLED]

3   Additionally, a more consequentialist argument
    was staged to support open access: the transfer of
    research knowledge into practical solutions in
    manufacturing, health care, policy, education,
    conservation, etc. could be much faster if research
    knowledge was more openly and readily available
    to everyone, not just academic institutions able to
    pay subscription fees.   [CONSEQUENTIALIST]

Various formats of open access are currently in use. **Golden open access** means free availability for readers, but a so-called APC (article processing charge) is usually levied. In normal language, this means the employer of the researchers or the financer of the research has to pay for publications. **Green open access** allows free publishing of the final prepublication version of the article in a repository of a university or another institution, usually after delay period of 6–24 months.

Many established journals have chosen to provide at least a version of open access to their articles. In addition, public funding agreements more and more frequently require publishing in open access journals.

The ethical questions of open access publishing are complicated and benefit from guided dialogue within the research community. One way to approach them is to assess open access according to ethical approaches:

- Openness and transparency are key research values.
  How well do different publishing formats apply
  these principles? What type of publication system
  would best support openness and transparency?
  Who has a right to dictate/require how and where
  research results are published? Is it fair that you
  can buy the open access option for money? Many
  of these questions are directing to those who are
  responsible for the whole research environment at
  the local and global level.   [PRINCIPLED]
- What are the harms and benefits of different
  publication pathways to all stakeholders (individual
  researchers, universities, publishing houses,
  society's decision-makers, consumers, etc.)? From
  this perspective, which publishing format should
  be prioritised?   [CONSEQUENTIALIST]
- How do our publishing choices reflect our values
  as researchers? Which motives would be the most
  admirable and virtuous?   [VIRTUE]

AUTHORSHIP

Authorship is an essential question for every researcher. Who is included and in which order is an important question. Different fields have their own traditions around authorship and the order of authors. On the face of it the question is simple in all fields: authors are those who have significantly contributed to the manuscript and research described in it. If the question of authorship is not discussed explicitly, people taking part in research may be left with different expectations around authorship and their role in the process. Authorship matters to everyone as it defines research ability and academic merit, as well as responsibility for the results.

Guest authorship is an authorship not based on actual input into the research or writing process. In these instances the researcher receives academic credit when it is not due. The authorship can lead to considering the guest author as an expert in areas where that is not the case. This can lead to decisions around funding, career opportunities or expert roles that are not based on actual knowledge or research experience. Guest authorship may occur with consent by the author or without their knowledge. In the first instance, the guest authorship may result from pressure by some people to be included as authors due to their position or potential to damage/support the careers of other authors, maintenance of relationships between different groups or colleagues in the same institution, desire to increase chances of being published or offering a gift or return of a favour to someone. When the guest author is unaware of the authorship, the reason is likely to be based on desired kudos of having an established name in the paper or presenting a collegial connection where none exists.

Journals typically provide some guidance on authorship and increasingly require authorship statements to clarify the role of each author. Many of these guidelines are based on the so-called Vancouver Guidelines, which were originally created by the editors of the International Committee of Medical Journal Editors (ICJME). According to these guidelines, four conditions all have to be met for someone to be included as an author:[5]

1   substantial contributions to the conception or design of the work; or the acquisition, analysis or interpretation of data for the work;
2   drafting the work or revising it critically for important intellectual content;
3   final approval of the version to be published; and
4   agreement to be accountable for all aspects of the work in ensuring that questions related to the accuracy or integrity of any part of the work are appropriately investigated and resolved.

Ethically essential importance is attached to defining the terms 'substantial', 'critically' and 'important intellectual content'. There is room for multiple acceptable interpretations and opportunity for disagreements to develop between interpretations. These create the potential for disagreement on who should be an author. It appears essential to establish an ongoing guided dialogue around the question of authorship both within research groups and within the research community.

Transparency is again a good guidepost. Agreeing on authors at the beginning and adjusting the list as the project and writing take shape will help to reduce confusion and disagreement. Further, writing authorship statements and being explicit regarding everyone's role in relation to the published manuscript will endorse fairness in the academic community.

The question of the order of authors has several realisations depending on the number of authors and the research field. A publication with two or three authors having similar roles in the study differs from a publication based on the work of several researchers having heterogeneous tasks and statuses in the process of research. A special case is articles based on large experiments, which may have dozens or hundreds of authors who have taken part in various functions in the project. The main options in the order of authors are:

- alphabetical order;
- the order is drawn by lot;
- the order changes if the same authors write frequently together (*Johnson and Smith* becomes *Smith and Johnson* in a following publication);
- the order reflects the significance of the authors – the most important contributor is named first; or

- the order reflects seniority or other rank (usually the senior supervisor or project leader is the last-named author).

The question of the order is not one of right or wrong. Here again transparency reached by dialogue is the key to an ethically grounded choice. One thing is to negotiate this among the authors; another thing is to make the creation of the order of authors clear for the reader if there is a risk that she or he might interpret, for example, alphabetical order in the wrong way.

PEER REVIEW

Most academic manuscripts will go through a peer-review process at some stage. The process does not always look the same, but the idea of having your peers evaluate the work is commonplace in most research work. Here, we will focus on publishing in peer-reviewed journals as it is the most common form of academic publishing.

Manuscripts go through a number of filters before they are published. The first one is the editorial review that determines whether the manuscript has any potential to be published. As a result, the manuscript is either rejected or sent for review, typically to two peers who have expertise in the field covered in the manuscript.

With the increase of open access publications, the review process is going through a transformative process. An open peer-review process in which names of both the reviewer and author are openly shared has now challenged the traditional double-blind process in which both the reviewer and the author were anonymous.[6] Anonymity is typically suggested as a way of promoting neutrality in the review process, as well as creating a safe space for reviewers to be critical towards the work of their peers without having to fear for consequences. How well anonymity can be protected is dependent on the size of the field. In small and specialised fields it is very difficult to find a reviewer who would not recognise the author or group based on the content of the manuscript.

The open review process has been suggested to promote fairness and align with the core principles of transparency and openness. In addition, the review process is time-consuming; making it public provides credit to the author of the review as well, together with recognition of the important contribution the reviewer can make to the quality of the final paper. Similarly, no reviewer is able to hide behind anonymity to reject or criticise a manuscript without good reason, and thus the quality of the review process is improved. On the other hand, the open review system can be challenged if particularly junior academics are reviewers as they may not be able to criticise the work of senior peers for fear of losing face or credibility. In addition, knowing who the authors are may unduly influence the review process. Making a choice of whether to support open review or not is based on an understanding of the key concepts of transparency and anonymity, as well as the values placed on them.

In addition, estimates of benefit and harm in each system to the research community will influence the choice. An interesting question for dialogue would be to explore what types of benefit and harm are incorporated in each peer-review system, how they could be measured and compared, and which system would better support the research community we wish to develop.   [CONSEQUENTIALIST]

The choice of reviewers has specific ethical considerations. It is clear that the choice is an essential part of a quality research process, and at least the following considerations should be included in the selection:

- **Competency.** Does the reviewer have the competence to review this particular manuscript? The definition of competency may be challenging. Similarity in research publications is often a key criterion. Does that mean the responsibility for the review should be shouldered by more experienced researchers only? Should we trust authors' suggestions on competent reviewers or would that lead to too much potential for bias and favouritism?
- **Conflict of interest.** Is the reviewer's own research too similar to the research being reviewed, which could lead to a competition between the reviewer and author? In this instance it could be advantageous for the reviewer to reject or suggest substantial revisions in order to gain an advantage over the unpublished research. The competitive nature of research and the role of publication as an indicator of academic excellence make this an essential question of fairness. Simultaneously it requires a balancing act with the competence of the author. The evaluator's own field of research should therefore be similar enough and different enough to the assessment of the present study.
- **Commitment to a schedule.** Jobs and theses may be dependent on approval of the submitted manuscript for publication. Thus the time taken to review becomes an essential element of fairness and should be considered when selecting a reviewed. Time is a sensitive issue: forcing acceleration of the review process may lead to deterioration of quality; however, if the process takes too long, it risks publication occurring elsewhere first, slows down the transfer of knowledge within the research community and into society, and delays the academic recognition and credibility of the authors. The balance between experienced academics, who are likely to have less time for reviewing but better ability to review, and younger academics with possibly more time but less experience, can be difficult to optimise.
- **Previous experience.** What are the experiences with each reviewer – have their reviews been informative, clear and reliable? Good reviews promote good research, are a credit to the journal and improve the authors' abilities.

One interesting small ethical question relates to the reviewers making a suggestion to reference their own research in the manuscript they have just reviewed. This could add further support to the argument or it could just be fishing for citations. This would be difficult to justify ethically due to the unfairness an inflated citation index could have in the allocation of resources or career opportunities. The journal editors and reviewer may, however, form a symbiotic relationship in which the reviewer is encouraged to suggest further references to other articles published in the journal, and the editor will allow suggestions for personal references as well.

We will return to ethical questions concerning peer-review practices in other chapters of the book.

***

Publishing is at the heart of research. It is also an essential part of being a researcher. Because it is such a central element, everyone attaches values, norms and expectations to their own publishing process, as well that of others. Research ethics guidelines focus on publishing for this very reason. The value and importance of collectively exploring an issue grow with the significance of the issue in the overall context. For this reason, guided dialogue around publishing can guide both individuals and, more importantly, research communities to make better choices around questions of authorship, choice of publication forum, developing peer-review systems and balancing the needs of different stakeholders. The changing context in different writing processes and the expanding nature of research publications invites us to engage with the questions throughout our own research projects as well as throughout our research careers.

Case study 1: where to publish?

The choice of the publishing forum is far from a simple question. This issue is likely to be considered by using a consequentialist approach: the researcher or group of researchers should find a journal or publisher which is 'maximally prestigious' but at the same time achievable and quick to publish. However, this straightforward reasoning may be hampered by other factors, for example:

1   **Reputation.** Does the publisher belong to the band of 'evil actors' in the publishing world or to the group of those who behave well? Should this influence the decision?
2   **Open access.** What are the rules for open access availability of published papers? How do they influence the selection? Is this a rule that overrides all other considerations?

3   **Scope of the journal.** Does the journal publish papers with broad themes or does it represents only a narrow research field? Which is considered a greater benefit?
4   **Personal experience.** What are your personal experiences or experiences of colleagues with that journal or publisher?
5   **Contact person.** Do you already know the chief editor, a member of the editorial or advisory board of the journal?
6   **Favouritism.** You have your own pet journal and you would like to publish there. Is that justifiable?

These questions represent different aspects of ethical thinking. Do you typically consider these questions in your decision-making? What kind of data can you consider to further define the impact of these aspects of harm and benefit? Should a department/faculty/university have a publishing strategy, or should these issues be solved purely at a personal level as part of a researcher's autonomy?

Case study 2: limits of vague expressions

Consider the beginning of a text: 'In the Western countries sexual behaviour has faced a revolution during the last decades.' In this sentence there are four meaning-carrying components: *Western countries, sexual behaviour, revolution* and *last decades.* Strictly speaking, each of them is ambiguous in the sense that the reader can understand them in different ways. Which countries are meant by 'Western countries'? One can understand 'sexual behaviour' in different ways. 'Revolution' used as a metaphor gives an idea of big changes, but how big are they? Are the last decades the last two or three, or even more?

Sentences like this are typical for media texts, but you can see similar ones in scientific articles. Are they acceptable if the author and the readers understand the sentence in a similar way? If the reading of the text differs substantially from the meaning the author wanted to express, is the reader responsible for that or the author? To what extent does the answer depends on intentionality of the vagueness of the text? You are not allowed to mislead the reader, but what can we do about accidental misunderstandings taking place? Do you agree with such an interpretation? If you had to justify your opinion to other people, which arguments would be valid and worthy?

Case study 3: who should be an author?

Professor Hasina, as part of her large international funding project, collaborated closely with four other research groups. The research groups had signed a data-sharing agreement in accordance with open science principles. Hasina's group had collated data on urban aerosol particles and had access to similar measurements made by the other groups in their respective cities. Post-doc Sofia was given the data set to analyse and prepare it for publication.

It was agreed that Sofia would be the first author and the research group leaders from the other groups would also be included as authors, together with Hasina. Sofia spent approximately six months gathering the data, going through it and merging it all into one large data set. She was able to start the analyses and did all the preliminary analyses before she went on maternity leave. Before her leave, Sofia sent her results to all the groups involved and she received comments from two out of four group leaders.

After Sofia went on leave, the responsibility for the research was transferred to Rohan, a second-year PhD student. Rohan was busy with another project; six months passed before he could work on Sofia's data. Rohan worked on Sofia's analyses and started writing the manuscript. At this time Rohan noticed a significant weakness with the data. He and Hasina decided to try another methodological approach. A senior researcher in statistics was brought in to help with the analysis, and she worked closely with Rohan for a number of weeks to analyse the data.

When Sofia came back from maternity leave 12 months later, Rohan had completed the analysis and written the introduction, methods and results. At this point the manuscript was also shared with the other group leaders; one of them sent extensive feedback while the others only acknowledged the manuscript. Rohan and Sofia worked together to finish the article within the first month of Sofia returning to work. The article was predominantly based on the methodology used by Rohan.

- Who do you think should be included as an author in this manuscript?
- Who do you think should be the first author?
- What guidelines and/or principles apply to this decision?

At this point Sofia suggests that her colleague, Rami, from a university she had visited should be included as an author as well. Rami has an impressive research record in immigrant urban experience and there is significant potential for future collaboration. Hasina supports Sofia's suggestion and points out to Rohan that he would be well-placed for a post-doc at Rami's university if the collaborative project developed favourably. Sofia and Rami had discussed this research and some of the comments made by Rami were incorporated into the discussion of the manuscript at Sofia's suggestion.

- What consequentialist arguments could be used to support the inclusion of Rami as an author?
- Are there consequentialist arguments to suggest Rami should *not* be included as an author?
- What principles would support Rami's inclusion or exclusion?
- What options does Rohan have in this situation? What about Hasina?

Other authorship cases:

1 The research was dominantly based on laboratory work. Sofia and Hasina designed the research methodology. An experienced lab technician, Veronica, carried out the actual work and Sam supported the analysis from the statistics department. Sam's support and development of analysis software was essential for the results. The head of the project, Erik, followed the research closely and supported Hasina and Sofia in theory work. Sofia wrote the first version of the manuscript. Hasina read the manuscript several times and made corrections. Sam read and checked the section relating to statistical analysis. Erik read the last draft but made no changes. Veronica did not participate in the writing process. In total, Sofia spent approximately five months on the project, Hasina three weeks, Veronica four months, Sam a week and Erik maybe a little less than a week. Who should be an author and in which order should the authors appear?

2 Ester did her Master's thesis with Erik. Erik worked closely with Sofia as the topic aligned well with his own research work. Erik designed the data retrieval methodology from an existing database and the analysis was based on Erik's original idea. The resulting analysis was of publishable quality. Regarding authorship, there are multiple options: (1) Erik writes the article based on the analysis himself and either asks Sofia's permission or not; (2) Erik writes the article in his own name and refers to the Master's thesis as part of his article; (3) Erik asks Sofia to write the article and he edits the article in preparation for publication – authors could be listed as either Erik and Sofia or Sofia and Erik; (4) Erik and Sofia write the article together and the author names can be either Erik and Sofia or Sofia and Erik. Consider each option and their possible ethical justification. Is any option ethically unacceptable? How much does the fact that Sofia is interested in applying for a PhD influence the decision? One of the foundation questions relates to an analysis on who 'owns' research done at Master's level?

Case study 4: an ideal conference

In this chapter we have discussed ethical issues which arise in publishing research. Organising conferences and presenting papers at them includes some interesting questions for which one needs to use ethical tools. Organisers of conferences and other scientific events cannot avoid thinking of the ratio of quality and quantity. If we restrict the number of papers and select the presenters by using strict criteria, we get a high-grade and interesting scientific gathering. On the other hand, offering the opportunity to a maximum number of researchers is more equal and fair, especially when we bear in mind that, in many cases, the acceptance of a paper or a poster is often a prerequisite for a travel grant.

The *quantity–quality balance* is not the only dilemma for organisers of a conference. Similar questions are:

- the topics of accepting papers using the scale 'anything goes' or 'strictly sticking to the specific topic of the conference';
- the general structure of the conference: the organiser must decide how many plenary papers, how many parallel section papers and how many posters;
- the time provided to the presenters and to discussion;
- the content of the programme outside the scientific presentations (banquets, dinners, excursions).

The topics of research rarely change radically. Therefore, presentations of researchers often partly repeat what has been said earlier. It is impossible to count the share of old and new. Theoretically we can estimate that 80 per cent consists of old and 20 per cent of new. It is reasonable to describe to the listeners the context of the new findings. Consider the following cases using *consequentialist* and *virtue* approaches:

1   Professor X has given a paper in a small symposium. A researcher attending the symposium is organising a large international congress and asks Professor X to keep the 'same' presentation as a plenary lecture in the opening session of the congress.
2   Researcher Y has made an important scientific finding. The article based on it has been accepted by a good journal. Now Y is given a section paper at a conference.
3   Doctoral student Z has presented a paper in a small seminar in her doctoral school. Now Z is given a paper in an international conference. There are two of her supervisors and three doctoral students of the group in the audience.

4   University lecturer Q has not attended scientific conferences for some years. Now he has a section paper on a topic which has been studied very little. He is going to present quantitative results which are based on a rather small data pool.

NOTES

1   There are several ways to approach the question of scientific truth...
2   Other used terms are *divided publication* and *repetitive publication*.
3   E.J. Huth (1986), Irresponsible authorship and wasteful publication, *Annals of Internal Medicine* 104, 257–259.
4   P. Suber (2012) *Open Access*, Cambridge, MA: MIT Press (http://legacy.earlham. edu/~peters/fos/overview.htm).
5   ICMJE Vancouver Guidelines (www.icmje.org/recommendations/browse/roles-and-responsibilities/defining-the-role-of-authors-and-contributors.html).
6   A. Tattersall (2016), Open peer review, *Altmetrics: A Practical Guide for Librarians, Researchers and Academics*, ed. A. Tatersall. London: Facet (http://eprints.whiterose. ac.uk/100874/5/Chapter%2011%20-%20Open%20Peer%20Review%20Chapter%20-%20OA.pdf); D. Nicholas, A. Watkinson, H.R. Jamali, E. Herman, C. Tenopir, R. Volentine, S. Allard and K. Levine (2015), Peer review: still king in the digital age, *Learned Publishing* 28:1, 15–21.

Chapter 4

Supervising students

The main ethical considerations in doctoral training are:

1 Being one of the main tasks of universities, doctoral training should be given a proper position in teachers' workload and in formulas which determine university and faculty financing.
2 There is always a certain tension between the supervisor and the doctoral student due to various features of this relationship:

- The supervisor represents the past and the present traditions, while the doctoral student represents the future.
- For the doctoral student the situation is unique, while the supervisor has a lot of similar relationships.
- The supervisor and the student share a common goal, but have their own roles.
- The relationship is based on a distinct power relationship, which is expected to shift during the PhD process.

Ethics by guided dialogue typically requires researchers and research communities to consider the following key ethical questions in doctoral training:

- Are the selection criteria of doctoral students appropriate?
- How should the balance between common guidelines and rules, and individual needs of the supervisor and the doctoral student be achieved?
- What is the appropriate procedure if the supervision process fails?
- How should fair evaluation of doctoral theses be guaranteed?
- Is the number of annual doctoral degrees elaborated, at the research policy level, from the point of view of all stakeholders, including the doctoral student?

Practically all established senior researchers have doctoral students. Supervision of the highest academic thesis is a central part of senior researchers' work, especially in universities. Training of the next generation of researchers is an important part of the function of universities. Universities are in most countries the only institutions that can offer researcher education and accept the academic degree based on that. It is also worth bearing in mind that doctoral theses comprise a large part of the total amount of research done at universities.

However, when discussing the significance of doctoral training, it is essential to see beyond the produced dissertation. From a societal point of view, a more important result of doctoral training is the highly qualified citizens who brings their academic knowledge and skills to various sectors of society. It is reasonable to expect that these people are an important driving force in a modern knowledge-based society.

The interaction between the supervisor and the student prompts multiple ethical questions, which often arise from the imbalance in the relationship.[1] The supervisor role is invested with power and responsibility regarding the progress of the student's studies and about the development of their future as an independent researcher. Because research is more and more often done in groups, the supervisor has to be fair towards all doctoral students. This complicated relationship can be jeopardised by the fact that the supervisors usually lack any formal training in supervision. The research community, respecting expertise, has traditionally thought that it is enough if the supervisors are recognised and competent researchers. Sometimes the only 'training' they have is the impression built on the basis of the work of the previous generation of supervisors.

Adopting the role of a supervisor is one of the rites of becoming a member of the research community. Sticking to the traditions created through generations gives depth and stability to the work, but at the same time this can hinder necessary reforms and unnoticed transfer of old bad habits to a new generation. Some ethical questions in doctoral training spring from a clash of old and new courses of action. In these situations the members of the community have to decide whose opinions, values and desires dictate the supervision process.

As in many other countries, also in Theland, the number of doctoral degrees has increased rapidly. The research-funding formats have led to the financial importance of supervising doctoral students. The 'overproduction' of doctors is a topic of debate both in the academic world and in the wider society. Asking how to define the appropriate number of new doctoral degrees and who should make the decision generates an interesting ethical dialogue. When approaching these questions it is important to consider who is responsible for the substantial growth in the number of doctoral degrees. Is it a consequence of egoistic policy by universities or is it based on the real needs of society? Alternatively, it could be a reflection of a society where the ability to stand out as educated is pushed further up the academic progression – when a significant proportion of society now completes an undergraduate degree, differentiation is achieved by completing a doctorate.

CONSEQUENTIALIST

When approaching the question of an appropriate number of PhD students by using the consequentialist approach, it is important to determine who the stakeholders are and how harm and benefit is identified for each. Here we meet a decision-making challenge: as a stakeholder group, the doctoral students are most affected by the doctoral training policy, but they have the least ability to influence it. This is typical in ethical decision-making – the decision-making power and the majority of the impact are divided between different stakeholders. This ethical imbalance increases the responsibility of decision-makers to give extensive, if not also primary, concern for those stakeholders most affected by the decisions.

Another issue that worries (or should worry) people is the quality of doctoral theses and that of doctoral training as a whole. Are the standards for accepting dissertations falling, as is often suggested? And if the answer is *yes*, is it just an inevitable consequence of the increased number of doctoral students? It is impossible to give an unequivocal answer to this question because we lack reliable data. In addition, doctoral training is currently more than just the thesis. The importance of developing leadership skills and project management abilities is now a standard part of doctoral students' studies and learning goals. The question of what a doctoral candidate should be able to do is an equally important ethical question to asking how many doctoral degrees the society should aim for. Both of these require broad evaluation of multiple stakeholders (universities, students and the whole country or the international research community) and clarification of values/goals considered in the decision-making.

The main theme of this chapter is supervision of doctoral theses. This supervision relationship is key in the research community, both procedurally and financially. Other supervision relationships, e.g. at the Master's degree level, share many of the ethical questions with doctoral supervision.

Our discussion begins with three important elements of ethical reasoning, as described in Chapter 1: identification of stakeholders; rights and responsibilities; and defining options in the context of doing research work. We will then explore the idea of ethics by guided dialogue through cases and examples. As elsewhere, the different approaches are labelled [CONSEQUENTIALIST], [PRINCIPLED] and [VIRTUE].

Identifying stakeholders

Primary stakeholders are, for obvious reasons, the **supervisor** and the **doctoral student**: the doctoral dissertation is produced through their cooperation. There are some differences between research fields in the role of the supervisor, but some general aspects remain the same in all relationships. The supervisor has already defended his or her dissertation and is, thus, as a researcher more experienced than the doctoral student, and has in succession and in parallel several students to be guided. It is possible, though, that the student is a more talented researcher than the supervisor, but this does not change their roles in the process. The supervisor also holds an official position as a representative of the department and/or faculty. In the case of multiple supervisors, this representative role is usually given to one of them and the other supervisors have different subject-specific roles.

In practice, personal characteristics determine how the relationship develops. In contrast to supervisors, doctoral students are in a unique period in their lives. To apply for a postgraduate position is, for a young person, a major decision, which in many ways dictates subsequent life decisions; in the career of a senior researcher supervision of a single student plays a much smaller role. Thus the primary stakeholders come to the situation from very different premises, which increases the risk that, despite a common goal, they may differ in desires and ways to reach it.

The student and supervisor do not work and interact in isolation. **Other doctoral students** and **research colleagues** are secondary stakeholders. The relationship between the doctoral students can be of great significance as well as conflict-prone. Other doctoral students provide an important reference group with which it is easy to discuss problems related to the dissertation. On the other hand, these people are probably future rivals in terms of applying for the same positions and grants.

Doctoral students may experience rivalry already during their studies if they need to compete for their supervisor's time, travel grants or possibilities/duties not related directly to their own work. The supervisor's colleagues may see the supervisor as a rival in the competition for the name (i.e. having a discovery named after them) and fame – or, on the contrary, they may be thankful for the contribution she or he made to the results and visibility of the department. This is a challenge for each work community: to envy the success of a colleague or to be proud of it. Truthful soul-searching often reveals both emotions in most of us. Is it wise and polite to show envy or hide it?

In universities, the superior–subordinate relationship play a less important role than in many other workplaces, but if the supervisor has, for example, the head of the department as a **superior**, he or she is, of course, a stakeholder.

PRINCIPLED

Competition is an inherent feature of academic life. Thus, one can ask to what extent success in supervision should influence university teachers' salary and what the indicators for measuring it are. What are the general principles that should be followed in salary policy?

CONSEQUENTIALIST

If the number of doctoral degrees is a relevant indicator in this issue, one can ask how this affects readiness to cooperate in supervision. This is a general question when using any indicators at an individual level. Does the use of strict quantitative indicators harm cohesion and collegiality in the research community? Do we benefit in one thing but produce harm in another respect? How do we evaluate the balance of benefit and harm in that case?

VIRTUE

The superior of supervisors represents the university administration and its principles. A good superior has a fair relationship with subordinates. But does fairness mean avoidance of any competitive elements in coaching and leading? Or does it mean strict and transparent indicators in salary policy? One more aspect of being a good superior, according to academic traditions, is to give teachers and researchers, especially senior ones, full autonomy in their work. Does such reasoning lead to the conclusion that in the academic environment we do not need superiors or that we should minimise their role?

Faculty or an equivalent body is an important stakeholder. The faculty takes the doctoral student, accepts the thesis, and sets general rules for the whole process of doctoral training. The number of doctoral degrees may also be a criterion in the formula, which has significant influence on faculty funding. The faculty is a secondary stakeholder. It works at a collective level and the responsibilities and decisions concern a larger number of people, while the supervisor and the student meet as individuals and are therefore primary stakeholders.

External referees and **opponents** of doctoral theses play a central role in the quality assurance of doctoral dissertations. They have a lot of power. However, their influence is one-sided: they affect the outcome of the dissertation, but the supervisor and the doctoral student have marginal influence over them.

The target audience of a dissertation is the **research community** as a whole, which makes it an important stakeholder. Fellow researchers of a certain field read every scientific publication with a critical eye and may also use it as a foundation of their own research. The research community plays a distant role in issues concerning various phases of doctoral training by creating traditions and activating discussion around the principles of supervision and other constituents of doctoral training.

Writing a doctoral thesis is typically a project of the whole **family**. One can come to such a conclusion when reading the prefaces of theses and listening to speeches at banquets. New doctors thank spouses, children, parents and other people in their personal life for support, patience and even sacrifices. While they appear as stakeholders for the doctoral candidate, it is not clear to what extent other stakeholders should consider them in their ethical reasoning. Working on your doctoral degree can be considered to be equivalent to employment and the considerations towards the family of the candidate need to consider rights to parental leave or right to have holiday time, but beyond that further ethical reasons are needed for including this stakeholder group in decision-making.

Doctoral students now complete much research and will have a social impact following the completion of their degree; thus it is reasonable to consider **society** as a stakeholder when it comes to considering harm and benefit in relation to doctoral supervision. Society is a collective stakeholder and the impact is only a potential one. Therefore its role in making ethically guided choices needs to be carefully considered in respect to the other stakeholders.

Understanding rights and responsibilities

Doctoral studies include a lot of ethical questions that are linked to the rights and responsibilities of the stakeholders and how they are balanced. This reasoning starts with the very beginning of the whole process: has the doctoral student the right to select his or her supervisor? That possible right is balanced with the supervisor's right to select or reject students. The student–supervisor relationship is delicate, and many conflicts can be perceived as one party considering the other as not fulfilling their responsibilities, and thus the injured party feels their rights have not been respected and supported.

Let us look at this using an extreme example. The supervisor and doctoral student have ended up in a situation where their views on methodology or an ethical issue are totally opposed. This opposition has led to a serious collision and breakdown in the supervision relationship. In this instance, does the doctoral student have the right to leave this research group or even the university and seek supervision elsewhere? According to the general freedom principle of academic work, the answer should be *yes*. However, this freedom may not entail an ability to move with all previous data or even the research question, which can have a significant impact on the opportunities the doctoral student has. Breakdowns in relationships are sometimes unavoidable, and for these reasons discussions at the beginning on data ownership, exit plans from the group and responsibilities of each party are also ethically sensible steps to take. In addition, shared understanding will assist research work and reduce potential emotional drama if it is necessary to discontinue the doctoral studies.

The **doctoral student** has, of course, responsibilities. The main requirement here is intensive work on the thesis and completion of other necessary parts of the doctoral studies. If the doctoral student works on a project that is only financed for a limited time, the demand to proceed with the work is very high. The time pressure becomes especially demanding in a situation where some problems occur in the personal life of the doctoral student, such as health problems, or when there are serious methodological or other research problems that could not have been predicted.

However, the relationship we are dealing with is reciprocal, so we have to think of the ethical rights and responsibilities of the **supervisor** as well. We usually list only various responsibilities for supervisors, but they also have rights. Supervisors have a right to decline a doctoral student accepted by the faculty – or do they? The answer is not always clear. On the one hand, nobody will benefit from the situation where senior researchers are forced to be supervisors against their will. Alternatively, the decision can be taken from a broader perspective considering fairness of supervisory workload within the department or faculty. If one senior researcher has significantly fewer supervisory duties compared to department colleagues, it may be considered ethically justifiable to reduce their right to reject students.

Rights and responsibilities are regularly conflicting, which creates friction and challenges in the supervisory relationship. The availability of the supervisor is one of the key rights doctoral students consider they have. This translates into a responsibility of the supervisor to inform the student early enough about changes in the guidance schedule. It is impossible to know about an acute illness beforehand, but plans to spend a longer period abroad, maternity leave or leaving the university seldom appear suddenly. On the other hand, the supervisor has a right to privacy. The importance for the student of having information and the delicacy of that information for the supervisor can be difficult to balance. A written code of conduct for supervision can help to clarify the differences in rights and responsibilities and assist in guided dialogue around the key issues.

The supervisor's responsibilities are often outlined in lists of aspects of good supervision, including encouragement, support, setting reasonable expectations and establishing a strong research plan.[2] The situation is unique in the sense that supervisors typically have no formal training in supervision and there are very few explicit contracts or guidelines to the work that is so vitally important in the immediate and broader academic context. Guided dialogue can assist both individuals and departments/faculties in forming a clearer understanding, and possibly even some guidelines to support the supervisory process.

Superiors of supervisors have responsibilities, especially in situations where something goes wrong. In the academic world there is a high threshold against intervening in the work of colleagues. We can view the superior's role from both principled and consequentialist perspectives. Consider, for example, that the head of department is aware that a supervisory relationship has become problematic and that it affects not only the supervisor and the doctoral student, but other people in the research group.

- Do you think the head of department has a right to intervene even when no one has made a complaint? Or do you think there is a responsibility to do so?   [PRINCIPLED]

- One way to consider the responsibility is to evaluate the harm and benefit of intervening or comparing the harm and benefit of different ways of approaching the situation. How should the head of department balance harm and benefit experienced by different stakeholders if the supervisor, student and colleagues would all experience the intervention differently? Would it be more difficult for the head of department to intervene in the supervisor's work if the supervisor is a well-known researcher and higher in the hierarchy of researchers than the head of department?   [CONSEQUENTIALIST]
- Or in ethical terms, do you think research excellence has weight in ethical analysis in a way that would appropriately justify negligence in other areas?   [PRINCIPLED]

Universities have different forms in organising doctoral training. The main responsibility may be given to **faculties, departments, graduate schools** or other structures. Despite the overall structure, there must be a certain formal body that has responsibility for the practicalities of the process. Regulative measures may be taken in the form of official statutes or rules, or they are given in less strict guidelines, recommendations and handbooks. There are several issues where ethical considerations are either explicitly considered or implicitly included. These issues are included in the answers to the following questions, for example:

- What are the appropriate criteria for accepting doctoral students?
- How is the supervisory role defined and agreed upon?
- What are the time limits for taking a doctoral degree?
- If the thesis consists of published articles, how many of them are needed and which journals are accepted as fora for publishing?
- What is the procedure in selecting the official opponent for the thesis?

Transparent rules diminish conflicts caused by differences in understanding of the rights and responsibilities, but variation in actual situations will always challenge the interpretation or lack of rules. If the supervisor has too little time for the work with a doctoral student, is this an acceptable excuse to prolong the time it takes to achieve the doctoral degree? Can a brilliant paper in a prestigious journal compensate for the number of papers required for a doctoral degree? Is it okay, if the doctoral student and the supervisor do not sign an annual plan, but agree on the work only orally?

Defining options

Let us take three examples of weighing between options. In the first case there are two options: to accept or not to accept the invitation to be a referee for a doctoral thesis. The decision may be affected by various circumstances. How well does the topic of the thesis match with the research interest of the referee? How busy is the referee with other duties? Does the referee know beforehand the supervisor of the doctoral candidate? Have the universities evolved regular collaborative contacts? When searching for an answer, different ethical approaches may be helpful in providing perspectives, which will assist an exploration of the options from multiple directions:

- What is beneficial for the referee/doctoral candidate/university/research community as a whole? How would harm and benefit differ for these stakeholders? Would potential referees be justified if they considered primarily their own interests/harm/benefit? [CONSEQUENTIALIST]

- What aligns best with the general principles of the research community? Which principles would be most appropriately referred to here? [PRINCIPLED]

- Does an ideal researcher accept the invitation? What is the ideal balance between different activities for a senior academic? [VIRTUE]

In another example one must decide not only what to do, but also how to do it. Consider the following situation: the doctoral student turns to the faculty and requests a new supervisor. There are several options here, including: negotiate with the student and the supervisor to try to resolve their problems; investigate who is guilty for the clash and, after that, if no solution can be found, find another supervisor for the student; or provide another supervisor immediately without any further investigation just on the basis of the student's request.

- Which of the options is beneficial from the viewpoint of the doctoral student/supervisor/ faculty that is responsible for smooth doctoral studies, not only in this particular case but also in general? Is this case considered in isolation or in the broader perspective of how it could influence other students and supervisors in the future? [CONSEQUENTIALIST]

- Are there binding rules tied to rights and responsibilities in the faculty guidelines that dictate what to do or what cannot be done? [PRINCIPLED]

- What would be the response by a faculty that
  wants to be a first-class doctoral studies provider?
  What does the decision say about the person or
  the faculty making the decision? What values
  would be reflected in the decision and are they
  values the parties want to be associated with?   [VIRTUE]

There may be situations where the doctoral student wishes to discontinue the doctoral studies. Thus the options are to continue or to leave. For such a radical decision, there may be various reasons: their partner is moving abroad, total loss of interest in research, severe illness or a brilliant job offer:

- The decision to leave doctoral studies is
  definitely not what we expect an ideal doctoral
  student to do. However, leaving may be
  supported if we consider the student more
  holistically as a person, family member or citizen.   [VIRTUE]
- The faculty surely has guidelines for the
  procedure, but not any sanctions; the student is
  free to end their studies.   [PRINCIPLED]
- The consequentialist approach leads to clear
  differences in consequences: such a decision is not
  an easy one for a doctoral student, but for good
  reasons she or he has come to this conclusion.
  From the point of view of the supervisor the
  situation is undesirable, especially if the student has
  been among the best ones or holds a significant
  role in the group. For the faculty, the departure of
  a doctoral student is a loss, the significance of
  which depends on circumstances – for example,
  are there sanctions if the faculty does not produce
  a certain number of doctoral degrees? However, in
  the reasoning of the case we have to consider the
  other option as well. If the doctoral student
  continues the studies against their will, there is a
  risk that the studies will never be completed
  despite major efforts by the supervisor and faculty.   [CONSEQUENTIALIST]

Options are often highly context-specific. An ethical dilemma develops when all options require stakeholders to choose between core values/goals/rules. In most cases an option that protects the rights and interests of most stakeholders can be found. Ethical dilemmas, on the other hand, allow us to explore our fundamental ethical standpoints and make decisions from a clear value position.

In the rest of this chapter we utilise the steps of defining stakeholders, rights and responsibilities when we scrutinise three phases of doctoral studies: selection of the student; conventions in supervision; and graduating.

SELECTING STUDENTS

Research fields differ a lot in the numbers of Master's degree holders who want to continue to doctoral studies. It may vary from 5 to more than 50 per cent. These differences, naturally, influence students' thinking: in some fields doctoral training is an obvious option; in others it is an exception that needs more justification. The fields differ significantly also as to the needs of society to have doctoral-level specialists. In most countries an academic career is possible only for a small number of new doctoral degree holders. But there is a big field-wise divergence in work opportunities for young doctors outside universities.

It is very difficult to estimate the desired number of people with researcher training over a span of 10–30 years. The labour market undergoes significant changes quickly, which inevitably leads to fluctuation in the demand for highly educated specialists in all sectors of industry and society. Another factor affecting the opportunities to find a job is the general attitude of employers towards doctoral degree holders. This double uncertainty is both a practical and ethical challenge for faculties, departments and individual researchers who are giving information about doctoral training. On the other hand, doctoral training should be an attractive option for the best students who have completed their Master's degree.

- In this situation there may occur a clear discrepancy between the benefits of the student and those of the department or society.   [CONSEQUENTIALIST]
- If we look at the issue from the virtue perspective, it is quite clear that a responsible faculty gives students a truthful picture of future potential.   [VIRTUE]

It is also hard to elaborate the benefits of doctoral training from the perspective of a single student. Doctoral studies take several years and one cannot be sure to what extent the doctoral degree will help with employment. Being too qualified for jobs outside university builds an extra barrier to future employment of doctoral students. Because it is impossible to make reliable calculations on this issue, we often base our choices on other grounds than future employment security. Research is attractive because it is perceived as a fascinating activity. It combines in a unique way deep theoretical reasoning and concrete solutions to a limited problem. One may think that the opportunity to learn new things and to become a member of a research community is rewarding in itself. These are very personal questions and matters of balancing individual values on what is worth spending time on. These turn ethical if we include other stakeholders as well and consider the choice of offering and accepting from the perspective of the department or society.

Recruitment of doctoral students is usually organised through an official application, which is then evaluated by the body responsible for doctoral studies. This procedure may have strict regulations and selection criteria, or be based on recommendations made by supervisory staff. Typically, an **unofficial preselection of students** precedes submitting an official application. Master's-level students may be encouraged to apply for further postgraduate studies by implicit and explicit encouragement or discouragement. Compared with official selection with strict criteria, encouraging and discouraging students is often private or even unconscious, so that the people involved themselves do not recognise the process and its meaning.

The hidden character of this kind of allusive communication creates an ethical issue in student selection. The lack of transparency creates a space for biases and discrimination to develop and to guide the student selection process. In the unofficial preselection, who gets the nod and who the shake of a head? Is it influenced by gender, temperament (nice and well-dressed student, noisy troublemaker, peculiarly dressed bohemian), family background (a child of a well-known person or professor from the same university, a country lad or girl) or another reason which is not spelled out. Everyone is entitled to their own personal views and desires, but they do not form a solid foundation for decisions taken at work. The first ethical challenge is to recognise the process. When recognised, we are able to examine whether the preselection steps are justified or not. This benefits both the candidates and supervisors. Decisions based on subjective preferences are likely to be unfair and create an image of the process as inappropriate. Very few academics would want to be associated with the image a hidden process creates. On the other hand, a proven ability to work together could reasonably be used as a preselection criteria – transparency would be the key.

The preselection process may also place the supervisor in an ethically complicated position. Consider the following possibility: the supervisor has a talented Master's student who has shown some interest in enrolling for a doctoral degree. The supervisor encourages the student and they discuss possible research plans informally, and there is a sense that their research interests could align well. Then consider, that during the selection process at the faculty level using official criteria, it becomes apparent that other applicants are more appropriate and meritorious. What should the supervisor do?

- Would it be virtuous to continue supporting the familiar candidate as a relationship has been formed and the application was largely a result of their shared planning and strong encouragement from the supervisor? Or would it be appropriate to align with the faculty process and claim neutrality towards the student?   [VIRTUE]

- From a principled perspective, would a
  supervisor have a right or even a responsibility to
  promote the familiar candidate, or rather a duty
  to remain neutral in the process?   [PRINCIPLED]
- From the consequentialist perspective, what
  would the benefit and harm be for the supervisor
  directly choosing between the two options?
  What about the student? Or the faculty? What
  would the benefit and harm look like and how
  would we be able to compare them?   [CONSEQUENTIALIST]

Official selection of doctoral students is quite another thing. It is based on applications and done by an authoritative body, which may be a doctoral (graduate) school, faculty or department. Selection criteria are (or should be) transparent, but this does not guarantee clear, unequivocal decisions. Possible criteria might be:

- previous merits;
- future potential as a researcher;
- personal characteristics (innovativeness, diligence, reliability, capability to work in a group, etc.);
- the theme of the dissertation.

The previous merits can be measured rather objectively on the basis of the applicant's Master's thesis, possible other publications and MA diploma. Even weightings between institutions where previous degrees have been obtained or where publications have been made allow subjectivity to influence the evaluation. However, usually more weight is given to other criteria that are much more subjective in nature. One can estimate an applicant's future potential by assessing the research plan and by interviewing the candidate. Recommendations or statements written by previous or future supervisors are a less reliable source of comparable information about the applicant.

The third set of possible selection criteria (personal characteristics) are even more complicated. If these criteria are used it is essential that they are made transparent; however, it is reasonable to ask how they could be fairly included. We have limited opportunities for evaluating and comparing personal characteristics, which makes fair use of them problematic. On the other hand, if they are known these criteria do often influence decision-making. Is it then acceptable to pretend that personal characteristics do not have any influence only because we are unable to quantify and measure them appropriately? The principled approach inevitably highlights the importance of transparent rules for selection criteria. If, for example, capability to work in groups is taken into consideration, it has to be mentioned beforehand as a selection criterion, and also the way it will be evaluated (on the basis of statements of previous supervisors and teachers, on the basis of interview, etc.) must be clear. A transparent system can be seen as aligning with core values and resulting in fairness of process. But if the system becomes overly structured and heavy, the ability for people to make authentic decisions is reduced, the cost of the process in time and resources increases and the resulting selection may not be improved regardless of the measurement used.

The last issue in recruiting a doctoral student is the topic of the dissertation. The basic three options here are:

1 The faculty (or graduate school) recruits only students to work in certain research groups on a topic fixed beforehand.
2 The faculty has determined a set of priority areas of research and the topics of applicants' doctoral studies has to match them.
3 The faculty is open to any research topics within the disciplines taught in the faculty.

The options may be scrutinised from the point of view of different stakeholders. *For the student* the safest option is the first one: she or he is more likely to get proper supervision and is able to be a member of a research community. On the other hand, the student may be forced to give up on a favourite theme, which may bring down motivation and innovation capacity. The last option includes elements of hazard: you cannot be sure of the level of supervision, although it opens the door for new and fresh ideas. *For the faculty* the first two options are more secure than the third, because there is a certain predictability in the needs of supervising and it is good for the faculty to follow a certain research policy. We can also examine the question from the point of view of the whole *research community*. Being a central constituent in building the future generation of researchers, decisions within doctoral training vitally influence the course research will take. Does strict concentration on a limited number of research topics endanger diversity of research?   [CONSEQUENTIALIST]

One of the general principles of research is freedom in the choice of topics. Researchers should be allowed to study anything they want. In this respect, doctoral students comprise an interesting group to think about; when accepting the topic of a doctoral thesis, graduate schools and faculties have to think of their research priorities and resources and expertise they have for supervision. [PRINCIPLED]

How should a 'good' *supervisor* respond when a student proposes a topic that goes outside the supervisor's basic expertise? Does the supervisor try to change student's mind or does the supervisor advise the student to find another supervisor, perhaps in another university? Is the supervisor obligated to explain any personal situations, such as time available for supervision (health problems, another big project, plans to go abroad soon, etc.)? How does an ideal *faculty* act in accepting topics of dissertations? Is it preferable to be rather strict in this matter in order to build a solid foundation for future prosperity, or should the faculty think more of the current applicant's needs? [VIRTUE]

In the end, the selection process needs to compare the different criteria and prioritise them in order to make transparent decisions. For example, if one student scores higher in terms of merit but has proven difficulties in working as part of a group, and the other student has proven group-working skills but lesser merits, which student should be selected? Meritocratic decision-making has been a core value in academia, though there might be reasons to revisit this as the academic world is rapidly changing and the skills to succeed are changing as well.

Legalities can influence the selection as well. Let us consider the following situation. The supervisor has received project funding and is able to pay for one doctoral student to work in the project. According to all agreed criteria the best candidate for the position is pregnant and cannot participate in the project for the first year. All timelines have been designed and communicated with the funder, which now expects the doctoral student to commence at full capacity as the project starts. Would the rejection of the pregnant applicant be inappropriate from an ethical perspective in this context? The decision requires comparison between the equal rights for employment for women and all the contracts, plans and workload of other project workers. How would you decide if there were no legal restrictions?

A further ethical consideration relates to funding for doctoral studies. If a prospective student needs to write a funding application, how much should the potential supervisor participate in the application process? There are multiple stakeholders to consider: the student, supervisor, other applicants, funding body and the department. The doctoral training is a learning experience and thus would it be possible to consider the application process to be included in that learning process? Or does the application process precede the actual doctoral training in a sense that the supervisor should not take part in it for purposes of fairness and equal opportunities? There may be guidelines and rules around this, but if there are none the decision will be based on values, traditions and goals of the supervisor above any other stakeholder.

CONVENTIONS IN SUPERVISION

One of the most important and difficult questions during doctoral studies is **time management**. For the student it is about distribution of time between concrete work on the dissertation, attendance of seminars and conferences, various courses included in doctoral studies (pedagogy, management studies, etc.) and personal duties and needs (family, friends, hobbies). From the supervisors' point of view the time management question has different dimensions. They have a much wider range of commitments and interests and their formal role includes many responsibilities.

The most valuable thing supervisors can provide to the student is their time. The circumstances of supervision vary. In laboratory conditions the supervisor may see the student practically every day and supervision is realised as a set of brief encounters. When there is no routine of daily contact, appointments have to be organised separately. When thinking of the forms and frequency of the encounters, we have to bear in mind that concrete guidelines and advice for carrying out research are not the only things transferred to the student, but also tacit knowledge on behaviour in the research community.

What is considered as an adequate amount of supervision will depend on the context and individuals, as well as the stage of the doctoral journey. The right to supervision can be paired with a responsibility to provide supervision – though both the right and the responsibility have multiple ethically acceptable interpretations. The key would be communication of expectations and abilities. Clarity increases the success of the supervisory relationship, which in turn contributes towards improved outcome for all stakeholders. Some dialogue is necessary for defining these rights and responsibilities in each specific context.

An important ethical question in supervision is equal attitude towards all doctoral students, as most supervisors will have more than one student to supervise. Equality could be interpreted in different ways:

• The supervisor gives all students guidance and advice to exactly **the same degree or the same amount.** Equality is taken to mean the same as equal shares. This may seem to be too mechanical a principle because conducting research and writing papers or monographs on the basis of it consist of different phases so the need for help varies.

- The supervisor distributes her or his time according to the **needs of students.** This may lead to a strong imbalance in supervisor attention. The weakest students get almost all the attention and the most talented have to manage largely on their own. On the other hand, from a utilitarian perspective we can argue that it is not reasonable to use supervisory time for students who do not need supervising.
- **Gaining the maximum benefit** principle would mean that major attention should be paid to the best students who grasp things quickly and are able to conduct high-level research.
- **According to the merits** principle differs from the previous one by paying attention to the past. This principle may be expanded to other positive things by awarding for cooperativeness, punctuality, initiative or other qualifications important from the point of view of the group.

As a rule, supervisors instinctively use different strategies but it is useful sometimes to stop and think about one's operational models.

Apart from supervision, there are many other situations in which the supervisor in one way or another shows her or his trust: when assistance is needed in organising a small seminar; when one should meet an important guest at the airport; or when the faculty needs a representative of doctoral students in a working group. All these actions take time from a student's main activities but, on the other hand, they enable the student to become acquainted with the way the university and research community work. That is why students may regard them more as a privilege than a burden.

As mentioned above, the supervisory relationship is based on a power imbalance. The supervisor has significant power over not just the supervisory relationship, but also the atmosphere and working patterns in the research group and the department. This power can be used in different ways. One way to explore this is to define some stereotypes and consider which would most closely align with a virtue ideal. How would you rate the success of a supervisor who is highly ambitious and controlling, with assumptions on efficient output and regular overtime, but who in return will open doors to great opportunities, introduce the students to key people in the field, and actively mentor them on career options? Alternatively, at the other end, how would you evaluate a supervisor who has a caring and soft supervisory style, where long discussions are held including the research topic and other interesting personal and social themes? The atmosphere is supportive, work pace is reasonable and the level of independence is high. On the other hand, there are very few extra opportunities and the group does not advance career plans.

These opposing stereotypes can also be evaluated against their ability to achieve goals for doctoral supervision. The challenge is to define these goals. Is the goal a structured and timely graduation, or broad intellectual growth? Only after the goals are known is it possible to consider options for achieving them. What do you think is the aim of supervising doctoral students? Guided dialogue may be helpful in forming a shared understanding and creating the best possible supervisory relationship with transparent goals and ways of collaborating.

It is important that power and responsibility go hand in hand. The supervisor has significant power and thus carries ethically more significant responsibility in the supervisory relationship. This could translate into transparency and clarity of aims, processes, ways to manage challenging issues and the willingness to deal with challenging issues before they develop into problems.

The powerful position of supervisors also gives them a significant responsibility as role models. They do not only impart factual knowledge, but many ethical, moral and social codes of behaviour. These would include defining what is considered plagiarism in their field, what is required for authorship or how to manage outlier data. As most of this passing of knowledge is implicit, the role of ethics courses, for example, is to guarantee that all essential elements have been covered and no bad habits are transferred without the student being able to appropriately judge whether they are habits worth adopting.

As funding for doctoral training is increasingly provided for a fixed period, doctoral students contributing to teaching or arranging conferences, for example, becomes an interesting ethical question. These activities are beneficial for developing skills and building networks, but at the same time they significantly challenge the ability to complete the doctoral degree within the given timeframe. From the consequentialist perspective this becomes a complicated exercise of identifying harm and benefit for each stakeholder, particularly the doctoral student. Ethically it is also important to consider who has the right to make decisions around how the doctoral students utilise their working hours. An ideal scenario is built around negotiations for the mutual benefit for all stakeholders. When the decision-making process breaks down we can wind-up, at one end, with a student that has no academic experience or skills outside the immediate research ability, and at the other end a student who becomes almost a personal secretary to the supervisor and is not able to complete their studies within the planned timeframe.

PROCESS OF GRADUATING

There is significant variation in how countries and universities conclude doctoral studies and allow students to graduate with a doctoral degree. In Theland the manuscript of a dissertation is given to two external reviewers and an oral examination is held with a third reviewer.

Dissertations are now almost typically formed from published articles with a new introduction and conclusion rather than a monograph. Most faculties will have guidelines on the number of published articles, the role of the student in each (possibly depicted by the authorship order), the quality level and the type of journals in which the articles need to be published. These guidelines provide a minimal standard for a doctoral degree. All guidelines will leave room for contextual consideration and the overall understanding of what should in reality be required for a doctoral degree can vary greatly between different stakeholders:

- What has been the student's role in the research (assuming studies carried out in a research group)?
- Should additional articles be attempted?
- Should articles in a higher-impact journal be submitted?

Different stakeholders, the supervisor and student in particular, can have different goals in the process. For example, one has a goal of prompt and efficient graduation and the other to achieve as high-quality publications as possible. When the goals are not aligned, it is necessary to either choose whose goals are given priority or to seek new shared goals. This process of aligning goals is highly influenced by the power imbalance between the student and supervisor. The student is often at the mercy of the supervisor both in the ability to evaluate what is truly important and in the hierarchical sense of the relationship. At the same time, the parties are given an opportunity to explore values relating to the core of the doctoral supervision – what is the relationship between the two in terms of equality and power and how these core values will determine the process in case of disagreements. The supervisor is a supervisor for a reason, but what powers are invested in that role does not automatically follow from the supervisory status?

Even when the goals align well, decision-making can be difficult as no one has the privileged information to say which choice will best lead to the desired goals. It is impossible to know which publications and work experience will best assist in finding employment following graduation. Would it make more sense to do the minimum for the doctoral degree and focus on publications in the post-doc period, or should the doctoral degree itself be of the highest possible academic quality, even if that takes longer to achieve and includes greater risks? Risk-taking is inevitable at times and different stakeholders may have different risk-taking abilities and desires.

If the doctoral dissertation is not based on published papers, but is written as a monograph, the definition of complete becomes more complicated. Completeness is closely tied to ambition and standards; a perfectionist would never consider anything complete. The overall goal of doctoral studies is to develop the student's ability to independently participate in academic discourse in the field. Therefore, the decision-making on completeness of the dissertation must include the student. The supervisor should have academic expertise to guide the decision-making process, which itself can be a valuable learning opportunity. Once again, if a shared decision cannot be found, we must determine who has the right to decide.

The next step is the submission of the doctoral dissertation for review. Different universities have different systems and traditions for the choice of reviewers. In many cases the supervisor has an opportunity to influence this selection process.

The following aspects would be part of an ethically robust process in selecting reviewers:

- How well is the reviewer respected in the field (this may impact the reputation of the department/faculty)?
- How experienced is the reviewer in the field of the dissertation (to guarantee ability to provide a high-quality review)?
- What are the previous experiences of the reviewer in this role (the quality/extent of the review, keeping to deadlines)?
- What is the willingness to take risks (choice of familiar and safe vs a new person; possible impact on reputation in using the same reviewers repeatedly)?
- Are they national or international reviewers (risk of international reviewers not understanding the process in Theland)?

The answers to these questions depend on the goals, values and traditions held by the department, supervisor and, to some degree, the student. Is the overall aim of the selection to maintain existing connections, have an easy and smooth review process or earn academic respect? Would these be acceptable goals for choosing a reviewer? Is the appropriate focus on the fair treatment of the doctoral student? Would these other goals align closely enough with the main focus? A win–win option is typically ethically unproblematic, but if a chosen reviewer is not academically appropriate but would support collaborative plans of the department, the decision would be difficult to justify.

The next step is the interpretation of the reviews. Ethical issues are minimal if the reviews align and are straightforwardly supportive or unanimously reject the dissertation. A rejection at this stage will invite the supervisor and student to consider the future of the degree and possible steps to reach their goals. The situation is considerably more complicated if the reviews are inconsistent or suggest further work before acceptance. At times of very diverse reviews, the faculty may choose to obtain a third review to help make a decision.

It is commonly accepted that the supervisor has no role in the review or grading of the dissertation. Ethically the position can be problematic if one of the reviewers or opponents unofficially asks for a comment or opinion on the dissertation.

- Would the most appropriate decision be to decline making a comment using principled approach?   [PRINCIPLED]
- Or approach it from a consequentialist perspective by commenting on a very general level, thus maintaining and supporting academic relationships and communication?   [CONSEQUENTIALIST]

Doctoral supervision does not necessarily end at graduation or submission of the dissertation. The future of the graduating student is often shaped by the supervisor. Encouragement, introductions and time spent to form post-doc plans are likely to have a significant impact on how the future will look for students. Will they stay in academic research? Will they stay in Theland or move to another country? Will they seek to utilise their learning from the doctoral journey or move on to other types of tasks? Reflection on virtues will help in identifying the appropriate role of a supervisor at this stage. And again, when there is substantial power and ability to influence, it corresponds with responsibility for its appropriate use.

* * *

The supervision of doctoral students is a key process both for individual researchers as well as for the research community as a whole. This relationship also has a great impact on how the research community develops as it is often the conduit of passing ethical traditions and norms to the next generation. Each aspect of the supervision relationship has open ethical issues. From selection to graduation, engaging in guided dialogue can both transform the relationship as well as generate growth of individuals and the research community. Because of the nature of the relationship, the responsibility to initiate guided dialogue is likely to be with the supervisor more than the student. Sometimes the dialogue may benefit from a larger group and allow the benefits to flow into the entire department or research group. It is always the right time to start guided dialogue around supervision practices.

Case study 1: choice of doctoral student

Professor Erik has secured further funding and is able to bring in a new doctoral student to his existing group. The doctoral student should be competent in urban environment issues, with special attention to people's behaviour. Erik receives the following applications. Consider what criteria are appropriate for selecting a doctoral student and how to apply those criteria fairly and transparently while maintaining a reasonable selection procedure in terms of bureaucracy and time needed for the selection.

1   **Anila:** previous studies are in urban studies; received 5/5 for her Master's thesis in her home country. Anila lives permanently in Theland with her husband, who is a local. She is 31 years old and has been at home with her two small children for the past four years. Her Master's supervisor described her as diligent and reliable, though shy and quiet.

2   **Jonas:** previous studies in urban studies; received 4/5 for his Master's thesis, which he did at Erik's department under a different supervisor.

He is 28 years old and single. Based on previous experience, Jonas is bright but not particularly hard working. Known to drink too much at departmental parties; he is the nephew of the dean.

3   **Olga:** previous studies in sociology, but not matching the current research proposal. She received 4/5 for her Master's dissertation in her home country and has moved permanently to Theland, where her husband is employed as a lecturer in the same faculty. Olga is 25 years old with no children. She is very motivated and eager and willing to work hard.

4   **Ying:** previous studies in urban sociology and pollution; received 5/5 for his Master's degree in his home country. Graduated from the same university as the current doctoral student Feng. Ying is 24 years old and single. He has stated a strong interest in science fiction and heavy metal music in his application. Feng states that Ying is hard working but very introverted.

5   **Tina:** previous studies in sociology, but not relating to the current research project. Graduated with a Master's degree from another university in Theland with 5/5. Tina is 30 years old and recently married. Her Master's research was of exceptional quality; she has appeared in the media to discuss her research and comes across as highly motivated, intelligent and professional. She has existing teaching experience and has had success in preparing funding applications. She also has experience in working in the public sector on urban policy.

6   **Willem:** previous research experience in environmental sociology as a research assistant in Erik's group. He has a Master's degree that he studied for under Erik, for which he got 3/5. Willem is 26 years old and single. Willem is very popular in the department as he is good-looking, cheerful and a great listener. Willem is motivated for the doctoral studies and has always done all his work diligently and well.

Consider the decision from the perspective of different stakeholders, including the applicants, the professor, the existing team, the department and the research community. Consider the rights and responsibilities of each stakeholder in this situation. Also reflect on your own experiences and what characteristics you may give weight to because of positive or negative experiences and how appropriate their inclusion is in your decision-making. Would you be willing to make these transparent decision-making criteria?

You may rank the applicants from the perspective of different stakeholders and explore any reasons why the lists are likely to look different. How can you ethically justify the differences and how would you choose whose list is the one to adopt?

Case study 2: choice of supervisor

In reality, it is often not possible to choose a supervisor from a large pool of options if the doctoral student has a defined research plan or is not willing to move to another country. However, the choice of supervisor is an important aspect and most applicants have an idea of what a good supervisor would 'look like'. In reality, no one is perfect and this case is designed as an exercise to explore what is essential for everyone in building a successful supervisory relationship.

Consider the following potential supervisors. Which would you pick as your supervisor? What criteria can you recognise as key for you? What do those criteria reflect in terms of values you hold in relation to yourself, the doctoral studies and rights and responsibilities in the supervisor–student relationship?

1   **Marko:** graduated four years ago; he is 34 years old and has no previous supervisory experience. Marko is very successful in his own research career, with an impressive publication list, and he has been invited to prestigious committees in the field and has international collaborations and funding. Marko is quite shy and gentle in the way he approaches other people.

2   **Alexander:** 46 years old and a very popular teacher in the faculty, but only two of his doctoral students have graduated. He is known to be very supportive but not a demanding supervisor. Most people find him very inspirational. Alexander has a limited international reputation, though he does have a reasonable publication record in both national and international journals. You have met Alexander and you shared an instant chemistry and felt comfortable with his four current doctoral students as well.

3   **Rika:** 55 years old and very hard working. She has the most doctoral students to her name in the department and her own research publications are largely based on collaborations with her students. She has a sunny, easy-going personality. Rika has nine other doctoral students at the moment, working around three different research questions.

4   **Vincent:** 56 years old and internationally well-known, with multiple top journal publications in recent years. Vincent is a very experienced supervisor and is known to be demanding and requiring full commitment from his students. He is very critical and focuses on every detail. He is known to have a temper and people are careful not to annoy him. Vincent travels extensively to meet his international commitments and uses his connections to assist his students to develop

their careers. His students are known to have been successful in their academic careers following graduation. He has seven doctoral students at the moment.

5   **Maria:** 62 years old. She has a great academic career of her own, but has recently scaled back on her activities due to ill health in her family. Maria is known to care deeply about her doctoral students and their overall well-being, and to fight for their opportunities and funding if need be. Maria will make sure all projects run smoothly and there are no surprises in the process. She is known to have extensive moody and dark periods. She currently has five doctoral students.

6   **Karl:** 60 years old and a head of department. Karl is very well known in his specialised field in Theland, with multiple media connections. Karl has supervised 30 doctoral degrees and has a solid reputation as a supervisor. He is an old-school academic with a distant and slightly arrogant demeanour. He has nine doctoral students at the moment.

Case study 3: rights and responsibilities in the supervisor relationship

Doctoral studies are based on collaboration between the doctoral student and the supervisor. People have various expectations of the role of the student and supervisor in this process. These differences can be based on traditions, the academic field, or personal experiences and attitudes. Consider the rights and responsibilities of both the supervisor and doctoral student in the following stages of the doctoral journey:

1   discussion on the meaningfulness of doctoral studies – future prospects, the abilities of the student, employability, etc.;
2   choice of research topic;
3   securing research funding (knowing possibilities, writing applications, etc.);
4   attending conferences (choosing where to go, securing funding for attendance, preparing presentations);
5   patterns of supervision (how often to meet, what is discussed, how problems are presented and solved);
6   approaching potential ethical problems in the supervisory relationship;
7   determination of the completion of doctoral research;
8   post-doctoral opportunities.

Case study 4: disagreement with supervisor

Disagreements between people with shared goals are quite common. The supervision relationship is significant and disagreements within it are therefore noteworthy and deserve ethical consideration. Disagreements between supervisor and doctoral student may concern:

- ethical questions in handling test animals or persons, artefacts or data;
- preference of applied methods;
- orientations to theory or collecting research material or data;
- general attitude to practical applications;
- sufficiency of material, background literature, published articles or repetitions of experiments;
- practicalities of supervision.

How to solve these disagreements? Which of them are true ethical disagreements and which could be based on different traditions and expectations? How many could be simply resolved by more open communication? Who could help? In solving these problems, is it necessary to try to find who is responsible for them, or just to try to find a way out of the situation? Are there questions where it is clear whose perspective has priority? When would it be reasonable to change the supervisor? When should the doctoral student leave the university and find another one?

NOTES

1   E. Löfström and K. Pyhältö (2014), Ethical issues in doctoral supervision: the perspectives of PhD students in the natural and behavioral sciences, *Ethics & Behavior* 24:3, 195–214; E. Löfström and K. Pyhältö (2015), 'I don't even have time to be their friend!': ethical dilemmas in Ph.D. supervision in the hard sciences, *International Journal of Science Education* 37:16, 2721–2739.

2   R. James and G. Baldwin (1999), *Eleven Practices of Effective Post-graduate Supervisors*, Melbourne: University of Melbourne (http://melbourne-cshe.unimelb.edu.au/__data/assets/pdf_file/0004/1761502/11practices.pdf).

Chapter 5

Recruiting academic staff

The main ethical considerations in recruiting academic staff are:

1   Recruitment of professors and other academic staff influences many people's lives and the effectiveness of universities. Therefore, it is one of the most important decisions a university makes.
2   The academic pyramid has a large base but only a few PhD students can reach the top of it. This means heavy competition for academic positions.
3   Being such a significant element of academic life, it is important to have clear regulations and rules. Ideally they reduce the number of unclear cases but leave space for contextual application and judgement.

Ethics by guided dialogue typically requires researchers and research communities to consider the following key ethical questions in recruiting academic staff:

*   How to balance previous merits and future potential of applicants?
*   What is the relationship between mechanic quantitative data and peer review in assessing research merits?
*   How much weight should be put on teaching skills?
*   Is the interview an important part of the selection procedure?
*   To what extent should personal qualifications be taken into consideration?
*   Are language skills (English and/or the language spoken in that country) an issue here?

More and more researchers work in various sectors of society outside universities, but an academic career remains the main goal for many young researchers. These days academic freedom has limitations due to the eagerness of universities to determine research strategies and focus areas. Still, in comparison to other specialist jobs, a professorship provides exceptional opportunities to exploit one's creative capacities by adopting new research ideas. Educating young talented people is another rewarding part of professors' and university teachers' lives. Additionally, the social status of professors is still very high in many countries. Therefore, it is not a surprise that many PhD candidates dream of becoming a professor one day. As a result, even those not yet applying for senior positions are interested in their selection procedures and criteria.

Recruitment of professors and other academic staff is important not only for individuals but also for universities.[1] Selecting a person, who will lead research and educate the next generation of academics for years or decades to come is of paramount importance. On that account, the academic community likes to speculate on these choices beforehand and argue over decisions afterwards. Although the recruitment procedure of professors is at the very core of academic traditions, the selection criteria are not static and typically new criteria are added to the list.

Professors have a key position in universities, both in practical terms and from an image perspective. They symbolise the very essence of universities. Therefore, selection criteria for professors reveal a university's values and desires, whether that is intended or not. A university sends a strong message if it chooses to focus only on research merits and excludes teaching and other skills as selection criteria. Similarly, each concrete choice for new staff can be interpreted as signalling something: we prefer young/experienced scholars, people from abroad/our own alumni, researchers with wide competence/researchers with deep knowledge in a narrow field, scholars representing mainstream research/scholars with exceptional ideas. Every particular choice of a new employee is based on a bundle of various factors, and it may be difficult to say which of them is the decisive one. People not taking part in selection may exaggerate the role of a certain criterion. That is why it is important to articulate all phases and elements of the process as transparently as possible.

Being such a central element of academic life, recruitment of personnel is worth paying attention to from an ethical perspective. The aim of this chapter is to highlight some essential questions we meet in this context. There are usually a great number of applicants for each vacant position – sometimes dozens, at other times more than 100 applications can be received. Therefore, it is rarely the case that one applicant is the best, regardless of which criteria are applied. In such a situation we inevitably meet with competing arguments and opposing points of view; in other words, we need ethical tools and transparent dialogue to handle the complex situation in a way that the whole community is able to trust the fairness of the process.

Identifying stakeholders

First, we will explore stakeholders in the recruitment process and their relationships with each other. **Applicants** are evidently primary stakeholders here. The decision influences their lives directly and immediately. The impact of the decision varies depending on the field, other opportunities, and the applicant's position and attitude. In some instances, particularly if vacant positions are rare, a failure to be recruited can have significantly detrimental impact on an applicant's academic career and future plans.

Colleagues of the recruit are also primary stakeholders. New recruits will inevitably affect the dynamics, effectiveness and atmosphere of the work community. Naturally, future colleagues make a less important group of stakeholders than the applicants themselves, because the influence is less direct. Members of the community also have an opportunity to influence the way the newcomer will be adopted as a full member of the community, and sometimes they have a role in the selection process as well.

Students, both present and future ones, comprise another important stakeholder group. Students become increasingly more interested and involved in a recruitment process if one of the applicants already works in the department. Students' activity may be realised in various letters and statements for an applicant who has a very positive or very negative reputation as a teacher or supervisor. Regardless of the selection itself, the new member of staff as a teacher and supervisor will influence students' lives.

The recruiter is also an obvious stakeholder. There are two different meanings of the word: the institutional employer and the individuals involved in the recruitment process. It has been said that universities make only two important decisions: which kind of students they choose and which kind of teachers they employ. The individuals who take part in the recruitment process at its various stages – being a preparatory group or decision-maker – meet ethical questions as they consider and weigh different selection criteria and directly apply those to the merits and experience of the applicants. Although clear conflicts of interest have to be ruled out, the people involved in the process are likely to know some of the applicants beforehand, which raises further ethical questions of bias and equal treatment of applicants.

A common practice in academic recruitments is to use **external experts** who provide peer reviews on the research merits of the applicants. Their role is important but not decisive. If their opinions have no influence on the selection, one can question why they are asked for a statement. If their opinion determines the final decision, one can ask what the role of the recruiter is. Obviously, there is space for ethical reasoning here.

An interesting question in the recruitment process is whether **previous position holders** are allowed to be involved in the selection of their successor. According to academic traditions in most countries, the answer is: *no*. We seldom think about what kind of ethical reasoning stands behind this tradition. Is it just a part of general principles of the community and a characteristic of a good professor, or can one see in it a reflection of benefits from the perspective of certain stakeholders (e.g. applicants or the university)?

If the position is financed through the state budget, **tax-payers** are indirect stakeholders as well. Quite another case is a position established through a donation made by an individual, an enterprise or a foundation. There may be different rules regarding the extent to which the **donor** is allowed to participate in the determination of the sphere of a professorship or recruitment decision. Ethically it would be interesting to allow a body external to the university to have a strong say on the direction of research and/or recruitment of new staff. This would affect the independence of universities and their staff in a way that may not be desirable.

Understanding rights and responsibilities

Responsibilities in the administrative unit (faculty, department or another administrative level) conducting the recruitment process may be divided into **collective bodies** (e.g. faculty council) or to **individuals** (e.g. dean). It is their responsibility to make sure the procedure runs smoothly and according to the valid statutes and regulations.

Every member of any administrative body involved in the recruitment process is obligated to announce any kind of conflict of interest with any of the applicants. The concrete rules for this may vary country- or university-wise, but usually they include close kinship, previous supervision relationship, research collaboration and grave scientific opposition. There may be some time limits for these formal 'conflict of interest' rules, e.g. a research collaboration during the last five years. A member of a body may also self-exclude due to other reasons – for example, if she or he has had an affair with an applicant when they were studying. The general idea of conflict-of-interest rules is to remove doubts about impartiality and objectivity. The observance of the rules may not eliminate partiality entirely, but gives a more solid ground for credibility of the decision. Having responsibility means also that the decisions should be made in the best possible way. 'Best' often means to select the candidate who will benefit the subject/department/university most, or that it follows the given rules and principles of fairness most accurately. There may occur situations where the best option is not to take any of the candidates and to reopen the position at a later time.

Rights and responsibilities of **applicants** should be manifested in an open document that is approved by an appropriate administrative body. These include general right to a fair and transparent selection process. This would mean that the selection criteria mentioned in the job announcement is complete and is applied in practice. On the other hand, applicants do not have a right to express their opinions about the scholarly sphere of the position, but they may be asked whether they accept the external experts who are planned to give their statements on their research merits. Applicants are responsible for giving honest account of their merits in their CVs and in other application documents (list of publications, plan to develop the field, teaching philosophy and portfolio).

External referees have the right not to take the task, but if they take it they must give a proper statement within the given time limit. The referees have the right and responsibility to express their honest opinion of the applicants. They have the responsibility to base this opinion on analysis of the documents they have received. If there are problems in getting a statement, the faculty has to consider whether to take another referee or to try to proceed with the process without that statement – both being unpleasant options.

Exploring the possibility of using assets other than academic merits in recruitment, we can consider the old tradition of giving priority or some other favourable consideration to applicants from the same university or department. Some of these researchers have worked in the department for years, with the expectation of an upcoming retirement and opportunities for career advancement included in that. It could even have been a tradition in the department to groom a successor and promise a position following retirement. This situation may be approached from various ethical perspectives.

The balance of harm and benefit in this tradition does not fall equally between stakeholders. The most benefit would be experienced by the home-grown applicants. The best outcome from the university's and faculty's point of view is less obvious – there is a benefit in choosing a known and safe option and nurturing loyalty and tradition. On the other hand, it is always profitable to have as many good candidates as possible and to be able to choose from the largest possible pool. Also, it is possible to experience harm with the safe option with a lack of fresh ideas and being stuck with a second-rate choice just because someone has put in years of waiting. Similarly, the community may experience harm if their expectations and traditions are not respected and they feel lack of respect and loyalty from the university. This tradition is likely to produce only harm for outside applicants. The research community at large is likely to experience more benefit by open recruitment where ideas and people are able to meet and align in new and exciting ways.   [CONSEQUENTIALIST]

The principled approach could be applied in two different ways. First, it would be necessary to be open and transparent about the selection criteria and to apply the criteria as honestly as possible. If preference is given to the home-grown candidate that should be openly communicated to other applicants as well. Second, we can ask whether this preference is an appropriate principle to adopt. This can be a reflection of other selection principles.   [PRINCIPLED]

Virtues can be considered for each of the stakeholders. If virtue is about integrity, motivations and how you wish to view your life, it would be interesting to consider what virtues would be supported by selecting an applicant who has waited long enough – is that how academics would wish to see themselves? How about the virtues a university would choose to uphold – would supporting and nurturing their alumni be equivalent or greater than seeking academic excellence?   [VIRTUE]

In the next section we will explore different options related to the recruitment decision in each step of the recruitment process.

TYPES OF POSITIONS

The recruitment process starts with the decision on what type of position is to be fulfilled. To some extent, this decision is determined by external factors, including funding options or national priorities. The external conditions reflect value decisions made by someone outside the academic institution. Within the institutions, there is typically an opportunity to determine the level of the position, skills required and the research focus.

The level of the position will reflect the focus and perceived institutional needs. As different positions have different profiles in research, teaching, supervision and administration, the choice of the position reflects the importance or perceived need in any of these activities.

There are some variations in academic positions in universities around the world, but they are more similar than different. The key academic position everywhere is (full) **professorship**, which is the highest position without further promotion. Professors typically teach the least and focus on research, supervision and administration. **A lecturer** is another academic position present in many countries. A lecturer has more teaching hours than a professor. There is some variation in the teaching load and responsibilities of lecturers. A **tenure track** position may have three steps or levels. Promotion to the next level depends on the merits the position holder is able to show after a fixed period (e.g. five or seven years). After two successful positions the person may reach a full professorship. A university may also have **post-doctoral** or other researcher positions, where teaching duties are typically minimal.

The scale of salaries in different positions has an evident consequence for the number of various positions: with the same budget, one can recruit more junior staff than professors. A consequentialist-based assessment can be made for whether there is a clear vision of what is expected to be achieved and whether there is a way of estimating which type of positions will best support that vision. If the focus is on research excellence, the recruitment will target high-level professors and positions for young researchers. If there is pressure to educate more specialists in a certain area, recruitment of excellent lecturers is an obvious option.

In most cases, a professorship is not established as a new position but has a history with previous professors. This has an effect on two areas: when the position can be opened and how its research sphere is defined. In Theland there are no strict dates for retirement. A professor can leave his or her position at any age between 63 and 80. From the faculty's perspective it would be ideal to know the exact date for at least a year beforehand in order to avoid interregnum, but officially the professorship holder can give notice a month before retiring. Here, the retiring professor should realise that sitting on the decision is ethically questionable.

Theland's universities have tried to make the retirement process more flexible by offering all willing professors an emeritus/emerita agreement, which enables a new kind of relationship between the retired professor and the university. It does not include any legal positions or obligations to teach, but enables some supervision and teaching if the professor is willing to do that. All professors planning to retire are offered an opportunity to give lectures, which will be video-recorded and then used in teaching.

Regarding the research sphere question, the situation is often as follows. The previous professor and her or his colleagues, perhaps students as well, do not want to make any changes in the sphere of professorship. They insist that they have worked well and there are no reasons to change the status quo. They may even think that any change in the field of professorship belittles the work that has been done by them for decades. A further argument, not always openly expressed, may be the existence of younger researchers, who have planned to apply for the professorship. The faculty/university instead sees that there are several grounds to redefine the position or even to move it to a totally different area. The main argument is usually reference to the changed needs of society. If disease X (e.g. poliomyelitis) is no longer an issue, why not open a position in food allergy, which is a growing problem. If German is no longer such an important language, but the significance of Chinese studies is rapidly increasing, there would be significant grounds to move the professorship to that area.

Another aspect of professorship relates to the breadth of the field. There are wide and narrow, specialised definitions. An extreme case for the first principle would be a professorship in physics, medicine or cultural studies, in comparison to a professorship in low-coherence interferometry physics, clinical neuro-physiology or ancient Arabic culture. The two options are based on different reasoning. With a wide definition of a professorship, we try to find the best person to develop research, while the narrow approach guarantees the best solution from the point of view of introduction and education. For example, if the faculty of medicine needs a person to teach anaesthesiology then a call for a professorship in medicine does not guarantee that they get one.

A decision can also often be made on offering a permanent/tenured position or providing fixed-term contracts, which may include options for continuation. Contracted employment allows flexibility and the opportunity to renew and easily get rid of staff that no longer fit the vision or who have not achieved at the desired level. The contract option may be considered to increase motivation and effectiveness of staff. On the other hand, permanent positions may attract higher-quality candidates, creating a space where academic freedom produces novel ideas and the continuity can create commitment, which can turn into energy to develop the institution. What we believe about different types of employment structures and how they guide employee behaviour is largely based on our assumptions about how people work, our values on what is important and reflections on what we would personally prefer. Each stakeholder group may have different views on how each decision would influence individual stakeholders or stakeholder communities. As a result, these decisions, unless tightly guided from an external source, are the result of value-based assumptions and reflections on different goals that individuals desire to achieve.

SELECTION CRITERIA

The decision on the type of position is closely followed by setting the selection criteria. The principled ethical considerations require the selection criteria to be both made transparent and followed during the selection process.

From a rule-based approach the key ethical requirement is adherence to transparent selection criteria. What the selection criteria should be is a more complicated question. It would include principled considerations regarding fair procedure and equal opportunity. While these are common requirements, their meaning may require further attention in each case. Interpreting fair opportunity may include consideration on who are equal applicants – can age, language ability or alumni status, for example, be considered an ethically appropriate way to differentiate candidates?   [PRINCIPLED]

Ethics by the guided dialogue approach encourages us to consider the selection process in advance and outline the values, goals and procedural steps as clearly as possible in order to avoid ethical challenges further into the selection process. For example, a clear process of a very strictly scored interview may seem like a fair merit-based selection process. But it can lead to an applicant with the right knowledge but totally unsuitable attitude being ranked highest. Similarly, a very poorly defined set of criteria can lead to subjective issues and opinions ruling the selection process, which would jeopardise the procedural fairness for the applicants. For example, listing selection criteria and other elements that can be considered in addition to the selection process is likely to assist greatly. Even more merit can be found when the criteria are directly linked with the values and goals of the employing organisation.

Let us look at the language question as an example of using guided dialogue to make a decision on selection criteria. It is worth paying special attention to the language skills question because it includes evident ethical questions. First, a short comment on the command of English. Almost all researchers in Theland speak English, but you can still find scholars in national fields (Thelandish history, ethnography, culture) who do not speak English. Is this a reason not to select such a person for a professorship? A more problematic question is whether to require command of Thelandish, which is very rarely spoken outside Theland. The solution to this question has a decisive effect on the selection process and the future work of the new professor. If the candidate is required to have a command of Thelandish at the time of selection, it means that scholars from other countries are not eligible for the position.

The language question may be approached from different perspectives.

One may think that the command of Thelandish is a question of principle: language is a central constituent in a sovereign and independent country and professors play an important symbolic and practical role in the social discourse on many issues. Another principle could be internationalisation, being mentioned in values of many universities: why should we hinder that by having outdated language rules?   [PRINCIPLED]

Considering the benefit and harm of the language
requirements, one may raise the following ones at
faculty/university level:

* The fewer language requirements we have the
  more (quality) applicants we get.
* If a professor does not speak the local language,
  it is hard for her or him to be an influential
  person in society.
* One teacher's lack of the local language means
  that her or his colleagues have to take on the
  administrative and other tasks that are conducted
  in that language.   [CONSEQUENTIALIST]

Because there are contradicting arguments on this issue, one might approach it
not from the principled point of view but thinking of the benefit and harm for the
university. A solution could be considering professorships case by case. There are
certainly fields where lack of local language command harms the ability to do the
professor's job. Primarily these include national research fields in such areas as
civil legislation, primary school pedagogy, social care, public health and nursing
science, where a professor is expected to be an active and influential player in
society. Quite another situation occurs in physics, biology or psychology, where
we usually have a wider range of professorships and most elements of the research
are international. One could imagine that having two or three professors not
speaking the local language does not make a big difference. Of course, the
problem of shifting some tasks to a local language speaker remains. An intermediate
solution is to demand that foreign researchers learn the local language within a
certain period of time (e.g. 2–4 years). Sometimes this works, but in a totally
English environment without systematic assistance it is very difficult to find
enough time and motivation for that.

From the consequentialist perspective, setting criteria
brings in broader considerations on the benefits of
other stakeholders. What does the department/
university wish to achieve through the new
employee? Assumptions are then made on what
qualities and skills will best support the achievement
of the set goals. In this situation the employer is
traditionally highly self-focused and considers their
own interests above the interests of all other
stakeholders.

Possible criteria based on a consequentialist
approach on the language issue include:

- What language skills are required for teaching based on the type and amount of teaching expected by the applicant? What are the topics of teaching? The level of students being taught? Is there a need for previous experience in the specific area or is it sufficient to have some teaching experience or training?
- Supervisory experience? How does experience translate to ability and how is that ability measured and compared between applicants? Is it suitable for supervision to be in English only?
- Research ability, area and plans. Is there an ability to gain external funding? Is language an essential factor in doing or sharing research results?   [CONSEQUENTIALIST]

Special attention should be given to the wording of any criteria. Items described as *essential* or *desirable* criteria may later become important in the process from the perspective of procedural fairness.

PHASES OF RECRUITMENT

Once the position and selection criteria have been confirmed and applications have been received, recruitment enters a stage where the values and goals identified earlier are applied in practice.

Let us look at this situation through an example. A department in the Capital University of Theland is recruiting a new professor, who is expected to spend 40 per cent of their working time on research, 40 per cent on teaching and 20 per cent on administrative tasks, and include the role of responsible teacher of a certain study package. The selection criteria include quality of research, relevance of research, future potential, teaching experience and skills, and language skills (must be able to teach in Thelandish).

A **recruitment committee** is responsible for the selection process. At the end of its work, it makes the proposal to the rector about the person to be selected. The recruitment committee consists of five professors, three from neighbouring disciplines (two from the same faculty and one from another university) and two from other faculties of the same university.

The recruitment process consists of three stages. In the first stage the recruitment committee makes a short-list of candidates by removing those who do not fulfil the core selection criteria on paper. The second stage comprises **review panel** work. The review panel is asked to give its opinion on the quality of research carried out by the short-listed candidates and only on that. At the third stage the candidates give a public lecture in front of students, which is evaluated with the help of specialists in university pedagogy. They give a statement also on the candidates' other capacities in teaching and supervising. Besides that, the recruitment committee interviews all the short-listed candidates. They are given scores based on two criteria: relevance of research and future potential. The 'future potential' score comes from a set of characteristics: progressiveness of the research career; capability to get research funding; plans to develop research and teaching of the subject; and personal characteristics enabling advancement in the field. These issues are evaluated on the basis of interviews and documents provided by the candidates. The relevance of research is assessed in a similar way.

All stages and the final decision require a lot of ethical reasoning. Already the selection of reviewers for the panel is a challenging process. The aim is to find the best possible reviewers, who are capable of a fair and prompt assessment. Particularly, the issue of fairness suggests that it is valuable to consider whether the following questions might influence the process:

- To what extent must the reviewers be experts in the field the applicants are experts in? If more than one research area is represented, should reviewers share the same pattern of expertise?
- Does the gender of the reviewers matter? Should both genders always be represented? What about nationality?
- If some applicants have extensive publications in Thelandish, must at least one of the reviewers also speak or at least read Thelandish?

In our example, the recruitment committee short-listed eight candidates from the 28 applications. For 'quality of research', the candidates were given 3–5 points by the review panel. The review panel consisted of three external experts who stated that the scores they gave are a compromise as the panel members had various opinions on the merits of some candidates. A further challenge for the panel was the differing career lengths of the applicants. The panel noted that they tried to consider this issue by paying more attention to quality rather than quantity of publications. This was also already noted in the general rules of the procedure by limiting the number of publications to be assessed to ten. The panel reported that it has made all efforts to remove any subjective bias from its evaluation and based its work on the documents provided by the applicants.

The results of the review panel and other qualifications of the short-listed candidates are given in Table 5.1. It shows the candidates differ significantly from each other. Everyone excels in something. Therefore, the recruitment committee has a difficult task in selecting the best candidate.

The first thing to be discussed is whether the overall score is reasonable in this context, because the criteria may be given different weights. In fact, the differences in the scales of the marks (from three to five or from one to five) gives a certain priority to those criteria with a large scale.

A further obvious point of an ethical choice is the language question. Should the two best candidates be excluded on the basis of the lack of command of Thelandish, which was mentioned as a necessary requirement? Both Emilia and

Table 5.1 Qualifications of short-listed candidates

Name (years of experience)	Quality of research	Relevance of research	Capacity as a teacher and supervisor	Future potential	Language command	Total
Emilia (15)	4	3	5	4.5	N	16.5
Veronica (7)	5	4	2	5	N	16
Edward (19)	4	3	4	4.5	Y	15.5
Nahele (6)	5	4	2	4	Y	15
Lars (21)	3	2	5	5	Y	15
Tina (10)	5	1	5	3	Y	14
Akiko (9)	3	2	3	5	Y	13
Timothy (5)	5	1	1	3	Y	10

Veronica stated in their applications that they are ready and willing to learn to speak Thelandish; they said that will be able to teach in Thelandish in two years' time. Actually, Emilia is a native speaker of a language which belongs to the same language group as Thelandish. The language ability was set as a pass/fail criterion and many candidates may have opted not to apply because of it. So would the selection of one of these two candidates, who promise to learn the language, create unfairness towards other candidates and erode the fairness of the process?

Further, if Emilia and Veronica are excluded, the three next best candidates are all male. The department has a reputation as a 'boys club', with all the senior positions held by men; recruiting another male professor would appear to strengthen this already negative image when the majority of the graduate students are currently female. Can the gender criteria be ethically justified in this situation when the criteria for the selection and utility for the department appear to support different options?

Allowing factors other than what is presented on paper to influence selection creates a few common challenges. Even when no formal conflict of interest exists, the recruitment committee members are likely to know something of at least some of the applicants. They may have known them as colleagues, met them at conferences, have been their supervisor or are familiar with their public persona through the media, for example. As it is not possible to remove this knowledge completely, how should it be managed in order to create a fair selection? One of the challenges is that this information is ad hoc and there is a different amount of additional information for each applicant. Further, some of this type of information will be supportive of the application and some of it will discourage selection.

One way to approach this is to ask whether a recruitment committee member should share their personal information of an applicant with other committee members. Negative information would appear to have a greater impact on fairness. For example, should a committee member share that a candidate has been accused of sexual harassment in a previous institution, though no formal charges have been brought? This could have a significantly negative impact on how the candidate is perceived by the committee and guide the interpretation of all other information this candidate has presented due to the human tendency to find an anchor for all new pieces of information to be compared to. On the other hand, how would the fairness be fulfilled if the committee selects an applicant and there is knowledge that would strongly suggest the applicant is not able to fulfil the role properly due to personal chemistry, health challenges or an alcohol problem, while one committee member knew about these and did not share the information with the committee? Can all this be reflected in the 'future potential' score?

In this case, a member of the selection committee has had previous positive encounters with Veronica; everyone knows Edward as he currently works at the department, where he is not very popular due to his grumpiness in social interactions; and one member has heard of difficult collaborative experiences related to Lars. How should these be shared?

The length of career also raises discussion in the committee. Is it a relevant issue or is it more important to have a look at the 'future potential'? In fact, 'future potential' may be regarded as a summary factor including elements from all other criteria. One cannot have strong future potential without having produced high-quality research and without sufficient teaching and supervision skills. This raises the question of whether these selection criteria should be given different weights.

***

The selection process is so multifaceted that the above issues are often only a few among the multiple criteria considered and debated. Making the selection process visible allows values to become explicit. Guided dialogue is a method to unpack different aspects of the recruitment process and become more aware of both the values that guide the process as well as the potential ethical issues along the way. This strengthens transparency and openness in science and may build more robust and viable research communities. Not everyone is going to like a recruitment decision, but it is possible for them to understand it.

Case study 1: Capital University recruitment

You are a member of a recruitment committee in the case described above. Who would be your favourite candidate on the basis of your intuition? After that, try to consider the situation by using different ethical tools which include possible benefit and harm from the perspective of various stakeholders, especially thinking of the best solution for the university. Consider what would be the principles to be followed in this situation. Finally, can you name some characteristics for a well-functioning university from this perspective?

Case study 2: recruiting a professor of mockology

Another university in Theland is recruiting a professor in mockology. The procedure differs from that in Capital University. The external reviewers work as individual experts and give separate statements not only on quality of research but also on the future potential of the candidates. As a matter of fact, the career perspectives of the candidates are regarded as a major selection criterion. The recruitment committee sent the application documents of eight candidates to three reviewers and received the following reviews:

1   Professor Schenk (60 years old) is one of the best-known professors in mimiology, which is a sub-topic in mockology. He says in his summary that the decision is very difficult because each candidate has strengths and special skills. In his very thorough report, he highlights that giving different weight to different aspects of the position he has arrived at different ways to rank the applicants. He states that he has personal experiences of working with one of the candidates (Nikolas). After thorough consideration he has ranked the applicants in the following order: **Laura, Nikolas, Tom.** He points out that in the end he gave most weight to research experience and expertise in his evaluation.

2   Professor Johnson (41 years old) works across the Atlantic from Theland; she is one of the best-known professors in parodology. She has actively published in the top journals on her home continent. She notes that she does not personally know any of the candidates which 'in itself suggests none of them represent the international elite in the field'. Her short review concludes: 'Clearly the most upwardly mobile and internationally best-known researcher is **Susan** and for that reason she should be appointed to the chair unless there are reasons to object to her selection. The next best candidate is **Nikolas** and third is **Elias**, whose international reputation remains very modest.'

3   Professor Wong (55 years old) is internationally less well known than the two other reviewers, but she has actively collaborated with research groups in Theland. She has held positions in mockology with defamology as her key research interest. Professor Wong knows all the candidates but has had most to do with Nikolas and Laura. She also emphasises the challenges in the review process. After a lengthy evaluation of the skills and abilities of each applicant, she concludes: 'I believe the best potential for success as the professor of mockology is with **Susan**. The second best is equally **Elias** and **Laura** and third is **Tom**.'

All five applicants are given an opportunity to give a sample lecture. They receive the following evaluation: Excellent – Elias, Tom and Laura; good – Susan and Nikolas.

Consider the differences in the way the reviewers have approached the task and how their reviews may differ. Then consider how the decision should be made. What aspects should be highlighted and what other criteria should be specifically considered (administrative experience, funding track-records, supervisory experience, personality, etc.), or should the decision be based on expert reviews alone?

Case study 3: potential as a criteria

It has been common to consider the right of the best applicant to be recruited to any position. How would the selection process change if we reversed the process and primarily considered the right of the university/faculty/department to recruit the candidate they believe would advance the future of the institution? Reviewers would be asked to provide an evaluation, as has been done previously. But the focus would be different. There are at least two alternatives:

1   **Threshold.** Reviewers evaluate the ability of the applicant to function in the role. It would be a minimal threshold approach to exclude only those candidates considered unsuitable for the position. This would be followed by a panel choosing the candidate that can best benefit the department/institution.
2   **Estimate of potential.** Reviewers will rate and rank applicants. This time the review criterion is not what the applicants have achieved to date, but what skills and abilities they have to advance the research area and institution.

If you consider the stakeholders, who would benefit from this approach to recruitment? Would it influence the attractiveness of working in a university? Would it raise the quality and impact of research or rather reduce it? How would that influence postgraduate training? How would it influence the division of labour between expert reviewers and decision-makers?

Case study 4: tenure track positions

Many universities have an increasing number of **tenure track positions**. The normal practice is: a fairly young researcher ('young' means in the early stages of a career) is recruited; after 5–7 years his or her merits will be evaluated; if evaluation gives the green light, she or he will be promoted to the next stage; after a further 5–7 years a new evaluation will be provided; if a green light is given again, the position holder will be promoted to full professorship. There are various traditions in naming the researchers at the three levels. One of them is: first assistant professor, then adjunct professor and then (full) professor. Tenure track positions are in some universities a popular, even the main, option in recruiting new people. The system sounds effective and profitable from the university's perspective: it gets a talented and ambitious researcher who is ready to put all his or her efforts into high-level research. However, in this system there are obvious ethical questions to think about if we look at it from the perspective of other stakeholders:

- Do the tenure track holders and the university/faculty understand the checkpoints similarly? Is the evaluation just a formality so that the normal merits of a researcher are sufficient or is the idea that the promotion is blocked for half of the tenure track position holders?
- Universities have different rules and practices as to the rate for promotion of researchers after the first or second stage. In one university it may be 50 per cent after the first stage and 80 per cent after the second ,while in another university the rates are 80 per cent and 95 per cent. Should the potential applicants for a tenure track position be informed about these figures?
- At what stage are teaching merits evaluated?
- Has the tenure track holder enough time for research if she or he has to teach as well?
- Is the system fair from the perspective of future young researchers if the university promotes only those researchers already recruited and does not open positions for newcomers?

NOTE

1   Academic recruitment is a research topic as well. For a general review, see H. Metcalf, H. Rolfe, Ph. Stevens and M. Weale (2005), *Recruitment and Retention of Academic Staff in Higher Education*, Annesley : DfES Publications. For a gender perspective, see M. van den Brink, Y. Benschop and W. Jansen (2010), Transparency in academic recruitment: a problematic tool for gender equality?, *Organization Studies* 31:11, 1459–1483. For a sophisticated mathematical method:, see B.D. Rouyendegh and T.E. Erkan (2013), An application of the fuzzy ELECTRE method for academic staff selection, *Human Factors and Ergonomics in Manufacturing & Service Industries* 23, 107–115.

Chapter 6

Funding research

The main ethical considerations in funding research are:

1   There is significant pressure to apply for external research funding, because it not only enables research, but is also an important characteristic of a successful researcher.
2   Distributors of grants for research projects (research councils, private foundations) play an essential role in research policy by deciding which kind of research is funded.
3   Referees, being key persons in the process of selecting grant holders, meet big ethical questions in fulfilling their tasks.

Ethics by the guided dialogue approach typically requires researchers and research communities to consider the following key ethical questions in research funding:

- What is the ideal set of funding instruments from the perspective of development of research?
- Where is the line between a normal positive and optimistic tone and being misleading in describing the estimated results of a research plan?
- Who is the primary stakeholder in research assessments: the researchers in the application, researchers as a community, departments, universities, ministries or development of science as an abstract notion?
- In what circumstances is it justified for the financer to deviate from the expert panel's opinion and grading?
- How should one determine the conflict of interest cases in the course of the process?

If we compare the contemporary research world with that of 30 or 50 years ago, we see a huge difference in the significance of external research funding.[1] Our predecessors did research mainly as a part of their normal workload. Nowadays, more and more research is done with the help of external grants, which are an object of intense competition. This new situation has raised new ethical questions. Compiling a funding application is not an optional task, because external funding is often an obligatory condition for realising projects. You can get funding only if you are able to sell your ideas to the financers and their referees. As in selling cars or vacuum cleaners, you have to show that your product is better than the competition. It means that you have to praise the originality and importance of your research plan, but at the same time you are not allowed to promise too much. Experienced applicants have learned to think carefully of the needs of financers by accommodating their desires and wishes in the research plan.

The main forms of external research funding are **competitive funding** with open calls and **contract funding.** The former is more or less researcher-driven; the latter is driven by the needs of those initiating the research contract. In this chapter we consider mainly competitive funding; some ethical questions of contract research funding are also raised.[2]

In competitive funding financers organise open calls and researchers or research groups themselves determine the concrete topic of a project. The financer, being a research council, university or private foundation, may give some topical boundaries for projects to be funded, but leaves space for researchers to determine the actual research questions. Contract research or 'research on demand' takes place when an enterprise or institution makes a contract with a researcher or researcher group about conducting a specific study meeting their needs.

Each financer has rules and guidelines in selecting projects or persons to be financed. These parameters provide the framework for making actual funding decisions. However, there is always space for individual reasoning and consideration. These general guidelines, choices of eligible topics and previous funding decisions influence the application process. This is an unconscious or conscious learning process that helps researchers to write applications that are more successful.

The use of external referees is one of the cornerstones in the selection process. Here, we are at the heart of science. Ethical questions concerning peer review processes are seldom a topic of discussion outside the research community, but among researchers this is a popular theme for intensive discussions and debates. Due to the vital importance of funding, the research community must engage in an ongoing dialogue around the ethical issues that different funding strategies present.

Identifying stakeholders

Being an important constituent of the whole research world, funding mechanisms have several stakeholders. Primary stakeholders are naturally **researchers** who apply for research funding. Regardless of whether the funding application is successful or not, the researcher is affected by the decision. The impact can be dramatic. Sometimes failure to get external funding totally jeopardises the realisation of an important research project or even employment. Not all researchers experience the funding decisions in the same way. Often, young researchers without a permanent position suffer the most. For them, lack of financial support may even end their academic career. Even if we adopted a more community-oriented approach to funding and its consequences, we cannot override individuals. Researchers are, in the end, the ones doing the work and it is impossible to consider funding without considering how the decisions affects their opportunities, motivation and ability to do research work.

Researchers are not the only stakeholder who benefit from positive funding decisions. Competition concerns also **universities and departments**, whose prestige and sometimes financing depend on the amount of external research funding they are able to secure. 'Money comes to money' is true also in research. In some research funding instruments, an organisation may also be a direct applicant. In all situations, organisations are at least indirect stakeholders as the ability of its employees to gain external funding is in their interests. Therefore, universities have created and funded centres and offices which help researchers to write applications. They may even hire **grant-writers** who help researchers in verbalising their ideas in elegant and impressive language, which convinces financers and referees. These grant-writers are also stakeholders in this business, because their appreciation and, maybe their salary, depends on the success rate their applications achieve.

Financing organisations are important stakeholders. They are responsible for the procedures of selecting the proposals to be funded. In many cases the financing organisations also have the decision-making power to guide the type of research projects they wish to fund. There are also concrete individuals, functionaries and council members who stand behind the decisions, as well referees who are asked to write statements on applications. Senior researchers may act both as council members and as referees (not in the same case). It is relevant that they understand the difference between these roles. **Enterprises and institutions** are a special case among stakeholders. They typically sign project contracts with individual researchers and research groups. They play the role of a primary stakeholder when research is completed 'on demand'.

In addition, the whole **research community** is a stakeholder. Each decision made by a financer can be interpreted as a signal of something: of the attitude to various research topics, to gender balance issues, to the use of multidisciplinary approaches or to preferable age of applicants. Researchers are all continuously trying to sense what is trendy and sexy now because they want to be able to push the right buttons in the next call for research grants. Naturally, the influence of funding decisions on the whole research community is not direct, but there is no doubt it exists.

In the case of a state-owned financing body, **tax-payers** are also secondary stakeholders. They want to see that their money is not wasted but is used wisely. In fact, for a layman it is hard to comprehend the necessity to study many of the phenomena, which are normal topics of scientific research. Therefore, it is quite easy for the media to highlight funded projects which sound odd or at least unnecessary – it appears one could easily find better use for that money. The distance of citizens to research may be great in terms of understanding, but, on the other hand, everyone experiences the benefits of research results through policy changes, new products and better services.

The last stakeholder group is various direct **users of knowledge**. They benefit from research if the results are somehow transmitted to them. Research results can be transferred to companies, committees, decision-makers, professionals and service providers in a number of different ways. An increasing amount of focus is given to a quicker and more penetrating transfer of research knowledge. This is often referred to as social impact. Funding instruments take this into consideration in their request for applicants to extrapolate and plan the meaning and practicalities of this transfer. In many cases, specialised staff and organisations are now available to take part in this transfer process. They are all stakeholders as well.

Understanding rights and responsibilities

In the funding process, all primary stakeholders have rights and responsibilities according to the roles they play. Often the same people have different roles in different funding processes.

The first responsibility of the applicant is to follow the application deadlines. This is just a technical requirement, which is usually reached by blocking applications that are late. A much more serious responsibility is the correctness of application documents. Typically, these include at least a research plan, a CV and a list of publications. They have to be compiled honestly and according to the general guidelines. This is quite a clear requirement, but the observance of these guidelines is in practice not always easy. The challenge is born out of the desire to present everything to the best advantage of the applicant. The line between an optimistic account of the research proposal and a dishonestly inflated one can be difficult to determine.

The applicants have the right to be treated equally and fairly. This is a necessary aim, although we often have multiple interpretations of what is equal and fair treatment. The minimum requirement is transparency of different phases of the process. If successful, the funded researcher has the responsibility to use the grant in the way she or he has described in the proposal. However, plans tend to change during the research process. It is difficult to give exact advice on how significant the changes can be before permission is required from the financer. Usually in the guidelines they speak of 'minor changes, which do not alter the general aim of the project'. Again, the wording invites ethical reasoning around the concepts of 'minor changes', for example, which must be defined within each context. In addition, the grant-owners have the responsibility to report to the financer according to fixed rules. Many financers also require that they are mentioned in publications based on research they have funded. However, what are the sanctions if researchers do not follow this rule?

The **financer** has the right to select the proposals for funding. They also have the right to determine the procedure they want to use. Financers may have different practices as to justification of decisions they make. If we look at this from the perspective of the applicants, there is a difference in the 'blackness' of the box. The 'blackest' box is provided by an organisation, which gives the address where to send applications, and then after a certain period announces who received a grant without providing any justification for the decision or information on the names of referees. In fact, there are a lot of different practices: for referees it might be that they are not used, they are used but are anonymous or they are used and their names are given to applicants; for written statements it might be that they are not given, a statement written by referees is given to the applicant, a statement written by the financing body is given to the applicant or all statements are generally public. The black box ideology can be justified by the following argument: the less the organisation uses resources on the process itself, the more it can give as research grants. The transparency principle with written statements may be regarded as an advantage as such, because it increases the credibility of the process and helps researchers to write better applications next time. On the other hand, this may turn out to be a trap if future referees emphasise other things during the next round. When this happens, researchers may feel they have been misled.

The financer is a rather faceless organisation, but in fact individuals always make the decisions. Often the responsible bodies are called councils, which comprise researchers in certain fields. **Council members** are primary stakeholders. They come from different universities or research centres and are experienced researchers themselves. Nevertheless, as council members they *do not* represent any organisation or research field. This is a strict requirement for their work. If someone asks them to 'support grants from our university' or to 'make sure that researchers in our field get funded', they should answer something like this: 'I support all well-designed applications wherever they come from.' This principle is based on an understanding of fairness and equality that would require people to minimise any potential bias or conflict of interest in their work.

Another demanding ethical area for council members is professional secrecy, which is a distinctive feature of collective bodies. The councils are typically collective decision-makers, which means that all members stand behind any decision. However, there may occur a temptation to forget this principle and tell an applicant something like 'I tried to support your applications but the others were against it.' The council member may even say that Smith and Kim were against it. Such behaviour is unacceptable for at least two reasons. First, it breaks the confidence of the council members and is against the principles set out for the work. Second, the consequences of such a breach of confidence would have a negative impact on the research community by eroding trust in the funding system as well as creating barriers and cliques for genuine collaboration. Holding on to the confidence principle is important in its own right. The importance of maintaining confidence is further supported by the consequentialist argument.

Another aspect of secrecy relates to the possibility of misappropriation in the funding selection process. Sharing advanced research plans can be risky. In highly competitive fields, research plans, new methodologies and expected results are the foundation of research success. In the funding process these valuable documents pass through the hands of many, who would benefit from the advanced knowledge themselves. A significant amount of trust is placed in the hands of the council members and reviewers to treat the application documents in the strictest confidence. When misappropriation happens, it significantly erodes trust in the process. Misappropriation also creates an unfair advantage, which may lead publications, positions and future funding to be distributed inappropriately.

While the competitive funding structures are based on agreements and codes of conduct, **contract research** substantially differs from 'open' research by its legal basis. Rights and responsibilities of both sides are mentioned in the contract as precisely as possible. If something goes really wrong, rights and responsibilities can be solved in a court of law. This is rarely an option with competitive funding and any misconduct or breach of rights are dealt with within the system itself.

Do the secondary stakeholders, research community and citizens have any rights and responsibilities? **Citizens** probably have the right to expect that resources directed to research are spent in a wise and effective way. In contrast, citizens do not have any responsibilities towards the research community, unless we think they should somehow respect research results. Perhaps, one cannot demand this from citizens; it is the responsibility of researchers to gain such trust.

The **research community** has the right to expect to have an open and honest funding mechanism. A more difficult question is whether the research community has the right to determine the amount of funding they need. It is likely to be a wish, rather than a right, as research funding is only one of many societal activities, and political decision-makers have a right to decide on the share of research in a state budget. The research community's collective responsibility is to maintain a functioning research infrastructure. In addition, an open and transparent system would invite the research community to engage in developing the structures and participating in the processes that influence the resources provided for research endeavours.

Grant applications raise one more aspect to be discussed: who is responsible for the information about relevant sources of funding? This question is especially important for young researchers. If an interesting funding possibility is available for a young researcher but the researcher misses it because she or he does not know about it, is it okay to blame the senior researcher of the department (especially if this is the researcher's (previous) supervisor) for not informing her or him? When answering the question, one can turn to principles and virtues. Is there, in the academic tradition, such a convention that senior researchers should search for information about funding opportunities and share it? Does an ideal senior researcher act so? Or is it enough that a senior researcher does so sporadically when she or he sees something interesting? This is an example of a very small issue that can have significant consequences for one stakeholder group. The answers to this question also highlights the way we perceive membership of the research community as either a highly collaborative or an individual activity.

In this chapter we will explore different aspects of research funding as a sequence of the application process within the context of a fictional structure in Theland. Through this process we will highlight options in ethical decision-making and questions that may help in engaging in guided dialogue.

FORMS OF RESEARCH FUNDING

Competitive funding has various forms and traditions around the world. Despite some of the variation, the processes have more in common than not. In order to have a concrete basis for our discussion we will use Theland's research funding structure as an example. This is a rather typical structure with some peculiar features.

The first question to discuss is the general proportion of external funding in comparison to core public funding. In Theland it varies, rather typically, discipline-wise (Table 6.1).

In recent years the share of contract funding has increased in all fields, but especially in the social sciences and humanities (SSH). Social sciences and humanities field researchers have traditionally completed contract research for ministries and other public sector organisations. Currently, it is more and more common for enterprises to engage SSH researchers in contract-based research projects. This is likely to be a sign of increased desire to understand people's motives and behaviour as a vital element of success for many areas of business.

As we can see, the role of competitive funding is very important. The core funding also includes some competitive elements, e.g. bonuses for active publishing, while in general core funding is not based on specific expected outcomes or research plans. The share of competitive funding is a central issue in the whole research policy. Because it is so important, it is a topic for guided dialogue. We can consider it from perspectives of different stakeholders and through different approaches.

Table 6.1 Share of funding sources in some fields in Theland

Discipline	Contract funding (%)	Competitive funding (%)	Core funding (%)
Technical sciences	20	30	50
Medicine	5	50	45
Mathematics	8	30	62
Social sciences and humanities	12	24	64

A consequentialist approach allows and forces us to focus on what we are ultimately trying to achieve in any decision we make. Everything is aligned with this first decision. To be able to do this, we must identify what values motivate the goals we set. Through the identification of values and goals we can then explore how different stakeholders fare in each option and reflect the priorities between stakeholders. In the case of research funding, politicians as representatives of tax-payers form an important stakeholder group. Their ultimate goal may be to have research that will improve the society in the most direct and efficient way. They may also hold a view that competition is the best way to encourage the right kind of research. Some of them also want to steer research through competitive funding towards questions and topics that are relevant from the point of view of the needs of the society directly, while others believe competition itself will lead to the same desired outcome. The values underlying these goals and expectations of how to achieve them align often with neoliberal thinking. The emphasis is on economic development as a prerequisite for the welfare of people. Further, economic development is based on free individual choices in a competitive market setting.

The attitudes of **universities** vary. Universities as institutions typically hold knowledge as a value in itself, even when we do not yet know how to apply it, or may never know how it could be directly utilised or commercialised. How competitiveness corresponds with this value is not straightforward. The attitude of universities towards competitive funding may also be influenced by previous successes. The universities with strong research and funding records may be happy with a big share of competitive funding. Others may emphasise the benefits of core funding and the value of diversity and equal opportunities.

Even if there was a generic agreement on the value and importance of competition in research funding, it is most likely that different stakeholders would disagree on the best format of applying and distributing competitive research funds. Many **researchers** are by nature competitive and do not shy away from having to prove themselves, but all of them dislike continual grant application writing and assessing proposals of other researchers. Some of them use 15 per cent of their working time on these activities, which is a significant cost in itself. Researchers have also paid attention to the costs of organising calls for research funding. In most funding instruments 6–10 per cent of the budget goes on administration and other assessment costs. It is reasonable to ask how many projects you could finance with these funds and how you can justify their use on administrative tasks instead. Therefore, the actual benefits of competitive funding must be transparently compared with the costs of the system in lost time, resources, insecurity and the way it shapes the research landscape.

When concepts of positive consequences, like 'competition improves research quality', become widely accepted, they will be treated like principles or axioms. They are no longer questioned, not subjected to consequentialist analysis or considered from the perspectives of different stakeholders. The current research context appears to have made this leap from 'this is one tool to improve quality' to a principled truth, 'competition improves research quality'. The negotiations are then only around the best methods and channels for organising competition rather than on the fundamental merits of competition itself.

There are still researchers who totally object to competitive funding for the reason that it contradicts freedom of research. Freedom of research is thus given intrinsic value. This may be supported by an idea that more freedom would translate into more innovation so that at the end of the day society benefits most from the research. However, and importantly, this approach treats freedom as a key and inalienable aspect of what research should be and something that we cannot sacrifice to demands of short-term efficiency. Proponents of freedom and the idea of core funding may not be strangers to concepts of quality control and some checks and balances on how people use their academic freedom. However, the idea of freedom as something valuable in itself remains at the centre of the argument.   [PRINCIPLED]

In Theland there are two major state-owned research foundations, the State Research Council (SRC) and Theland's Technology Agency (TTA). They have a clear distribution of labour. The SRC finances research that leads to scientific publications, while TTA aims, by funding research, to help companies to obtain commercial benefits. Despite the name, TTA finances not only technology-oriented research but any research that can boost business. That may concern studies on consumer behaviour in a certain country, new management models or international trade legislation. The organisations differ in their procedures for handling applications: the SRC uses peer review with mainly foreign experts as referees in all decisions, while TTA does not.

There are also private foundations that fund research. One of them has unusual principles: the funded projects are not selected by researchers or other experts, but by internet voting. Voting is open to all who have donated to the foundation. The capital of the foundation was collected by crowdfunding. In other foundations the decisions are made by the boards, which comprise researchers from the relevant field. Some foundations ask for two external referee statements for each application.

The SRC funding instruments include four types of individual grants (post-doctoral researcher, senior researcher, distinguished professor and visiting professor) and two types of funding for research groups (general project funding, project funding for centres of excellence). In project funding, the leader applies for financing for junior researchers, not for her-/himself. The strategic funding section organises calls for programmes with specific themes.

The funding instruments of the SRC reflect (or at least should reflect) general aims stated in the research policy. The question of proportion of various funding instruments seems to be rather technical, but it includes an important ethical dimension because they treat different stakeholders in different ways (Table 6.2). Consider, for example, how different instruments treat junior and senior researchers. How should we consider the convergent ladder of researchers' careers when designing funding instruments? If only 10–15 per cent of those who complete doctoral degrees will get a position in a university, do the funding instruments work in the fairest possible way? In other words, is it justifiable to open a wide first step in the ladder when, after the doctoral degree, it narrows dramatically?

What proportion of the resources should be directed to flagship research through centres of excellence and how much to smaller projects that cover larger areas of research and serve as stepping-stones to centres of excellence? We can look at this question from the point of view of the whole research funding mechanism, or consider the benefits to state or society. Further, we can ask: how much we should invest in the future (post-doctoral grants) and whether rapid gains are more important (programme funding) than providing funding for core research? Obviously, we should find a good working balance between various aims. Is that reached in Theland? And how about your own country? All of these questions guide us to return to our basic research aims, our understanding of fairness in research careers, and our assumptions of which mechanisms will best guide the process for achieving what it has been set to achieve. These questions are at the heart of guided ethical dialogue.

In comparison to competitive funding, ethical questions are very different in contract funding. The university or research institute may encourage its researchers to cooperate with enterprises and other non-academic actors, but nevertheless, the situation is never simple. The researchers have to consider at least the following questions. How is cooperation with an enterprise in harmony with my duties and obligations towards the institution that pays my salary? Is there anything in my main position in the university or research centre that contradicts the demands of the research client? How much normal working time can I use on this cooperation? To what extent can I give up the general principles of openness and general

Table 6.2 Research funding instruments in the State Research Council in Theland

Funding instrument	Percentage of total funding	Success rate (%)
Post-doctoral posts	16	8
Senior researcher posts	12	12
Distinguished professorships	7	18
Visiting professor	2	25
Project funding	38	13
Centres of excellence	10	6
Programme funding (strategic section)	15	23
Total	100	14

availability of research results? What are the rules in using the university research infrastructure in this kind of contract research? Is it ethical to do part of the contract research as a Master's or doctoral thesis? Do the fees and other compensations go to me or to my employer? There are no clear answers to these questions. Research communities and employers should openly discuss these issues and, when appropriate, agree on general guidelines. Contract research holds the potential to change the way we do research, so we should approach it as transparently and openly as we can to gain an understanding of how it aligns with our vision for research in the future.

WRITING AN APPLICATION

The ability to write impressive applications is a key requirement for success in research. Along with specific skills, the application-writing process also requires applicants to make ethical choices. All the ethical choices are somehow connected with the dilemma between the need to be successful in getting grants and to be honest and fair from the perspective of all stakeholders. In short, writing applications can be a test for being a good researcher.

The first question to be decided is the **choice of topic** for an application. Researchers' work consists of themes that repeat themselves in different forms from study to study. For an application you have to split the set of various phases into a reasonable package to fit the funding scheme. In project funding with several researchers, the concretisation of the theme has consequences, especially for younger researchers who may have different research profiles. In practice this means that some of them are out and some others are in when the project starts. Therefore, it can be viewed as an ethical question regarding the extent to which younger researchers are allowed or obliged to take part in the process of compiling an application. The answer requires at least consideration of consequences for each stakeholder and fairness of the process itself.

The choice of topic is closely connected with further questions: what is the **composition of the research group** and who is the **leader** of it? Naturally, researchers first look at these questions from a consequentialist perspective: which line-up gives the best chance of being funded? This is quite a tactical approach that consists of a set of ethical questions relating to the various stakeholders. A certain combination of researchers may be beneficial for the university. The optimal choice may vary. In one situation it is reasonable to merge two successful research groups; in another, it would be wiser to split them into two groups. One can always ask who will benefit from these decisions: individual researchers, the department, the university or perhaps even users of research?

The question of the leadership of a research group is often rather easy. The most experienced senior researcher takes the lead. But when is it time for her or him to resign? Who will lead the whole group if two previous groups merge? There may occur other reasons to change the leader. If in a call the financer wants to also see younger researchers as group leaders, is it acceptable to put one of them in that position although the senior researchers is actually still leading the group? Eventually we have to determine the line between acceptable strategy and dishonesty.

A challenging question in planning applications is the rather widespread demand to do **multidisciplinary research** instead of using the methods and traditions of only one discipline. Such an ideology can be embedded in any kind of research funding. It is especially popular in phenomenon-driven programme funding. It takes time to rebuild a research group by amalgamating researchers from multiple disciplines, but it may be the additional spice that attracts the funding. Most importantly, it may lead to new scientific openings that could not be achieved in a traditional way. Enlargement of a research group affects many researchers. Very rarely will all stakeholders benefit from the new situation, at least in the short term. Therefore, the situation calls for ethical reasoning and iterating the questions on core aims, key stakeholders and the timeframe within which benefit and cost are evaluated.

A call for **programme funding** with a strict theme is a challenge for a researcher whose research does not exactly fit the scope of this or any other programme. In such a case it may be difficult for applicants to resist the temptation to mask their research proposals with elements that show a link between the theme of the programme and what the group promises to do, although in reality these links are vague. This re-casting is quite common. For example, if the available funding is for multi-ethnicity research and you have only studied a small ethnic group in New Guinea, is it appropriate for you to submit an application? Which factors affect your decision? Your personal willingness to expand your research profile? The possibility of finding other researchers with a wider experience in multi-ethnicity research to join your group? The estimated success rate (probability to be funded)? Or something else? Is it ethically grounded for a researcher to apply for a grant if her or his research experience or the research topic does not match the criteria? In one sense it is not the fool who applies, but the one that would fund such an application. The ethical problem appears with the extent of re-casting. If the application becomes untruthful and deceitful then we have lost not only our core principles of honesty, fairness and transparency, but also wasted everyone's time.

Difficult situations may appear when a research group is taking part in a larger **international consortium** with partners from several countries. The larger the joint endeavour is, the greater the risk of problems. All details need to be negotiated: the concrete topic and the name of the project, distribution of labour, distribution of resources and who will act as the coordinator. If something goes wrong, participants face difficult decisions: leave the whole project or try to negotiate? In a big consortium there are many stakeholders who have put an effort into the joint endeavour. What will be their reactions if we leave the consortium? Should we think of the future as well? Have we broken relations with the other partners forever? This decision typically combines both questions around rights and responsibilities as well as consequentialist considerations, particularly for the individual stakeholder but for the whole group as well. The transparency principle would guide us to open this discussion to find a solution that best supports more than one stakeholder and allows everyone to hold onto their core principles and values.

The position of coordinator may give some 'points' to the department, but often researchers avoid this task because it translates into a lot of administrative work. But if a big international consortium is in danger because no one is willing to be the coordinator, should you sacrifice yourself? The question can be considered from the perspective of different ethical approaches: who will benefit from the decision and who will not? Whose benefit takes priority? Are there principles that should be noted (e.g. rotation of such tasks between universities)? How does an ideal researcher act in such a situation?

Some researchers say that compiling the **text of the application** requires verbal acrobatics. Indeed, words (and figures) are the only tool you have at your disposal when you try to convince the referees. Your main message is: it is worth financing our project because it is innovative and brings new insights to a relevant scientific question.

Speaking of acrobatics has a more concrete meaning by referring to the dilemma of finding a balance between a too optimistic scenario for new scientific findings and realism in reaching them. One can approach the question from the principle of being honest and truthful. However, applying the consequentialist approach, you may come to the same conclusion. If you accurately describe also the possible obstacles and risks of research, your proposal may sound more considered and raise more confidence among those who decide on funding. In practice, the line between truthful future expectations and excessive optimism is far from clear. The possibility of different interpretations begins with single words. A methodical 'innovation' or a 'totally new' approach may sound to a referee as unnecessary and unjustified superlatives. Words like 'possible' in the description of results for some means 'possible but rather unlikely', but for others means 'rather probable'. When speaking of the usefulness of the expected results, common expressions are: they may lead to commercial innovations; they can be utilised in industry; they make a good foundation for development of practical applications. Do these expressions mean that one cannot guarantee any kind of utilisation of the research results? If so, is this the right way to put it?

Researchers are by their nature optimistic. We tend to deceive ourselves when we think of the prospects of our research. In a way, we behave like gardeners, for whom overestimation of the future yields is a driving force to work hard in the garden. Such over-optimism is a natural part of human thinking and should be separated from deliberate misleading, but for a referee or financer it is impossible to see the difference between them. Clear excesses can be recognised but slight overstatements are more difficult to see. The personality of the applicant and that of the referee play a role here as well.

MAKING A FUNDING DECISION

Funding decisions are of great significance to applicants; they may direct the career of one or more persons up or down. For the funding body, the decision is routine and repeats itself at regular intervals. Frequent occurrence of these situations does not diminish the significance of ethical questions that arise during the process of handling applications; on the contrary, it makes ethical reasoning even more important. We will discuss ethical questions that appear in making funding decisions in the context of Theland's SRC. After that, we will take a brief look at procedures applied in foundations.

As described above, the SRC has seven funding instruments. The mechanism of handling applications is the same in all of them, but the emphasis on different selection criteria varies slightly. When the call is closed, the first step is to split applications into thematic groups of 6–20 applications in order to organise their review. This seems to be a rather mechanical task but in fact there are several decisions to be made. One of the most relevant questions is how to handle multidisciplinary projects. Are there enough of them with similar themes to make an expert panel for them? If not – as is often the case – how can it be guaranteed that these applications get a fair treatment? Who will suffer if the multidisciplinary nature of the project is a burden for an application? Maybe not only the applicant, but also the progress of research as a whole? Collaboration and bridging across disciplinary boundaries is one of the often cited aims of research activity. This is typically in the hope of more comprehensive and transferable results. The translation of this principle into practice takes place through funding decisions. For this reason, the alignment with stated principles and aims and how they are supported need to be clear and transparent to allow the community to grow and to trust the systems that support it.

The second step is selecting 4–8 members for each thematic panel. Again, different options are available: famous researchers or experienced evaluators, established senior researchers or also representatives of younger generations, specialists within a narrow field or generalists, old acquaintances or new faces. A big question is the coverage of thematic subfields. Applicants usually would like to have a 'precision expert' who represents exactly the same research area. On the other hand, for the work of the panel it is better to have experts with wider expertise. The selection can therefore reflect the priority of interests, utility (speed/cost) or an interpretation of fairness/equality.

Because Theland is not a very big country, the SRC prefers foreign referees in order to avoid conflicts of interest. A domestic expert is more likely to experience personal benefit or harm if her or his colleague in the same field is funded or not. Naturally, a conflict of interest is also possible in the case of foreign experts. The SRC has some technical criteria to avoid this, e.g. an expert must not have had recent cooperation with one or more applicants; 'recent' is interpreted as a joint publication during the last five years. However, strict rules can never cover all cases of conflicts of interest, as discussed in Chapter 5. In addition, you cannot see in any official documents the most serious form of conflicts of interest, which is a planned cooperation between a referee and an applicant. This is a clear case where the referee should tell about such a connection and decline the honour. This is important for the purposes of maintaining transparency and fairness. The decision either builds or erodes trust.

Panel members' work consists of two phases, deskwork at home and panel meeting in Theland. Deskwork means writing a preliminary statement about 2–5 applications. As a rule, each application gets such a statement from two panel members. For that task there is a rather detailed instruction and a form with five questions: innovativeness, feasibility, previous merits, networking and social impact. In each item the referee gives a grade (1–5) and writes a short justification (3–8 sentences). The statement ends with an overall mark and a general review. For the reasons described below, the social impact issue is located in the assessment form after the overall mark.

Let us look at these criteria and how they reflect different aspects in ethical decision-making.

Innovativeness does not accidentally take first place in the list of assessment criteria. For all funding of research, an ideal funded project helps researchers to make a breakthrough in science. Therefore, the most fundamental assignment for referees is to comment on this issue, because only an experienced expert is able to see the prospects of a research plan. However, this is also the weakest aspect of the peer-review system: are referees really able to accept that something that goes beyond the usual line of research is so promising that it should be funded? Researchers are, as a rule, very committed to the traditions of their own research fields. This often translates into a difficulty accepting clear deviations from that. Emphasis on innovativeness incorporates an assumption about research progress – that it takes place through leaps into the unknown rather than progress being a gradual step-by-step process.

Feasibility of a research plan means thorough design of the research to be conducted. It also includes an anticipation of possible problems and risks during the project. Because referees evaluate only the description of future research but not the actual act of research, this part of the assessment is linked to the capability of the applicant to write a consistent and credible research plan.

If the first two items are rather subjective, in assessing **previous merits** referees can rest on some evidence: publications (especially recent ones), visibility in the science world shown by citations, and previous projects and their results. According to the SRC guidelines, referees should not just mechanically count numbers of relevant publications or citations, but make a more subjective analysis based on available data.

Networking is an important component of a researcher's life. Domestic and international cooperation takes time but is also a stimulus for better research. In assessing this, referees have to make a distinction between real cooperation and cooperation only on paper. Networking for the sake of networking can reflect a value of the community and openness. This value typically rests on the core assumption of believing in connections as fertile ground for innovation and improving research quality.

Social impact is a tricky assessment criterion. In programme funding, social impact is a natural selection criterion. The strategic section uses two-phase assessment of proposals. First, the members of the section assess the social impact and then external referees assess the scientific quality, but only if social impact is higher than the threshold level. The consideration of social impact in the case of strategic funding is indispensable; the only thing to discuss is the way assessment is realised. A more fundamental issue is whether this criterion is relevant in normal (basic) research funding. Let us consider this from the perspective of various stakeholders.

Many **politicians**, as representatives of tax-payers, would prioritise funding that maximises social impact. According to them, the most direct and quickest path to practical implementation is the best way to benefit from research. Most **researchers** see the situation quite differently. They believe that any research has the potential to be profitable in the long term and that research is unpredictable and social impact cannot be guaranteed. They even think that society will benefit the most if they are given the opportunity to choose research topics themselves. The **research council** has an interesting position between these two 'camps'. They must try to understand both sides – politicians because they finance its operations, and researchers because they are its customers. We will come back to this social impact question in the next chapter.   [CONSEQUENTIALIST]

According to SRC guidelines, social impact is regarded as a selection criterion only in strategic funding; in other funding instruments referees give a score for social impact but it comes only after the overall mark as an additional point of view. It is said that it does not influence the selection of funded proposals. The purpose of having this evaluation in the assessment form is to guide researchers' attention to it. This is likely to assist in transferring knowledge once the research has concluded.

When panel members meet an official of the SRC is present. She or he plays an important role in representing the funding organisation. According to statutes, her or his task is only to give technical advice about the procedure. However, 'technical' easily becomes 'tactical'. It is not always clear when the official should interfere in the course of discussion. When a member of the panel has misunderstood the guidelines? When one of the panellists clearly has a hidden agenda and insists on the superiority of one of the applications even though all others disagree? Or should the official only follow-up the discussion and answer if panellists ask? If the council is committed to principles of independence, autonomy, fairness and even transparency, the official may have to adopt a role to uphold these principles and guide the panel to pay close attention to them during the process.

A panel at its best is an excellent form of working. In an ideal panel, members complement each other and reach the final solution as a joint effort. However, a panel may also be vulnerable if it comprises members who are not capable of teamwork and lack any flexibility in assessments. The chairpersons of panels are asked to give a short feedback on the whole process after the panel has completed the task. Officials give the council their feedback as well. Among others, they can mention whether some of the panel members have failed to be constructive and cooperative during the panel work. These persons are no longer invited to function as experts. These are fundamentally questions on whose voice is prioritised and heard, whose opinions carry the most weight. They circle back to assumptions on fairness.

After the peer-review stage the process returns to the SRC, specifically to the section of the SRC that handles the application. The distribution of responsibilities between referees and this section is clear: referees give a statement on each application and the section makes the decision on which proposals will be funded. One could think that the decision is easy to make on the basis of the referee statements. In practice, such a straightforward course of events is rare. In fact, there is a lot of space for choosing and all such choosing is linked back to values. One possible problem is discrepancy in the scales that different panels have used, despite the guidelines. If one panel has used the scale from one to five evenly and another panel has given five points to half of the applications, this does not necessarily reveal a difference in quality in the applications, but a discrepancy in the use of the assessment scale. Elements of procedural fairness must be taken seriously and mechanisms for managing them should be made transparent in order to build trust.

When assessing applications for centres of excellence and distinguished professorship programmes, an additional challenge is comparison of applications from different fields. Every panel considers and evaluates research plans in the context of a certain discipline or field, and grades them on that basis. However, the risk of having different assessment scales increases when we compare applications from totally different fields. It is possible that applications from fields having homogeneous understanding of good research will benefit, while applications coming from fields without such consensus will suffer.

Another question appears from the possible preference for certain assessment criteria. Let us suppose the situation shown in Table 6.3, where the SRC has made from 18 applications a short-list of four applications, two of which can be funded.

Table 6.3 Assessments of applications in a call of Theland's State Research Council

	Innovativeness	Feasibility	Previous merits	Networking	Overall grade	Social impact
Application A	3	5	5	5	5	3
Application B	5	2	3	3	3	5
Application C	4	4	4	5	5	5
Application D	5	5	5	4	5	1

After a long discussion, council members made four different proposal for the funding decision:

1 Applications A and D because they have the highest overall grade and the combined score is the highest; social impact is not regarded.
2 Applications A and C because they have the highest overall grade and in a toss-up situation one should consider social impact.
3 Applications B and D because the council has decided to put more emphasis on innovativeness, even if it includes some risks.
4 Applications C and D because they have the highest overall grades and have clear multidisciplinary elements, which is regarded to be a favourable feature of a research plan.

One can judge the choices from different angles. Who is the most important stakeholder in this reasoning: the individual applicant or the whole research community? Or should we think of development of research as a general aim? Does the decision influence the SRC's reputation and credibility? Does the preferred choice differ in different funding instruments: post-doctoral positions, senior researcher positions, project funding, centres of excellence funding, programme funding (where social relevance is used as a preselection criterion)? Does the overall mission statement of SRC, 'For the best of the humankind', help make the right decision? Interpretations of values, priorities and stakeholders will all entwine in this decision.

One more thing to think about is the so-called **balancing principle**, which is sometimes called the 'hygiene principle'. In fact, it contradicts all declared selection criteria. To explain it, let us think of the following situation. There are 50 applicants to a senior researcher post, 28 male and 22 female. After the first selection based on panel assessments, all six applicants are male. Actually, gender has not directly influenced the short-list but such a decision would send a clear signal of gender bias. Along with gender, a similar factor may be 'university' or 'subfield of research'. In the described situation the following rule is applied by the SRC:

If, after implementing general criteria of assessment, the list of selected applications seems to be one-sided from the perspective of gender, university or subfield of research, the council should apply the balancing principle. The principle should be used only when a high-quality application is available to be raised to the list of funded applications.

The use of the balancing principle is a very sensitive question. In the SRC it has been on the agenda for a long time. In the 1990s council members often used it in their arguments in meetings, but it was never explained in official documents. In 2000 the council rewrote its assessment criteria guidelines, which declared that no balancing principles are applied. After five years' experience, the council made a survey of its funding decisions. It showed that the number of funded applications made by female researchers increased, but the success rate was still relatively lower than that of male researchers. The share of the funded applications from Capital University increased during that period from 25 per cent to 31 per cent. Referring to the fairness and equality principle, SRC changed the guidelines again, which raised an animated discussion among researchers.

In **private foundations** the procedure of selecting the best applications is much simpler. They do not use tax-payers' money and have more freedom in their work. This is the process they prefer. On the other hand, according to the internal rules the will of donors should be put into action in the best possible way. In most foundations a single-phase procedure is used: the selected expert members of the committee make the assessment and the decision. One may ask whether this is justified. Or is it correct that private organisations have the right to make their own rules? Elements of fairness and transparency would probably apply even then. The transparency principle suggests that at the very least, all funding organisations would reveal their selection criteria and commit to their own process. The application process is time-consuming and all stakeholders deserve to know how their efforts will be assessed. Only then can they make a decision on whether to participate in the funding game.

Although private foundations have more freedom in organising the selection process, they may have difficulties in interpreting the will of the donor. Especially if the donation was received a long time ago, the purpose of the endowment may be difficult or even impossible to meet. If the grant is meant to be given to descendants of farmers originating from a certain village or to students studying a subject that no longer exists, the foundation faces significant challenges in delivering the grants. They have at least the following options: (1) not to give out any grants; (2) to give out a grant to any applicant, good or not, fulfilling the requirements; (3) to try to think what the donor, as the main stakeholder, would do in the current situation.

* * *

Research funding is an essential driver of research direction. It is often the way our values and general research aims become reality. These decisions also affect everyone in the research community. For these reasons, all choices and decisions related to funding are at least implicitly also ethical choices and decisions. The ideal of alignment, or lack thereof, between core values, principled aims and reality can be explored through guided dialogue. In order to discover alignment, first we should seek to understand what we think research is fundamentally about and why we do it. Second, we must be aware of the values we use in assessing how well different funding structures achieve our ultimate research goals. The values we hold, together with our understanding of how people are motivated and guided, become apparent in this process. Lastly, we need an open mind in looking at the complex reality and the different perspectives various stakeholders bring to it. Only then are we well prepared to agree on how we should arrange our research funding collectively and individually.

Case study 1: should I apply or not?

When we ponder the duties of people in different academic positions, it is worthwhile to ask a question of whether it is everyone's duty to apply for funding? Alternatively, could we consider that this responsibility is not universal and would be the responsibility of only senior academics, for example? We can approach this by considering responsibilities and roles or by considering benefit and harm of different options for different individual or collective stakeholders:

1   **Consequentialist.** Would I benefit if I applied for this funding? On the harm side is the time and effort given to the application process, which may be wasted and therefore would have significant opportunity costs. On the other hand, successful application would benefit individual careers, departments and possibly stakeholders applying or otherwise benefiting from the results. In a research group, if the senior researcher applies for funding, this could be a crucial benefit for the early career academics (i.e. PhD students), who may depend on this funding to be able to continue their work. The junior members may also consider the harm of the senior researcher spending significant time in preparing applications which always contain a risk of failure. The department or university may consider that the time and capacity of the senior academics is their greatest asset and resource, and applying for funding may or may not be considered a great use of that resource. In all situations the harm/benefit balance depends on the time required to submit an application in comparison with the potential size of the funding and the likelihood of succeeding. Consider where you would

draw the line where applying for funding is justifiable from the perspective of harm and benefit.

2   **Principles and virtue.** Does a senior academic have a duty to apply for funding? Can you be a good researcher if you have no external funding? What are the tell-tale signs of a good researcher when it comes to finding a balance between contract research and competitive research funding?

Case study 2: exploring the limits of honesty

When we prepare funding applications we always, whether consciously or intuitively, test the limits of sharing information honestly or expanding the truth unjustifiably. Because most people know that lying is not acceptable, we test the limits by choosing our words carefully without lying, but still giving the most positive image we possibly can. This applies to all parts of the application. For example, when discussing methodology we may refer to equipment 'to be purchased by the department' when no decision has been made to date. Or when discussing collaborative structures we may mention colleagues whose role we know will be absolutely marginal in the actual research process.

Possibly the most challenging part of the application process is placing the research in the context of other research work and the field in general. We do this in two different ways: on the one hand, we need to create a space to show that our research is answering questions that have not already been answered by other research; on the other hand, we need to highlight the merits of the planned results in scientific and possibly social terms.

Let us look at an example. Your research group is preparing an application which focuses on the isolation of a chemical extract from juniper needles. Positioning your research could have the following options:

- **Previous research.** Similar research has been completed in Norway. The results were published in a small Norwegian journal a year ago. It is the same chemical that had been successfully isolated from a rare tropical tree. The chemical is used by the cosmetics industry. Some research indicates that this chemical can invigorate skin cells, while the results are somewhat contradictory. Extracting the chemical from juniper needles requires a specific technology and the Norwegian research showed that this is possible. The technology is currently very expensive. Your research focuses on confirming the Norwegian results and exploring whether the process could be simplified and thus be made more affordable.

- **Expected results.** The research question is based largely on the ability to apply the results in practice. The potential application does have many conditions that must be met before it is possible: (1) Can the actual positive impact on skin cells be proven? (2) Is it possible to develop technology that is affordable enough for industrial use? (3) Can the conservation order of juniper trees be reversed or modified to allow commercial use?

How should these facts be considered in the application? Would the funding organisation influence how the facts are presented? How would you include the fact that the research is likely to be completed in only six months rather than the full funding period of 1–2 years? The rest of the time could be spent on further research on pine needles. However, before the juniper study it will be very difficult to provide concrete timelines for that research; how would you share that information?

Case study 3: contract research case

You get a tempting offer from an enterprise or a ministry to conduct a project 'on demand'. Consider which aspects of the proposal influence your decision?

1   **Why me:** are you the right person to take this project?
2   **What will I learn:** to what extent do you feel you will learn new things when conducting the project?
3   **Overall benefit:** can your colleagues/department/students benefit from the project?
4   **More money for something important:** is it profitable in financial terms?
5   **Topical or not:** how does the project fit with your research profile at the moment, the university's research priorities or in relation to the needs of your department?
6   **An important partner or not:** is the contractor relevant for your university as a counterpart also in the future?
7   **Normal requirements of scientific research:** can the results of the contract be published openly?
8   **What will I give up because of this:** are there some important things/research that I have to cancel/postpone because of the project?

When answering these questions, try to consider harm and benefit for different stakeholders. Are there any principles that override a consequentialist approach? How does an ideal researcher behave in this situation?

Case study 4: conflict of interest

Conflict of interest guidelines are designed to guarantee unbiased processes. The guidelines may determine you as having a conflict of interest and you must be excluded from a panel or as a decision-maker. You may also consider that you have a conflict of interest and exclude yourself, even when the guidelines do not suggest that. If these guidelines are too tight, the already difficult task of recruiting panel members may become impossible.

Consider the following scenarios from the conflict-of-interest perspective – do you think you should agree to review an application for project funding if the following apply:

1   The applicant is your second cousin. You have not been in touch for decades.
2   The applicant is a family friend of your parents and you see her regularly a few times each year in different gatherings.
3   You play hockey in the same team once per week with the applicant.
4   You went to high school with the applicant.
5   You dated the applicant at university and you lived together for a while.
6   You both sit on the board of a scientific society.
7   You worked at the same department where the applicant completed his PhD; you were not his supervisor. Now you work in different universities.
8   You have approached the applicant in the past and proposed a shared project. No specific steps have been taken yet and you have no previous collaborative projects.
9   You represent a different methodological approach to the applicant.
10 You and the applicant are both likely to apply for the same position as professor when the current professor retires next year.
11 You both applied for the same position last year and you were the successful applicant.
12 You and the applicant wrote a joint paper four years ago.

Consider for each scenario whether:

1   you consider that you have no conflict of interest and you will not raise the connection with the organisers of the review;
2   you believe you do not have a conflict of interest, but you still share the information with the organisation;
3   you believe you have a conflict of interest and you share that with the organisation and exclude yourself from reviewing the application;

4 you share the information with the organisation and ask them to determine if a conflict of interest exists.

Do you think the review process would benefit more from someone with a slight conflict of interest but strong expertise compared with a reviewer with no potential conflict of interest but weaker expertise?

NOTES

1 For discussion on this development, see: A. Geuna (2001), The changing rationale for European university research funding: are there negative unintended consequences?, *Journal of Economic Issues* 35:3, 607–632; H. Horta, J. Huisman and M. Heitor (2008), Does competitive research funding encourage diversity in higher education?, *Science and Public Policy* 35:3, 146–158.
2 On contract research and commercialisation, see: M. Perkmann, V. Tartari, M. McKelvey, *et al.* (2013), Academic engagement and commercialisation: a review of the literature on university–industry relations, *Research Policy* 42:2, 423–442; P.C. Boardman and B.L. Ponomariov (2009), University researchers working with private companies, *Technovation* 29:2, 142–153; D. Czarnitzki, Ch. Grimpe and A.A. Toole (2011), Delay and secrecy: does industry sponsorship jeopardize disclosure of academic research?, Department of Managerial Economics, Strategy and Innovations, Leuven University.

Chapter 7

Assessing research and researchers

The main ethical considerations in assessing research are:

1 There is a certain balance between how much time, energy and resources should be spent on assessments and to what extent we should trust that universities and researchers are effective and productive without continuous follow-ups.
2 Apart from intended consequences, assessments may have unintended consequences that may or may not be desirable.
3 Growing emphasis on certain criteria of assessment also increases the risk of manipulating the results to meet these criteria.

Ethics by the guided dialogue approach typically requires researchers and research communities to consider the following key ethical questions in research assessment:

- Who is the primary stakeholder in research assessments: researchers themselves, departments, universities, ministries or advancement of science as an abstract notion?
- Are the applied assessment criteria fair from the perspective of different fields and disciplines as well as different stakeholders?
- What is the role of peer review in research evaluations? Is its in-built subjectivity a harm or a benefit?
- Is it right that some researchers leave peer-review tasks to their colleagues?
- Should social impact be an essential part of research assessment? If yes, how can it be evaluated?

Various evaluations and assessments are an essential part of researchers' lives. They have always belonged to academic life, but due to external pressure to be effective and useful, academic evaluations have become more frequent and their focus has diversified. In previous chapters we have already touched upon some forms of research evaluation. In this chapter we will consider evaluations that concern research collectives, i.e. faculties, universities, research fields or even countries. In this context we will have a closer look at the two main methods of evaluation: peer review and use of bibliometrics.

The general idea of research evaluations is to identify and recognise quality and excellence in research. In the cases we have discussed in previous chapters, assessments have had a rather limited aim, selecting articles to be published, projects to be funded and people to be recruited. When assessing research merits of a larger collective of researchers, the methods are in some ways the same, but the purpose of the evaluation is quite different. In this chapter we concentrate on research evaluation with political or strategic goals at the university or country level. We will consider them from the perspective of the collective and also ask how these evaluations concern individual junior and senior researchers.

Regarding the collective of researchers, one can differentiate three major forms of assessment: **research assessments** of a certain administrative unit or research field, **financing formulas** for distribution of resources to universities and **university rankings**. One may think that these activities have very little to do with each other. Indeed, they have certain differences. Financing formulas are used and university rankings published year after year, while research assessments are conducted at intervals of five or six years or *ad hoc*. The purposes of these activities vary, as do the users of the analyses. But what is similar for all these procedures is the general goal of assessments: identification and recognition of quality and excellence in research.

There are several reasons for being aware of the process of evaluation. First, every researcher has to participate in these assessments. At the simplest level, they have to provide data or materials to be included in the assessment. The assessment criteria typically signal what is regarded as profitable and advisable at the policy level. The consequences of assessments are important. Research assessments implicitly guide how to do research and it affects research choices and behaviour. If only quantity counts, you will work towards more publications. If quality counts, you may strive for fewer publications in higher-ranked journals. So if an evaluation only considers highly valued journals, it is a short step to assume research is going to try to publish less but in better fora. Values are always included, though sometimes obscured, in the evaluation criteria.

Second, researchers are used both as external experts in evaluations and as members of steering committees that design evaluation processes. Both roles are very influential as measures taken on the basis of various assessments have extensive impacts on the lives of researcher collectives. Therefore, ethical questions gain even more weight.

Third, criteria used in research assessments are not stable, but are under continuous discussion. It is important that research policy-makers are not the only ones who set the rules and principles of assessment. Research communities at large should take part in these discussions, because assessment has a significant influence on research practices and priorities.

Identifying stakeholders

In research evaluation, researchers themselves are an obvious stakeholder as **objects of assessment.** It is their work that is under scrutiny, they have to provide data and written documents to be evaluated, and the assessment will certainly influence their lives in many ways. However, researchers are not a homogeneous group of stakeholders and they may have different opinions on desirable parameters and rules of assessment. For example, they can disagree on the selection of researchers to be included in an assessment of a university or faculty: only professors and other senior researchers, or junior teachers, post-doctoral students and doctoral students as well. This question is especially relevant if relative indications are used (e.g. publications per researcher or average number of citations per publication).

Apart from individuals, assessments concern collectives of researchers: research groups, departments, faculties and universities. The administrative body as an initiator of an assessment is also a primary stakeholder. It may be a ministry, university, faculty, research agency, federal centre of evaluation, or any other representative of authorities, that is responsible for quality and effectiveness of research. The initiator itself may also conduct the assessment, but it may also outsource the concrete realisation to a certain assessment centre or company. These then become stakeholders as well. The leaders of these organisational units (heads, deans, rectors) all play a certain role in the assessment process. They are in many ways end users of the assessments and they decide on possible bonuses or sanctions, which significantly influence researchers' work.

If the initiator of an assessment establishes a **steering committee** to lead the process, it will become an important and responsible stakeholder. The committee determines many details of the process, such as who are the objects of assessments, what is the time span, what methods are applied (peer review, bibliometrics or something else), how referees are selected, etc. All these questions include various ethical choices. Each actual decision is more beneficial to one group of stakeholders and less beneficial to others. Steering committee members may have a double role: they plan the rules of assessment but they can also be objects of it. This, of course, increases the need to rely on generally accepted principles.

Each assessment strengthens traditions or creates new ways to conduct assessments. Researchers who are not involved in them personally may also follow the results of assessments. They may make note of the criteria used in assessments and conclude that something similar is in store for them. So, the broader **research community** is a secondary stakeholder. **Policy-makers,** even if they did not initiate an assessment, may use its results. Sometimes the **media** are also interested in assessments and universities may actively inform of the results, especially if they are positive.

Understanding rights and responsibilities

It is obvious that **researchers**, being the objects of assessment, have the right to be informed on the rules and objectives of an assessment. They have the right to expect that assessments are provided in a way that treats researchers equally. This can be a difficult requirement because researchers may have diverse opinions about suitable rules and criteria of assessments.

It is quite obvious that permanent university or research centre researchers are obliged to take part in an assessment. They cannot think they are untouchable in this sense. It is researchers' responsibility to record annually their publications and other activities in a certain depository according to the guidelines of their employers. If in a research assessment some other data are needed, they have to provide these as well.

As was mentioned in earlier chapters, researchers asked to act as **external experts** have the dilemma of rights and responsibilities. They have the right to decline the request, but they may feel that as a whole they have the responsibility to take part in assessments because the practice of using peer reviews is an essential part of the general idea of the research community's work.

Fair treatment of researchers is one of the key question in assessments. Researchers have a right to be treated fairly. This translates to a responsibility for the **organisers of assessments**. The need to consider fairness applies both to the differences between research fields and to comparisons between branches and factions within research fields.[1]

As the question of fair and equal treatment of different research fields is crucial in any assessment, let us stop to consider it here. An option could be that all the fields should be evaluated in a similar way. Such a view seems to follow the equality principle and facilitates the possibility to say whether research in medicine in our university or country is of better quality than is research of mathematics or pedagogy. However, one can easily challenge this approach by arguing that research fields fundamentally differ from each other in publishing habits and general methodology. Comparing even similar fields like mathematics, physics and computer science or literature studies, linguistics and cultural studies is challenging as these fields have significantly different publishing traditions and patterns, and thus direct comparisons of any kind could be unfair and inappropriate.

Therefore it is reasonable to ask whether the comparison of the quality of research across disciplines is ethically sustainable at all. Should we weigh the value of publications only in the framework of a single discipline? Does the best publication in cancer research or theoretical physics represent as high scientific quality as the best publication in pedagogy or nursing research? One may try to approach this question by comparing similar statements in sports. A gold medal winner in the high jump is as good an athlete as a gold medallist in the long jump. On the other hand, to be the best football player in the world seems to be something more than to be the best water polo player because there are many more football players in the world than there are water polo players. Therefore, would the only acceptable point of reference for assessment be other researchers in the same field worldwide?

We can go further in this reasoning and consider subfields of research. All large research fields are heterogeneous in one way or another. Genetics is one of the hottest areas, and journals in genetics have the highest impact factors. From a social perspective, psychiatry is an equally important branch of medicine. However, psychiatry differs from genetics significantly in research methods and publishing habits. There are differences also between other medical specialities. Similarly, we see divergent habits, for example, in international law and civil law, in theoretical physics and nuclear physics, in bioinformatics and population biology, in logic, ethics and other branches of philosophy.

Defining options

The many details in assessment processes can be realised in different ways. For example: who will act as members of the steering committee and as referees? Where do referees come from (local, from neighbouring countries, from other countries)? How are researchers divided into groups (by department, field or some alternative)? What is the time span of assessment? These details influence credibility, fairness and cost-effectiveness of the assessment. Let us consider two concrete decisions from these perspectives.

Whether to conduct a research assessment of a university when there is no outside pressure to do so can be problematised, for example, in the following ways using guided dialogue tools.

'Positive and negative consequences' reasoning leads to some evident conclusions. A clear harm is waste of time: departments and individual researchers could carry out research instead of preparing materials for assessment. Assessments also cost money and people's time in administration. The benefits of assessment must be greater than these harms. The possible benefits could be:

1   Direct influence: the assessment provides information on the quality of research in the fields represented in the university. This can be used for internal resource allocation or organisational change.
2   Psychological effect: the assessment process signals to the researchers what type of research is desired and valued, and this may guide research towards improved quality.

3   Procedural influence: when compiling documents
     for an assessment, departments have to think of
     their achievements in research and values
     concerning publication practices.
4   Visibility within the research community: external
     referees visiting the university become familiar
     with research done by its researchers.
5   Visibility and appreciation in society: announcing
     the results of an assessment makes it possible to
     speak in public about the best fields in the
     university.   [CONSEQUENTIALIST]

It is impossible to weigh harm and benefit in concrete numbers, but a set of various points of view helps to decide whether an assessment should be conducted or not.

The other example concerns conducting a peer-review process as part of a general research assessment.

The starting point is to have a fair and credible assessment, which appropriately considers the inherent differences between disciplines. In adopting this principle, what should be the unit of assessment in relation to research fields? Let us assume that all 255 research fields categorised in the Web of Science/Social Sciences/Humanities are present in a certain university, which has decided to conduct a research assessment. Should the university establish 255 review panels to achieve credibility and fairness? Or is it enough to have 35 panels with 255 members covering all the fields? This is still quite a big number of panels and experts taking part in the panels. Another extreme would be 2–5 panels, each of which covers one large area of research such as medical or social sciences. These are the decisions that translate principles like fairness into reality. It is helpful to return to the basic principles during the design and decision-making process and to check whether the designed procedure truly aligns with the original principle and intention.   [PRINCIPLED]

At this point we are likely to re-introduce
consequentialist arguments as well. As the costs rise
together with the number of panels, we now face a
comparison between harm (cost) and benefit (fairness
and credibility). Some kind of compromise is likely to
be necessary. The credibility/fairness may be
achievable through intensive communication and
transparent guidelines that clarify principles and rules
of assessment even when the number of panels is
kept relatively low. What do you think?   [CONSEQUENTIALIST]

METHODS

Now we turn to methods used in research assessment of universities. In this
section we will discuss many issues, which may seem to be small practical details.
However, they deserve ethical analysis because their concrete solutions reflect a
certain hidden or explicit agenda and usually also influence the outcome of an
assessment. In particular the focus is on the definitions of fairness and equality
and how different details influence the outcome and consequently our perception
of how well fairness and equality of the assessment has been achieved.

First, we must decide the scope of assessment. Universities can conduct
assessments in administration, teaching, and/or **research.** In most cases there
is a difference in these assessments: assessments of administration and teaching
usually evaluate the processes, while research assessments target the results of the
activity, materialised in publications. Doctoral training appears to combine both,
so should it be part of a research assessment or is it included in an assessment of
teaching? The decision may be purely practical, but reveals at the same time
something about the university's background philosophy.

The next matter to think about is the **target collectives of assessment.** Are
existing administrative sections (departments or similar structures) a reasonable
unit for the assessment or should the researchers themselves get an opportunity to
create their own research communities for this purpose?[2] How do these alternatives
benefit different stakeholders – the university, departments and researchers? We
may even progress to consider whether administrative units reflect rather old
divisions between research fields and thus are unsuitable as units of assessment.

A research assessment can be conducted on the basis of **bibliometrics** and
other quantitative data by using expert panels (**peer review**), or as a combination
of these methods. In the latter technique, expert panels are given all necessary
background data but that material is only a starting point for their assessment.
Research fields differ in the way they trust bibliometrics. From the point of view
of fairness, which method is the most reasonable solution?

As to quantitative data, the basic indicator is the **number of publications.**[3]
Because publications vary, it is necessary to use some categorisation. There are
two possible dimensions in doing it. First, it is necessary to differentiate

publications for the scientific audience and those for other audiences (e.g. textbooks, newspaper articles, articles in expert journals). Second, a quality categorisation of publication fora is also needed. Some researchers think the impact factor, reflecting the average number of citations of articles, is a sufficient proxy for the quality of journals. Another way to determine the quality of journals is to use a peer-review method: a group of experts categorises the journals into needed classes. Similarly, a categorisation of books may be conducted publisher-wise. We can also add to the 'number of publications' indicator other supplementary components that place emphasis on quality – publications are taken into account only if they are, for example, published abroad or in journals mentions in a certain database (e.g. Scopus, Web of Science/Social Sciences/Humanities). As mentioned above, if any fairness or equality principle is followed, numbers of publications should not be compared to those in other research fields. The challenge is to define a 'research field', which may sound impractical these days.

Another common bibliometric indicator is the **number of citations**. According to a popular view, the number of citations does not directly reflect the quality of research, but is probably a reasonable proxy for it. In any case, citations tell something about the visibility of a researcher in the scientific world. The 'normalised citation rate per article' indicator tries to take into account differences between fields by comparing the number of citations with the average number of citations in that field. In creating that indicator, one should take into consideration also the type of publication (article, book, review article, etc.) and its age. Here again we are dealing with an assessment tool which is far from ideal because of the great variety of approaches and fractions even within a certain research field.

There are some indicators that combine both quantity (number of publications) and impact within the scientific community (citations). The current favourite is the Hirsch index (or **H-index**). If one's H-index is 20, that means this scholar has 20 publications which have been cited at least 20 times. The **i10 index** refers to the number of papers with ten or more citations. Usually these indices are used for individual researchers, but they can also be applied to larger groups of researchers, or even to countries, such as is done in SCImago. In the use of these indicators we face similar ethical and practical issues as when using other indicators mentioned above. Publishing habits and the coverage of databases in research fields vary and, therefore, a word of warning is needed: if we want to follow the fairness principle we cannot compare researchers' outputs by using only these indicators. These indicators are not value-neutral, and by providing a number or index they do not provide intrinsic truths. Each indicator has an in-built assumption of what is valuable and desirable in research.

A fairly new tool for assessment of researchers' work is **altmetrics**.[4] You can determine the method in different ways, but usually it covers other types of presence and visibility of a researcher in the academic world and/or society at large, not just what is shown by using traditional bibliometric tools as the number of publications or citations. You can be present and influential in different ways:

by writing blogs and tweets, by sharing videos, programmes and software code or by being mentioned in Wikipedia or other public arenas. There are also numerous platforms that can be used in distributing materials, data and opinions. Apart from general sites such as Facebook, Twitter, Instagram, Rabbit and Weibo, there are also specialist platforms built for researchers like Academia.edu, Research Gate and Figshare. By applying methods developed by altmetrics specialists we can count multiple forms of visibility.

The usage of altmetrics as a tool for measuring the merits of an individual researcher or a research community raises several ethical questions. If your publication is downloaded from Academia.edu, is this a merit for you equal to a citation? Is participation in social media nowadays a characteristic of an ideal researcher or is it still possible and admissible to be a traditional researcher who concentrates only on publishing in scientific arenas? Again, we have to think of the time pressure every researcher faces. On the other hand, some young scholars say that, in fact, networking with colleagues and other people and sharing materials and ideas not only takes time but, more importantly, generates energy.

The central ideology in **peer review** is that the community itself has the opportunity and expertise to determine what is regarded as valuable scientific contributions and what is rejected as being a matter of opinion or humbug. In the same way, the research community determines the features of high-quality research. Peer review can be given the following characteristics:

- It takes place as an internal activity of a research community.
- It is subjective.
- It is relative (research done by someone is compared to research done by other researchers).

Peer review can be criticised owing to the first two characteristics. However, a research community's starting point is that only it has the expertise that is needed in an assessment of research. Subjectivity is an inevitable feature of peer review. There is a lot of discussion and studies on problems in conducting peer reviews and the element of subjectivity is often part of the challenge. Therefore it is important that researchers used as referees understand their responsibility as reliable representatives of the research community. As described above, bibliometric data can be used as supportive material in peer reviews. However, it does not take away referees' responsibility. Any data can be interpreted in multiple ways; in fact, the whole idea of using peer review as an assessment method is based on the need to avoid blind application of statistical data.

As a rule, referees conducting peer review are experienced and esteemed researchers. For them to be asked to take such tasks is possibly an honour but also a burden as the review work takes time away from other duties. On the other hand, many researchers say the referee also benefits from assessments by having an opportunity to learn what kind of research is done and how research environments are organised in other universities.

FINANCING FORMULAS AND RANKINGS

Let us have a look at the **financing formulas** used by ministries in distributing resources to universities and the role of research assessment in them.[5] The simple logic is: the inclusion of an indicator into a formula means that this aspect of universities' activity is important. If the number of high-quality scientific publications is an indicator, doing research that leads to such publications is valuable. If writing books for the public or textbooks for schools is not mentioned there, it means this is not a desirable part of a university teacher's or researcher's work. Although the compilers and users of a formula may not think so, the indicators are easily interpreted from this normative perspective and they are likely to directly guide decisions made by academics.

Similarly, we can consider ethical issues in using financing formulas. They arise from problems in following certain principles and from the intended and unintended consequences among different stakeholders. In this example, we apply the financing formula used in Theland. This funding formula consists of the following large fractions:

- 50 per cent based on the degrees (Bachelor level, Master's level, PhDs) produced by a university;
- 30 per cent based on research output; and
- 20 per cent is strategic money (federal obligations, new openings and other special purposes).

Because we are concentrating on research, let us look in more detail at how research output is quantified:

- 20 per cent (i.e. two-thirds of the share given to research) comes from the number of publications: journals and publishers are divided into three categories in each of 24 research fields and the points scaled to represent categories 1–5;
- book chapters are counted as journal articles (the quality category is based on the publisher);
- a monograph (book) point is multiplied by four;
- the authorship is fragmented so that a publication is divided by the number of authors;
- the remaining 10 per cent is calculated on the basis of following criteria:

    1   2 per cent – number of articles published in *Nature* and *Science*;
    2   2 per cent – field normalised average number of citations per publication;
    3   2 per cent – share of publications among the highly cited 10 per cent in the field;
    4   2 per cent – share of publications with international co-authors;
    5   2 per cent – share of publications with colleagues from other departments.

Consistent use of any formula satisfies the
transparency principle. All stakeholders can
understand the rules of the game. **Credibility** does
not automatically follow. This requires a certain
consensus among all stakeholders about the set of
criteria. Unfortunately, this is seldom true. A further
important element of credibility is a reliable
categorisation of journals and publishers. Complete
agreement on ranking of best and least prominent
journals is perhaps impossible to reach, but if the
method of compiling these lists is plausible they can
be widely accepted. A possible method could be the
use of external (not domestic) expert panels for this
purpose, but this places domestic journals in a
potentially precarious position.

[PRINCIPLED]

The **fairness** principle is the most difficult to attain. In the list on the previous
page concerning the 10 per cent fraction of the criteria, the third criterion is field-
neutral in the case that the data on which it is based is equally representative for all
fields. The other criteria are more evidently biased due to differences in publishing
practices. The second criterion may seem to be field-neutral, but if the number of
publications is not field normalised then fields with high publishing records, such
as medicine and physics, have a much greater influence on the total number of
publications of a university than fields with less active publishing habits, such as
mathematics and literary studies. If we try to be very strict in realisation of the
fairness principle, we have to decline almost any indicator. There can, however, be
other reasons that support their use; they are better than nothing.

Typically, financing formulas are designed to increase
competition in a fair way by steering research in the
right direction. That is the **intended consequence**.
Besides that, there may be **unintended
consequences** that should be taken into account in
considering the rationale of the financing formula
used. An obvious question here is the overall
outcome of the use of data-based indicators. One
may ask whether any set of indicators can be
adequate to cover all aspects of research. The use of a
limited number of indicators may lead to a situation
in which researchers concentrate only on these and
neglect other parts of their work. An alternative
approach is to use, instead of bibliometric tools, only
peer review. Peer review has its ethical problems as
well, but many researchers would prefer it to

bibliometrics because it gives a more holistic view of
research than a limited number of bibliometric
figures. A further general question is whether there is
a risk that concrete quantitative indicators in research
shift university teachers' interest from teaching and
interaction with society only to research. [CONSEQUENTIALIST]

Each of the criteria have an evident positive consequence which is easy to support;
for example, cooperation between researchers from different fields is such a
desirable thing (indicator 5), but is rewarding this through a financing instrument
the right way to promote this kind of work? Other indicators lead to similar
reasoning when considering their benefit and harm.

A significant question here is whether research as a whole benefits from such
heavy incentives that steer researchers' work and publishing practices. If quality is
rewarded, it sounds good for the development of research, but if quality is
measured on the basis of citations and other quantitative criteria, does it actually
measure quality or, even if it does, skew the practices of doing research? Estimating
the true harm and benefit of these types of evaluations is difficult. However,
explicitly discussing the possible outcomes of different methods allows the
community to evaluate approaches and clarify its own values and directions they
wish research practice to take. Once the direction is clear, it is easier, though still
not easy, to design evaluation methods that maximise the chances of getting the
intended results.

In the first decade of the twenty-first century we saw an influx of worldwide
university rankings, such as Academic Ranking of World Universities (Shanghai),
QS, Times Higher Education (THE), HEECT (Taiwan), SCImago, Leiden and
some others. These rankings present similar ideologies to research assessments and
financing formulas: they are meant to identify quality and excellence. Rankings are
intended to be utilised by anyone: the media, the public, ministries, students and
researchers looking for the university to go to. Rankings are compiled by centres
specialised in this activity or by journals which want to attract public attention.[6]

The rationale of rankings, and the set of criteria used in them, have been
debated. Indeed, the principles of rankings of universities include many ethical
questions, and these questions are all the more significant because the media love
the rankings. The main points of criticism include: are the rankings a suitable tool
to compare universities with different aims and composition of disciplines? Is it
reasonable to compare whole universities, as there are stronger and weaker
departments in all of them? A third questionable aspect in most rankings is the
simplified usage of bibliometrics, which treats disciplines unequally. In this book
we are not going to elaborate on the methods used in various rankings because
they are far from individual researchers' influence. Instead, we pay attention to
some aspects of rankings that may appear in anyone's everyday life.

Makers of QS and THE rankings turn to thousands of researchers by asking
their opinions on the reputation of universities in their own fields. There are some

rules on how to do it; for example, you are not allowed to 'vote' for your own institution. The method is an interesting application of crowdsourcing. When invited to answer such a survey a researcher encounters some ethical choices. The first thing to decide is whether to accept the invitation or not. Motivations vary: *yes*, because it is my obligation or because it gives a possibility to influence the outcome of a ranking; *no*, because it takes time from other things or because I do not feel competent for such an evaluation. It is not easy to weight the motivational factors representing different ethical approaches and views of different stakeholders.

A further ethical question is, of course, how to respond to the survey. It is hard to defend any other way of answering than as honestly as possible. Any tactical moves are against virtue and principled ethical approaches. But are there different criteria in including universities on the list? Is it acceptable to base one's opinion on occasional acquaintances in conferences, or should one do some surveying among colleagues as well? Or should one visit homepages of relevant candidates and use that information as further evidence for the decision? We are again dealing with time management: how does an ideal researcher distribute her or his time between various obligations?

One thing in using rankings that concerns all researchers is their intentional and unintentional misuse. When a university or research field has received good results in a ranking, it eagerly distributes this information – and tends to forget the limitations and problems in compiling it.

SOCIAL IMPACT

The usefulness of universities remains a salient topic in research policy discussion. There appears to be a rough script to the debate: universities argue that every euro they receive from the state will generate five euro for the economy of the country.[7] In other words, we are effective and useful as we are, just give us some peace to do our magic. As for politicians, they demand from universities more explicit evidence of value for tax-payers' money. They want to measure the effectiveness of universities by quantitative figures.

It is important that researchers are able to discuss this issue, because nowadays it is so vital for the position of universities and research in society. The first task is to understand what social impact (other names for approximately the same thing are societal relevance/influence/benefits, usefulness, public values, knowledge transfer, third-stream activities, third mission of universities, Mode-2) is by having a look at the channels of influence, users of knowledge and some examples of how universities influence society.[8] Then we raise the question of measuring influence. The foundation of these considerations is the exploration of values both suggested as desirable regarding the role of universities in society and the values held by those who believe this valuable impact must be evidenced, proven and measured.

We start with some basic observations. A researcher can create patents and licences or open access materials, programs or prototypes. She or he can also write reports for authorities, textbooks for students, books for the public or internet materials for anyone. A researcher can also take part in state committees, boards of organisations and firms, and give public presentations in the media and at various events. All these activities may be visible and influential, but as a whole such direct influence is rather small in comparison to indirect influence. Researchers teach the next generation of specialists and these young people transfer the knowledge and skills they have learned to their workplace. This benefits society much more than direct influence by researchers themselves. Another indirect influence is through scientific publications. When publishing scientific papers and giving presentations in conferences, researchers enhance the knowledge capital of other researchers, who can then utilise this in their own research. The fact that researchers touch society mostly indirectly does not decrease their significance (see Figure 7.1).

There are three major user groups of new knowledge: the business (private) sector, public sector and citizens (see Figure 7.2). The **business sector** is eager to find innovations, inventions and new pieces of knowledge to improve their competitive position in the market. In concrete terms it can be a new or reshaped product or service concept based on advanced technology, new materials or new understanding of the needs of society/consumers ('green thinking', new living trends, new customer sequence), or a better localisation of the product by taking into account cultural features of the country concerned. Enterprises may benefit from new knowledge also in establishing a cheaper or faster production process, a better leadership concept (e.g. paying attention to the needs of multicultural personnel), or a more effective distribution channel (logistics, opportunities of mobile distribution). In return, the business sector may fund research directly either through specific and targeted contracts or through funding professorships, buildings and scholarships.

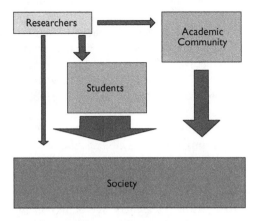

Figure 7.1 Channels of researchers' influence on society.

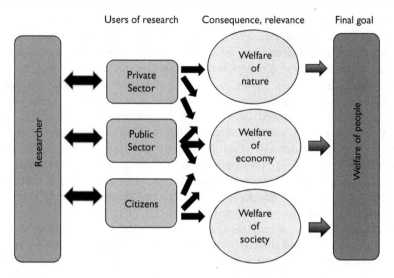

Figure 7.2 Interrelations between research and welfare.

The **public sector** can use new scientific knowledge in order to create better living conditions for citizens, to conserve nature and to create jobs. This translates to wise decision-making based on the newest evidence-based research. In concrete terms, it means regulative measures such as legislation, statutes, rules and top-down regulations, as well as effective administrative work. Although some services for citizens can be privatised, state authorities are largely responsible for the quality and costs of education, health care, transport, courts, cultural and leisure services. Societal innovations and improvements in decision-making and administration usually do not create more profits, but they allow reallocation of resources to improve quality of life.

Citizens can also be regarded as relevant users of scientific and other knowledge. The way ordinary people behave dramatically affects society as a whole. Usually we realise this when something goes totally wrong: when some people want to destroy society, nature or their own lives. As a matter of fact, society's success depends a lot on every citizen's concrete actions: how people educate their children, how creative they are at work, whether they are wise consumers and voters. Every piece of information adds something to people's worldview, which then regulates their behaviour.

Now we turn to considering how social impact can be measured. There are some points to be taken into account. The first thing is the **influence of other factors** beyond research in the chain of impact. The last question we touched upon, citizens' behaviour, is a good example to start with. Being a crucial element in society's well-being, citizens' worldviews are far from being a direct reflection of the knowledge produced by researchers. We build our understanding of the world at home and school. Then we add new pieces of knowledge to that by learning from each other and from our own experiences. The media is a strong player here, as will be discussed in the next chapter. So the path of new scientific knowledge to people's cognition is very complicated; though at most times it is undeniable, there are times when this connection is totally blocked by conservative worldviews and rejection of new knowledge.

Regarding innovations in the business sector, sometimes one can see a more or less direct link between scientific funding and a well-selling product, but these cases are very rare. Usually there are a lot of other factors that determine the success of a new product, such as administrative or legislative obstacles, investment capacities, the market situation, consumers' attitudes and production costs. When trying to find a measurable connection between quality of research and commercially utilised innovations, one has to bear in mind that, due to other factors influencing the process, only a small fraction of scientific findings are transferred to easily identifiable utilisations and many new products are launched without support from high-level research.

The situation in the public sector is similar: there are many factors that may influence the utilisation of scientific research. Two well-known tragic examples show one major obstacle. Research communities proved the severe health problems caused by smoking and the use of asbestos as a building material for years before this was reflected in legislation. The reason for this was obvious: heavy pressure from the business sector on the decision-makers.

While there may be little doubt that research influences society on multiple levels, there is equally no doubt that this influence is complicated and multifaceted. This makes measuring influence truly challenging. It is impossible to have clear measurements and quantitative facts. All measures will be based on assumptions, predictions and estimates. All of these have strong roots in values and life goals. Understanding this will help to reveal the measures of influence in a more complete context.

Another element in searching for measurements of social impact is the **timescale** of the influence. It takes perhaps weeks or months for a company to launch a re-shaped product or service concept. A new medicine or technological device based on high-level research might reach the market after years of intensive work and a complicated approval process. If one creates a new teaching method for maths, we have to wait for decades for its manifest positive influence. Evolution of thinking, e.g. the fact that the Earth is not flat but round, may take centuries. The longer the time span between new knowledge and its implementation, the more difficult it is to show direct causality between them. In most cases it is also true that the bigger the economic benefits or other consequences are, the more difficult it is to count them.

So, we have a dilemma: social impact should be somehow included as an additional aspect in financing formulas and research assessments, but the impact is often recognised only after a long period of time, and it is never achieved by research alone. In solving this dilemma, we have less than ideal alternatives: to leave social impact outside things that are measured, to settle for indicators that are clearly one-sided and biased, or to use peer review.

These questions will take us to the core of what we believe is the value of research. Typically, great value is seen in the social impact research creates. Now we have to seek reasons for why it needs to be measured. One of the reasons can be found in the current funding structures. If funding is distributed to those who excel, we need ways to determine excellence and measure all of its aspects. If we do not measure social impact in this context, it would contradict the fairness principle. If interaction with society is not taken into consideration at all, the researchers and departments that are active in that area will suffer. This may be dangerous also from the perspective of the needs of society, because the general rule is that if something is not rewarded it tends to lose its significance.

The second alternative has its risks as well. It is unfair to take into account only the short-term impact that can be more easily quantified. The famous quotation, said to be from Einstein, goes: 'Not everything that can be counted counts and not everything that counts can be counted.' Regardless of whether it really was Einstein who said so, the saying fits well with measuring social impact. You can relatively easily count numbers of patents, but there are reasons not to use this as an indicator. First, patents as such do not represent any social impact. In many cases they are used only to block other companies utilising new ideas. Second, and this is a more serious limitation in using patents as an indicator, they represent a tiny fraction of the social impact of research. In contemporary business, more and more innovations are based on open sources and on simply better understanding of people's needs and desires.

Could it be possible to make a list of various merits in interaction with society so that patents are only one of them? Compilation of such a list is not easy, but it is possible to itemise a rather large set of them: participation on boards, bodies, committees and working groups as a representative of a certain research field outside the university (companies, ministries, organisations); public presentations in front of various audiences; being invited to give presentations at professional events and seminars; books and articles for specialists or the public; interviews on TV and other forms of media; blogs and active participation in social media (Facebook, Twitter, etc.). Many of these activities can be quantified. However, two questions arise. Does it take too much time to register all of these activities? And can we ever list and quantify all possible forms of activities of societal interaction as they are often informal and invisible? The list could never be complete, which would further pose a question of its meaningfulness and usability.

Within the research community there is a long tradition of writing and reading referee statements. Therefore, although subjective by nature, the concept itself has a solid foundation. However, peer review is usually applied only to assessment of research merits. If this idea is transferred to assessment of social impact, some problems appear. The main one is the heterogeneity of the forms of social impact. There is a relatively wide consensus about hallmarks of good research, while such common understanding is lacking for social impact. Could it be, despite these reservations, possible to use peer review also in assessing social impact? It would be fairer than the usage of clearly biased indicators. For the credibility principle, there are doubts: are the referees, domestic or foreign, aware enough of the real impact of researchers?

Applying the consequentialist principle, we have to think of positive and negative consequences. A peer-review process as such and compilation of a description of these activities by the research community may increase the significance of this matter in researchers' eyes, which as such may positively influence their work. This is regarded as a desirable state of affairs: not all researchers are inspired in the choice of topics by societal and commercial needs, but all researchers, whatever they study, are capable and willing to think of possible further applications of the results they achieve. As to harm, the loss of time is perhaps not so significant. Is it too much if a researcher spends five or six of his or her yearly 1,600 working hours on this?

***

Assessments can drive the research process. They can influence direction, reward and punish, as well as reveal the purpose of research in society. Therefore assessments are never neutral or value-free. In fact, they are strong translators of values into practice. Understanding the values that in turn drive the assessment process is an essential part of aligning our core purpose with what we actually do. Guided dialogue can be used to explore what underpins the choices and decisions in the assessment processes. The dialogue can help to unpack what is meant by key concepts like fairness and equality, and allow for their more transparent and consistent application. Taking the bird's eye view of assessments is valuable for everyone in research. Assessments appear to be here to stay and we have the opportunity to use them to build stronger research communities.

Case study 1: proposals for enhancing research

All departments, faculties and universities everywhere want to gain more visibility and prestige in the scientific world. Sometimes they take special measures in order to get better results in obtaining performance-based resources or better ranking positions. The participants of a brainstorming event in Capital University of Theland made a list of proposals that could be used for enhancing the effectiveness of research. The following proposals got the greatest support in a democratic voting process:

1   All researchers and teachers are obliged to report their research activities in the depository of the university. Those with serious flaws in reporting will receive a 10 per cent reduction in their monthly salaries.
2   Researchers and teachers at the university are awarded with a small bonus for each publication belonging to the highest quality category.

3   The university will hire a consultant who will help researchers and research groups to maximise their publishing records by paying attention to: where to publish, in which language to publish, in which combinations of co-authors to publish, how to split research across publications.

4   Doctoral students are paid for helping senior researchers compile bibliographies of publications for reference lists.

5   Researchers are asked, always when appropriate, to cite researchers from their home university.

6   The university will hire a part-time world-class researcher whose publications will be included in the results of the university. His salary is equal to the salaries of four doctoral students.

Consider the harm and benefit of each proposal from the perspective of different stakeholders: teachers and researchers, the university, science. Ponder the possible concerns as to the proposal when reflecting on various principles: fairness between research fields, gender balance, credibility and reputation of science. What do you think? Do these fit within a well-functioning, ethically conscious university? What is core to universities doing their job well?

Case study 2: efficiency index of academic staff

The philosophy department at Capital University decided, in an open meeting of academic staff, to launch an efficiency index for academic work. The index is designed to create a transparent and fair tool for this purpose. The general idea is to take into consideration all possible aspects of activities. Each item of achievement gives a fixed amount of points, to be added to the total score of the academic staff. The main categories in the merit list are:[9]

1   Publications
   • Monograph abroad 20.0
   • Monograph in Theland 7.5; joint monograph of two co-authors in Theland 5.0; joint monograph of three or more co-authors in Theland 3.5
   • Paper in a leading international journal or book 6.0; with co-authors 4.0
   • Paper in other international fora 3.5
   • Refereed paper published in Theland 2.0
   • International congress or conference abstract 0.8
   • Book review in international publication 0.8; in Theland 0.3

2 Funded research projects
- International large-scale project as a leader 15.0; as a participant 6.0 (in Theland 7.5 and 3.0)
- International small-scale project as a leader 7.5; as a participant 3.0 (in Theland 3.5 and 1.5)

3 Conference presentations
- Plenary paper in an international congress 3.0 (local 1.0); in an international conference 1.5 (local 0.75)
- Section paper, poster or round table participant in an international congress 1.0 (local 0.5); in an international conference 0.75 (local 0.5)

4 Reviewing and editing
- Reviewing papers, theses, professorship candidates, universities abroad (0.5 to 2.5); in Theland (0.25 to 1.0)
- Editor-in-chief of a leading international journal or book series 1.5; a member of the advisory board 0.4
- Editor-in-chief of a less important international journal or book series 0.75; a member of the advisory board 0.2
- Editor of a domestic journal or book series 0.5; a member of the advisory board 0.1

5 Citations
- Citation in an international journal or book 2.0; in Theland 0.5

6 Supervision (when the degree is approved)
- PhD 5.0; Master's degree 1.5

7 Instruction in the university
- A new lecture course 3.0; an old one 1.0
- Seminar classes 3.0
- Invited lecture in a foreign university 1.0; in Theland 0.2

8 Academic administration
- President or secretary general of a scientific association 0.5 to 2.0; a member of the board 0.1 to 0.4
- Chair of a research council 8.0; member 4.0

9 Popularisation of science and research
- University textbook 8.0
- Secondary school textbook or popular science book 5.0
- Article in an expert journal 0.5
- Presentation in front of a non-academic audience 0.2

10 Media appearances
- Article in a central newspaper 0.5
- Interview in a newspaper or on the radio 0.2; on TV 0.4
- Other media appearances 0.1

11 Social media activities
   • Amount of appearances and followers on Facebook, Twitter and on other formats of social media 0.5 to 5.0
12 Social and commercial activities
   • Member of a board of a big company 1.5; of a small company 0.5
   • Chair of a state committee or working group 0.5; member 0.1
   • Active participation in the work of bodies and institutions of civil society 0.2
   • Expert and consultant role in the public or private sector 0.2

Consider this list of merits for academic work. You can use different ethical approaches.

• Who benefits from such a procedure? Young or senior scholars, the department, university or research community as a whole?
• Is there any harm in applying such a procedure? Is time spent in reporting all these details of work an issue here? Are there other unintended consequences? Is it okay if in teaching we use only quantitative indicators but in research also qualitative ones?
• The method used is meant to fulfil the transparency and fairness principle. Does it? Is it equal from the perspective of staff with different foci in their work?
• Does the procedure reflect what we could name as an example of the way a well-functioning university approaches this task?
• Is this a good example of applying the transparency principle?
• If we collect such information from individual researchers, can a compilation of these data be utilised in an assessment of a whole department or university?

Case study 3: faculty assessment

You are a member of an expert panel reviewing a faculty in another university. You are at the end of your week-long visit and finalising your statement. In this statement you are expected to give a grade for each department to summarise their research quality. The scale is 1–7. Each step on the scale is determined by the proportion of research that reaches good or excellent at the international level. You are in a process of jointly determining the grade for a department that most closely aligns with your own research. In the preliminary discussion the other panellists have suggested grades of 4, 5 and 6. Because it is very difficult to compare any department objectively with international research standards (which in themselves are challenging to determine), you find it difficult to decide what is a fair and justified grade. You decide to consider the decision using guided dialogue tools:

1   **Consequentialist approach.** From the departmental perspective it would be most advantageous to receive the highest possible grade. From the perspective of your own credibility, a stricter grading could be more beneficial. The researcher being assessed will always be delighted with higher assessments, but if they are unfounded and inflated the whole process loses meaning and everyone experiences harm. This could also lead to the panel members no longer being invited to carry out assessment tasks. The lack of justification in the process could also have broader consequences, such as the academic sector losing its ability to self-assess which is likely to lead to the need for external assessment of academic work.

2   **Principled approach.** Honesty is the key principle in this type of review work. If the review panel takes a biased approach, the entire review system will collapse. The challenge with honesty is the fear that others are not playing by the same rules. Game theorists have modelled these fears and how they may influence behaviour. In the review panel case the fear may be that departments or entire institutions are differently assessed. The results will always be used for comparison, but in reality they are not comparable.

3   **Virtue approach.** You consider what would be the hallmark of a good review panellist. How do they consider information, collaborate with others, define fair and honest procedure and align all with their core values?

Case study 4: dealing with control

Most research funding has in-built mechanisms for accountability to make sure resources have been appropriately used. Whether the funding comes from public or private sources, it makes sense for there to be mechanisms that guarantee efficient, honest and fair use of the research resources. On the other hand, no one benefits if these mechanisms take up an unreasonable amount of time. It is often challenging to find the balance. Researchers often experience bureaucracy and accountability mechanisms in the opposite way to how they are intended – they reduce the ability to use resources in their intended manner.

The benefit for the researcher (minimal control to leave maximal time for research itself) and benefit for the funder (maximum return for the investment in terms of research results) are not necessarily contradictory. Consider how you would find the balance from the consequentialist perspective. How much time should reasonably be devoted to reporting? How would you balance the needs of different stakeholders? How different are they in the end? Who should make decisions on the type of control mechanisms? How much can research processes be predicted and controlled by standardised mechanisms? If you considered principles – rights and duties – would they add anything to the discussion?

NOTES

1   See, for example: A. Mustajoki (2015), Measuring excellence in social sciences and humanities: limitations and opportunities, *Global University Rankings: Challenges for European Higher Education*, ed. T. Erkkilä, Basingstoke: Palgrave Macmillan, pp. 147–165 (www.palgraveconnect.com/pc/doifinder/10.1057/9781137296870.0017).

2   There were some unique features in the research assessment of Helsinki University: the participation was voluntary, researchers were ask to build researcher communities which were then evaluated, there were five categories of assessment. For more detail, see: www.helsinki.fi/arviointi2010-2012/eng/index.htm.

3   For a general introduction to research assessment indicators, see: H.F. Moed and G. Halevi (2015), Multidimensional assessment of scholarly research impact, *Journal of the Association for Information Science and Technology*, 66:10, 1988–2002.

4   For a recent discussion on altmetrics, see: H. Piwowar (2013), Introduction altmetrics: what, why and where?, *ASIS&T Bulletin* 39, 8–9; S. Haustein (2016), Grand challenges in altmetrics: heterogeneity, data quality and dependencies, *Scientometrics* 108:1, 413–423.

5   On financing formulas of universities, see: D. Hicks (2012), Performance-based university research funding systems, *Research Policy* 41:2, 251–261.

6   There is much literature on university rankings. The so-called Berlin Principles of Ranking of Higher Education Institutions can be found at http://e3mproject.eu/Berlin_Principles_IREG_534.pdf. Ideology of rankings and the methods of compiling them are discussed in many projects, e.g. the EU's Assessing Europe's University-Based Research Project (AUBR) (www.snowballmetrics.com/wp-content/uploads/assessing-europe-university-based-research_en.pdf); European University Association's University rankings and their impact (www.eua.be/Libraries/publications-homepage-list/global_university_rankings_and_their_impact_summary.pdf?sfvrsn=8). For critical analysis of rankings, see: T. Erkkilä (ed.) (2013), *Global University Rankings*, Basingstoke: Palgrave MacMillan; E. Hazelkorn (2015), *Rankings and the Reshaping of Higher Education: The Battle for World-Class Excellence*, Palgrave MacMillan.

7   See: www.kuleuven.be/english/news/2015/investing-in-research-universities-pays-off.

8   The new dimension in universities' role is often labelled as Mode-2 in contrast to the traditional Mode-1. The Mode-1 approach aims for new theoretical knowledge, the validity of which is tested within the academic community; the Mode-2 approach derives from problems important for society phenomena and is valued by usefulness of research. Mode-1 is discipline-oriented while in Mode-2 we often see cooperation

between different fields of research. There is a large amount of literature on this topic, for example: M. Gibbons, C. Limoges, H. Nowotny, S. Schwartzman, P. Scott and M. Trow (1994), *The New Production of Knowledge: The Dynamics of Science and Research in Contemporary Societies*, London: Sage; H. Nowotny, P. Scott and M. Gibbons (2001), *Re-thinking Science: Knowledge and the Public in an Age of Uncertainty*, Cambridge: Polity Press; H. Nowotny, P. Scott and M. Gibbons (2003), 'Mode 2' revisited: the new production of knowledge, *Minerva* 41, 179–194.

9   The case study is modified from the practice of the philosophy department at the Bulgarian Academy of Science.

Chapter 8

Interacting with society

The main ethical considerations in interacting with society are:

1 The researcher meets an environment where values and modes of operation differ from those they are familiar with.
2 Working with the media, decision-makers and the general public may take time from the main tasks of teaching and research.
3 There is a certain tension between 'globally' and 'locally' oriented researchers, and sometimes this tension sits in the minds of individual researchers.

Ethics by the guided dialogue approach typically requires researchers and research communities to consider the following key ethical questions when interacting with society:

- Does the third mission (interaction with society) belong to the core functions of universities?
- How is this interaction valued in recruiting new people and in awarding the best researchers and teachers?
- Is the influence from knowledge users and decision-makers a positive addition to research or something that jeopardises its core values?
- What are the desirable channels for expert work in society?
- Are there situations where telling openly is not ethically justifiable?
- Do researchers have more responsibilities than rights in interaction with society?
- How should a researcher position her/himself in social media?

Although research often takes place in the defined bubble of academia, it is not detached from society. Universities, its students, teachers and researchers are in fact an integral part of the wider society. As many think, universities represent and educate the intellectual elite of a nation. For centuries one of the core functions of universities has been to produce qualified experts to serve society in the many essential public positions.

Thus the interaction between research and society is not new, though the opportunities have increased significantly in the recent years.[1] The significance of universities and their research institutes has substantially increased as knowledge and expertise are even more centrally considered as the foundations of countries and economies.

In most countries the social role of universities has a legal framework. The framework typically defines the role of universities to include education and research. Interaction with society is typically regarded as the third mission of universities.[2] This interaction highlights the two-way nature of knowledge. Universities do not only disseminate knowledge, but the continuous dialogue with society shapes the understanding of how knowledge is used, what is needed and how new knowledge can be utilised by society.

Before having a closer look at the ethical issues in the interaction with society, we will bring up two issues that are of great importance when researchers enter the non-academic world: the role of an expert and the concept of scientific truth.

Expert role.[3] When researchers, working in the context of a rather closed community with its own practices and rules, step outside the academic world, they collide with a different set of values and modes of operation. Researchers have to relinquish the familiar researcher role and take on the role of an expert. After being trained to be fully authorised members of the research community, now they enter a world with other expectations and practices. If in their normal life the respect of colleagues is gained by high-standard publications on concrete research questions, in this new environment researchers act as experts who represent their entire field, and their worth is based on the ability to look at the common good. In most cases – this concerns both the media and the public sector as a whole – it is no longer so important who has produced the needed knowledge, the researcher her/himself or other researchers somewhere in the world. In this environment, the expert is first expected to amalgamate the results of the entire academic community. The next task is to apply this knowledge to a question which is real and important for society. In the research community, writing review articles is usually given to the most experienced and prominent researchers, while the task of knowledge transfer is given to the researcher who is available at that moment and is able to express the knowledge in an understandable way. In the academic world you concentrate on facts and research results; interaction with society typically requires interpretations and explanations, even speculations on something which is not scientifically proven. From an ethical perspective, the expert role poses at least two fundamental questions: who is suitable to take on the role and to what extent can a researcher stretch the limits of her or his scientific expertise?

A further demand in the expert role is a command of a new 'language'. In the academic environment, researchers express themselves in a language that is strictly codified. Interaction with society takes place in a different language. One may think that it is not a big problem, because that language is more 'normal' than scientific jargon. Indeed, it is required to use less complicated language than that of scientific writing. However, it a challenging task to talk about research to a new audience, because researchers are used to speaking and writing to a different audience. Researchers are used to discussing scientific topics with their colleagues, who share more or less similar background knowledge. When speaking to non-academics, researchers have to gauge what the audience knows about the topic. Although researchers theoretically understand the huge difference in levels of knowledge, they tend to forget this in the course of interaction. When taking part in conversation, people regularly try to avoid cognitive effort by speaking the way they usually do. This can lead to an inappropriate approach to the recipient.

The concept of scientific truth. A big issue in the expert role is reliability and the correctness of the given information. The academic world has stringent criteria for publishing. During researcher training we learn, through systematic instruction or as a piece of tacit knowledge, what can be regarded as scientific truth.[4] The statements you make in your papers have to be proven by using methods acceptable in the given research field. The situation is quite different in society: decision-makers and the media do not have time to wait for exact results; they want to get the best possible answer to their question today.

The definition of scientific truth varies discipline by discipline, but there are some basic types. Pythagoras' theorem is a good example of consistent and firm truth as it states that in a right-angled triangle the square of the hypotenuse is equal to the sum of the squares of the other two sides. This statement is true now and will be true also in the future. There are rather few truths of this type in science. We meet much more frequently truths which are the latest words of science but not the last ones. Darwin's theory of evolution was a revolution in understanding the history of species. It was for a long time the only truth that was accepted by the research community, because it was based on a large amount of reliable evidence. However, in recent years research in the field of epigenetics has forced us to rethink Darwin's theory in its strictest form. So, what was true 20 years ago has been revised. Another example: every year we get new and more reliable theories about the birth of the universe and its expansion, and we are apparently approaching the final solution to these questions, but we cannot be sure that the understanding we have now will never be questioned.

A further type of scientific knowledge is probabilistic. Intensive research brings us new tools to understand various phenomena better and better, but rarely leads to a final solution to them. Nowadays, we know much more about cancer and about the influence of genetic background to people's traits than was the case 30 years ago, but obviously we can never reach such a level of knowledge that explains these things in every case. In addition, it is not uncommon for researchers to hold contradictory opinions and these discrepancies seem to be a rather consistent feature in some fields. Such questions are, for example, the relationship of culture and language and the effectiveness of clear felling of forests.

Many researchers are comfortable and satisfied with the struggle around different truths and the probabilistic nature of science. However, people outside the academic world often find this situation confusing. Many have the impression that in comparison to beliefs, scientific truths are correct, reliable and stable. For some people, it is hard to understand that the best scientifically proven material for hip endoprosthesis was previously metal but is now ceramics; that the most healthy dose of red wine is two glasses per day while it was four glasses a month ago; that some researchers say that global warming over the next 50 years will see temperatures rise by 2°C, while others argue this will be 5°C. The very essence of scientific truth is beyond one's comprehension: beliefs appear more stable than scientific truths, which can be reformulated against new evidence. People, both citizens and decision-makers, desire definite answers to their big and small problems or the things they wonder about. This dichotomy of what research can provide and what the society desires creates a challenging relationship. 'Black and white' thinking helps people to navigate in the complex world, and they are disappointed if they do not get such answers from researchers.

After this short introduction we will consider some basic forms in researchers' interactions with society, namely contacts with the media, the general public, and the public sector. But first we turn to our regular steps of identifying stakeholders, understanding rights and responsibilities and defining options.

Identifying stakeholders

In interaction with society, the **researcher** is a key stakeholder. Researchers' approaches vary in this matter and influence their stakeholder status and subsequent rights/responsibilities. We can differentiate two major types of researchers: the first one may be called '**local**' and the second one '**global**'. Globally oriented researchers see themselves as members of the international research community and therefore they think that this is the major, if not only, reference group they belong to. These researchers judge their own success, and also the success of their colleagues, in this context. Locally oriented researchers want to be recognised and respected in their immediate environment. This goal makes them put efforts into teaching and societal impact. In most researchers you can find both of these approaches, though in varying degrees. All researchers and university teachers have to determine their attitude and desire relating to the need or obligation to go outside the academic world. In making this decision, they have to consider, besides personal interests, the opinions of colleagues and the wishes of their employer.

In all non-academic interactions the researchers, in one way or another, represent also their **department**, **university**, **research field** and the entire **academic community**. A well-known academic with a significant public role may generate a positive image for the entire department. Similarly, a very poor public image of one may have a poor impact on how the whole department or research field is perceived. Research is increasingly a more collective activity, so it appears appropriate to also consider the immediate research community, when making choices regarding how to interact with media or society in the broader sense.

Depending on the type of interaction, other stakeholders will vary. When researchers act as experts, the institutional counterpart – **media, public organisation, department or ministry**, etc. – as well as persons representing them – **journalists, workers, civil servants** – are primary stakeholders. When having a public lecture or writing a popularised book or an article for a newspaper, the **audience** and the **readership** are primary stakeholders.

In many cases the **whole nation** or a certain part of it can become an indirect stakeholder. Think, for example, of situations where a researcher is playing an expert role in a committee, in a parliament hearing session or in the media, when authorities are planning new regulative actions for a vaccination programme, school reform, food recommendations, business hours or priority areas in research policy. Some of these contacts may not be public, but their secondary impact may be significant to many.

Weighting harm and benefit for secondary stakeholders is a challenging task. We have to decide whether we should go that far in our thinking or whether we could leave considering further consequences to the authorities. Let us imagine the following situation. A researcher is used as an expert in evaluation of environmental harm in a large mining project. There is an obvious risk that if the environmental statutes are all considered applicable in the case, the mine will be closed, resulting in unemployment of up to 5,000 people. Can researchers, when giving their expert statements, leave this aspect of the question untouched and concentrate on the environmental facts based on scientific knowledge? This serious ethical question should be discussed among researchers.

It is also worth considering non-human stakeholders. Researcher engagement may have direct and significant impact on entire **ecosystems** or more specified cohorts of **animals**. Preservation of **artefacts** may also be influenced by research input, which would invite us to consider the needs and interests of inanimate objects. In this situation there is often tension between commercial goals and cultural values.

An important question to consider is the general attitude of researchers to other stakeholders. Sometimes you can see rather gregarious examples of the so-called information deficit model when researchers drip-feed pieces of knowledge to those who know less.[5] Such a behaviour has created an impression of arrogant academics who are not able to conduct real dialogue, but want to stand above it. One can ask whether such an attitude is acceptable to an ideal researcher. In the long run, it may also harm science and its prestige in society.

Understanding rights and responsibilities

When discussing the rights and responsibilities of researchers in interaction with society, it is important to distinguish two modes of action: researchers as initiators of the contact (**active role**) or as responding to requests from society (**reactive** or

responsive role). Many researchers are eager to share their scientific breakthroughs in one way or another. Whether media representatives consider these breakthroughs newsworthy will depend on multiple factors and not necessarily on the scientific significance of new findings. The same issue concerns publishers when they evaluate book manuscripts. Media houses and publishers have the right to not publish material they have received, no matter how important it could be.

Not all researchers are willing to talk outside the academic community about their work, but all universities are. They have special PR units that try to find a public space for any piece of newsworthy results their researchers have managed to produce.[6] The improved visibility is expected help researchers, departments or university through increased reputation, credibility and perception of excellence. Similarly, researchers may seek a wider audience to promote a certain research field or method, as well as to improve their own visibility and thus career options. All research presented in the public sphere may also influence financing bodies' decisions on priority areas of research. Here, one can see a relatively straightforward utilitarian approach in engaging the wider audience and the institutional decisions may be made without much consideration of rights and responsibilities.

The challenge in this consequential approach is hidden, for example, in the temptation to overestimate the significance of the scientific findings or future potential of that particular research direction – an attitude that ultimately raises the question of honest behaviour. The situation differs from that when we are selling our research idea in a grant application. The non-academic world is much more credulous towards new fantastic findings than academic referees are. Therefore, the researcher's responsibility for reliability must be considered differently in different spheres.

We are dealing with quite another situation when researchers play a responding role – for example, when the media has turned to them with a certain request. In such a position, many researchers start to question whether responding to the request is their **duty**. The moral sense of duty can develop from an opinion that the researcher should be at the service of the public good. Or a researcher feels obliged to reduce misconceptions, prejudice and superstition among people. This duty can be experienced as an unfortunate burden and distraction that just has to be done. If, on the other hand, the duty is experienced as a meaningful part of research work, the researcher may see the interaction with society as a natural part of her or his work. A perceived sense of duty, regardless of its origin, does not require responding to every request, and the definition of what the duty entails would be part of the ethical thought process to be completed both by the individual and the research community to set parameters on when the interaction should take place.

Another rights-based ethical inquiry relates to the 'permission' to participate in the public debate. Very few people, if anyone, are lone heroes in research as research results are increasingly more collectively achieved. Does this mean that permission should be granted by a supervisor, head of department or leader of the research group prior to accepting an invitation to be interviewed by the TV news or before speaking at the University of the Third Age? This question is linked with the principled views and considerations regarding the position of researchers, their rights and responsibilities within the research collective. Even though research is collective, researchers are individuals and personalities who are accustomed to a strong sense of autonomy in their research work. In this context, it may sit poorly to limit and manage their right to express their views and share their understanding in public. This question can be approached by looking at the benefit and harm of either allowing full freedom or limiting it in certain ways. Alternatively, it is possible to start with a principle of freedom/collective decision-making and possibly set some rules that limit the principle. For example, it may be assumed that each researcher is freely allowed to discuss issues relating to their research, but if they wish to comment on departmental matters such as a recent case of plagiarism or recruitment of a new professor, they need to discuss it with the boss first. Or is even this against the value of academic autonomy?

Sometimes researchers, who may have had bad experiences with the media, are reluctant to take part in public discussion, although they feel that it would be their duty. They may feel that their opinion has been overridden or given in a context where experts have been compared as equals with non-professionals or politicians. Researchers may also feel that it is impossible to be objective in the media because the discussion atmosphere is so polarised. This happens especially in questions which concern large groups of people, such as protection of animals, alcohol policy, status of minority languages and cultures and food recommendations. Researchers in these fields, after receiving a lot of hate mail, may think they serve society best if they concentrate on research.

From the perspective of public sector involvement – for example committee work – rights and responsibilities of selecting members to these bodies raises ethical issues. Often the same people are repeatedly chosen for various positions. In this cycle they gain more and more experience and become more and more desirable candidates for these roles. This 'law of aggregation' is common in most activities and raises a number of ethical questions: Is it acceptable or should something be done to change the situation? Does it lead to reasoning that these tasks are the responsibilities of only a few people while others may think that this is not their business? Is it acceptable that important decisions are made by only a few? Does fairness require offering these positions to as many people as possible, including younger and less experienced members of the research community?

Responsibilities relating to interaction with society are very complex. At the most basic level they have a responsibility to communicate truthfully and accurately about research results and to refer to sources of information. This is challenging when research discourse is translated into common language. The researcher may often feel that truth and accuracy are lost in translation, while the media, politicians or the general public seek simpler truths. And how to refer to the sources of information? Is it essential to refer at such a level of accuracy that it is possible to trace it back to the original source so anyone could read the scientific text as well? Should the names of the researchers always be mentioned? Would the reliability of information be threatened if the expert wishes to remain anonymous? Does the media have a right to get a statement from an expert when they want to? Would it be appropriate to state whether an expert does not wish to comment on an issue? While these are important questions, they sit more in the field of journalism ethics than research ethics and they are mentioned here mainly to raise awareness and consideration.

Would a 'good researcher' respond positively to requests to sit on a committee, to be interviewed in the news or to work with an enterprise? Or could being proactive and taking research results to the wider audience in some shape be an essential part of researchers' virtue? If we see research in the light of informing society and being part of finding solutions, the virtues of a researcher are likely to include ways to make research evidence known and applied.

Often the expert role includes an opportunity to promote the interests of particular groups, and researchers need to think of their role in this context. For example, if a postgraduate student is a member of a committee looking at research career development, is their position to promote the interests of postgraduate students and trust that others are chosen to promote the interests of researchers in different stages of their career? Or is it more acceptable or desirable to understand the task from the most neutral and inclusive position? And how about highlighting issues from one's own research area/field? How possible is it to represent others outside one's own research field and collegial group? These questions require an ethical decision on whose interests are primary in each situation. Pushing for personal interests may have some short-term positive consequences, but may not be as ethically justifiable from the virtue perspective or even consequentially if the focus is on longer-term well-being of research communities. Another view on possible consequences: supporting personal group interests too forcefully will probably result in being left out when the next working group is established.

Another ethical question related to committee work is compensation of members. If no remuneration is available, it is often justified by the voluntary nature of committee membership and the non-material benefits associated with being a member of the committee. Some may also suggest that such memberships are part of being a researcher and an academic. On the other hand, memberships are time-consuming. Even if the member is paid by the university (i.e. from public funds), is it acceptable to assume that an extra job is paid extra? One possible solution would be to pay the department/faculty for the time spent on the committee, as they are at least partially paying the opportunity cost.

Ethically it is also interesting to consider when a researcher has a right to label him/herself as an expert and thus give extra weight and significance to anything that is being said from the position of expertise. For example, if nuclear physicists speak up about nuclear power, it is reasonable that they claim to be experts. However, if they make comments about immigration policy or marketing of functional foods, they can no longer claim any expertise to back up their comments. If they are commenting on energy policy in general, the situation is more borderline.

As the definition of expertise is not clearly defined, and probably cannot be either, it may be helpful to also consider the social consequences. It is important to ask if there is any reason to consider speaking outside one's expertise as harm, particularly if no claim of expertise is suggested. Is there perhaps a risk that commenting outside one's core area of research diminishes the role of the expert? The situation gets even more complicated if we look at it from the perspective of the media, which tends to turn to faces familiar to the public; these are known as flip commentators.

Defining options

When researchers are asked to give an interview or to join an expert panel, they typically have two simple options: to answer *yes* or *no*. A similar situation arises when researchers consider whether to write a blog or a textbook – either they will or they will not. In reality, there are some further options, including whether to recommend the task to a colleague. Although there are not many options to be considered, there are plenty of factors that influence the decision. Let us clarify this through an example.

Researchers can receive different requests to participate in the media:

- A professional profile article in a science magazine with the title 'This is what I study'.
- An interview in a special-interest magazine (for example a zoology professor in a hunting magazine, or a statistics researcher in a sports betting magazine).
- An interview on TV news (for example, 'Is the current warmer weather a sign of global warming?', 'Is it possible that more WWII mass graves will be found?', 'How does the Spanish election result affect European politics?' or 'How dangerous is the current epidemic?').
- An expert comment in a newspaper, topics as above.
- Participation in a TV current-affairs programme.

To better understand invitations by the media, the following considerations are often helpful:

- **Who is asking?** Is the journalist familiar or a stranger? Which media outlet does the journalist represent (e.g. mainstream media company with a good reputation vs a low-quality press (aka yellow press) vs unknown new media company with upcoming online distribution formats)?
- **How long does it take?** Is it necessary to do preparatory work or is it possible to work with existing knowledge? Will the interview require travel? How long does the interview/recording/writing take?
- **Current workload?** Is the researcher in the middle of the busy teaching or research period that would be difficult to take time from?
- **General attitude towards the media in the workplace?** Do colleagues and superiors encourage it or is there a critical attitude?

Similarly to invitations by the media, committee and working group invitations are often best understood by considering what the options offer and require, particularly in addition to the above list:

- What is the harm and benefit balance of working outside the normal research environment to all stakeholders? What is, in the end, the best use of our brilliant research minds? What are the benefits of accepting an invitation for me, for my department, for my field or for the scientific world? Is it a waste of time for me or can I learn something as well? Can I or my department later benefit from the new contacts I will gain?   [CONSEQUENTIALIST]
- Is there a sense of duty to participate? Do I have a right to agree/disagree?   [PRINCIPLED]
- How would an ideal researcher behave in these situations? Do I feel better if I participate or is the contrary true?   [VIRTUE]

Time and money are further points to be considered when deciding on activities outside teaching and research itself. Researchers experience the transition out of the research world in many different ways. Some see it as a great opportunity to promote the understanding and utilisation of knowledge, while others see it as a necessary evil or distraction from research work. Regardless of the attitude we have towards these activities, time is likely to feature significantly in the decision-making. All new activities have an opportunity cost – we have to let go of something important, typically the full schedule of teaching, supervising, administration and doing research itself will have to change if we are to engage with society to any great extent. This common task of setting priorities reflects values and concepts of a 'good researcher'. These decisions can be further complicated by payments and public interest attached to the expert roles. Ethically the questions are often also framed around defining rights and duties to take research evidence to a broader audience and seek its application in society.

Now we turn to consider special features in interactions with the media, the general public and public sector.

THE MEDIA

The media are not the end user of knowledge, but in modern society they are a central source of knowledge for many. The importance of the media has steadily grown over the past few decades. Simultaneously, schools, churches and state administrations have lost their role and authority as the fundamental sources of knowledge and information. The media are in many countries highly commercial, and have an increasing mandate to entertain. Consumers of the media are often attracted by provocative means. The media typically play the role of a filter when it collaborates with academics. They distribute only partial knowledge produced by researchers to their audience. In this process, research must be truncated and simplified to make it accessible (Figure 8.1).

Media and academic publishing share the role of distributing information to satisfy the need to know more about the world. The methods, on the other hand, are very different, if not contradictory (Table 8.1).[7]

For these and other reasons, the relationship between researchers and the media is fragile and rigid. Typically, the media sets the rules by which their sources of information have to play and thus researchers end up in a foreign landscape. Contradictory aims and practices raise various ethical questions regarding the role and goals of researchers in the media. Many researchers think the media should adopt a way of thinking which is more typical in research. However, this desire is unrealistic. It is not the media's role to determine how researchers should do their work and vice versa – the research community cannot determine how the media should work either.

The most challenging aspect in media interactions is likely to be the demand to give unambiguous 'black and white' answers to complex questions. The media aims to deliver to their readers and listeners clear and simple truths, which will create catchy headlines and obvious conclusions. This is in direct contradiction with the way the research community discusses their work. The very nature of scientific understanding of proof and disproof makes it impossible for anyone doing research to state that they have found the absolute truth of the matter as was discussed above. This is often difficult to express when a researcher faces questions of 'is it' or 'isn't it' the truth? Researchers are likely to use phrases such as 'research suggests', 'we have reason to believe' and 'we have strong evidence' or just 'we need more research before we could answer this question'. The

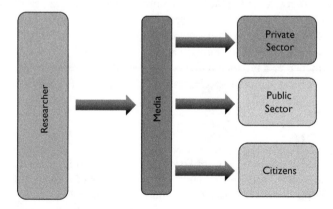

Figure 8.1 The media's filtering role.

Table 8.1 Differences between science and the media

	Science	Media
Time span	Typically at least months, if not years	Between hours and a few days ('For today's news…')
Language and style	Terminology typical for the specific field of study; accuracy is important; usually in English	To be understood by most, be readable and attract interest, often in a local/native language
Relationship between the author of the text and the knowledge behind it	Researchers produce texts based on their own research	Media professionals produce texts based on knowledge produced by the academic community
Hallmarks of a good text	Should bring something new to the joint stock of scientific knowledge	Should interest and entertain the target audience, often 'average citizens'
Type of information	New generic knowledge to reflect a larger truth	Context-bound knowledge with personal perspectives or societal relevance
Reliability of information	Only tested and reliable information is published	Possible to publish opinions and speculations
Sustainability of knowledge	Is valid until further research confirms or refutes it	Can be questioned immediately by anyone, including laymen, without any need to prove one's opinion or just on the basis of personal experience
Motivation to publish	To share information, claim ownership of results, develop scientific knowledge	To educate or entertain people, for financial gain, to be first to claim a scoop

audience or the media want clear yes or no answers. So when a journalist asks whether the increase in allergies is a result of increased levels of hygiene, or whether it is possible to find life on Mars, or whether all world languages originate from a single foundation language, researchers are likely to avoid straight answers. Instead of that, they will explain various theories and contradicting evidence relating to these issues. For the journalist this does not fit with the task at hand – it would be poor journalism to write all of that in the newspaper. It is essential to draw conclusions, distil a message and create a story; even if from a research perspective there is not one simple truth to be told.

Concrete news on research has traditionally concerned findings and results of a specific project. Competition to be the first has forced newspapers to make pieces of news which are in fact premature, such as 'In tomorrow's scientific journal X the research group led by Professor Y from Capital University will talk about the new evidence on the influence of Z to the appearance of lung cancer.' Another new habit in media reporting are pieces of news which do not concern results of research but plans to study something, especially if the project has got substantial funding. In fact, such advance reporting seems to be beneficial for both researchers and the media because results are regularly duller and more routine than expectations and plans at the beginning of a project. However, a negative consequence may be that among the audience – the general public – such reporting on research may feed excessive optimism regarding the possibilities of science. Instead of using the consequentialist approach, we could think of what is right according to the principles of research and how an ideal researcher behaves in these situations.

When working with the media, at the centre of many decisions is the risk of being misinterpreted. From an ethical perspective, one of the questions relates to responsibility. Could the researcher be morally responsible if the media and its end users misunderstand the research results – or does the responsibility lie with the media and/or audience? For example, epigenetics is difficult to interpret. If the researcher explains that environmental conditions with certain restrictions can influence the DNA of future generations, this could be interpreted as a departure from the Darwinian theory of selection. Or, if research results suggest that moderate alcohol consumption reduces the risk of cardiac infarct, would publishing this evidence be responsible if it increased the consumption of alcohol, particularly among those with the tendency to already over-consume it? Therefore, an ethical question becomes much more complex as we do not know what is the best way to discuss results to gain the best outcome for all stakeholders.

Let us test how different ethical approaches support making choices in challenging moments during encounters with the media.

Considerations from this perspective start with the basic question of consequences: does contact with the media harm or benefit the researcher's life/career? Interaction with the media could be a welcome source of publicity, which can help to sell a book that is being written, maybe help that little bit in getting a job one has applied for, or even make a funding application stand out. A TV appearance can work as an advertisement, and the researcher gets an opportunity to promote their expertise and knowledge. When including the research community and society as stakeholders, the benefits could include distributing the latest and the most correct knowledge to help decision-makers, or to generate interest in research work. The stakeholders could then be many, even if the impact on each may be small.   [CONSEQUENTIALIST]

To know whether these benefits are 'worth it' requires us to consider the cost or harm side of being in the public eye. The research community may see frequent media appearances in a negative light – being selfish, seeking attention or covering the fact that the research itself is mediocre. From the community perspective, the harm could result from simplification of matters in the media threatening the reputation of the research community.

The attitude of research groups and researchers will strongly influence how the research community deals with any kind of publicity. Is it a case of someone sacrificing their valuable research time to take on this role and thus sparing others, or is it a coveted position to be envied by others not as much in the limelight? The outcome of such reasoning is largely based on how benefit and harm are attached to these activities. It is impossible to quantify the harm and benefit of being the publicly known 'face' of a particular discipline. However, looking into them collectively will increase transparency, which is likely to lead to an ability to manage media activities better within the research community.

Applying the principled approach, we can ask whether interaction with the media is seen as a responsibility of a researcher. It is reasonable to ask whether everyone in research is expected to take an active role in society–research interactions. Maybe it is possible to consider a division of labour within a department or discipline to nominate different roles to fulfil this principled duty to actively communicate with society – some may be focused on international issues, some may have more domestic duties. [PRINCIPLED]

The media are often keen to give credit to an individual, a face to the discovery, rather than to deal with large collectives. This common trend can also be observed in media coverage of politics and sport. This raises the question of fairness within a research community: is it acceptable that a single representative of the group speaks for everyone – and also gets all the credit?

Media contacts are a good example for discussing the changing characteristics of an ideal researcher. Do the expectations and attitudes differ now from those of 20 or 30 years ago? Are there differences in answering this question among young and senior researchers? [VIRTUE]

CITIZENS

How researchers interact with society also affects the so-called 'general public'. As a stakeholder, 'the public' is very heterogeneous and shapeless. However, as a collective they make up society and are the engine for future development.

Many people are professionals in a certain area and become a target group for information directed to that specific community. Most people play the role of parents, and in that capacity transfer knowledge, beliefs and values to the next generation. Almost all people are citizens with the right to vote and consumers who make dozens of everyday decisions, which influence the course of the economy and their own welfare. As discussed in Chapter 7, the influence of research on these issues is typically indirect, but nevertheless important. Often, the impact is wider than the specific audience. For example, when speaking in an event outside the research community, the primary stakeholders are typically the participants of the event; however, there is most likely a much broader secondary stakeholder group formed by those whom the participants share their experience with. A book may have a similar effect when read by a limited number of influential people. It is important to understand the scope of impact a researcher can have when we are estimating the distribution of time desirable for these activities.

Researchers often decide individually according to their own priorities and desires whether to engage with the wider audience. However, researchers may also be encouraged by the university or research group to do that. In some fields (e.g. local history, social politics, law) a book may be simultaneously an academic publication and a popular text. In this way the book serves two purposes. Is this desirable? It is possible to think that this is something we should aim for as it brings research results to the wider audience more immediately. This may also assist in avoiding inaccessible and complex writing styles and traditions which will reduce the readership to a small, expert group. On the other hand, is this the right way to develop research?

Textbook authors have similar dialogues with the editor as appearing in the media produces with the journalist – how to manage the level of accuracy and reasonable detail in a text that also has to be readable and accessible to students. With book writing, time pressures are usually less significant, while simultaneously the importance of accurate and correct information is highlighted, because thousands of students may use the book for a number of years.

Writing popular science books or textbooks – particularly if they are financially profitable – raises an ethical question regarding the use of working hours to write them. There are ethical arguments for and against. Because teaching is one of the three core functions of a university, writing books can be part of normal university working tasks; on the other hand, the working hours have already been compensated for and gaining a second income from books appears as double dipping. The time required for writing books meets the all-too-familiar case of opportunity costs. This leads us back to discussing the core tasks of researchers – should they include engaging with a wider audience? Could there ever be a duty to do that?

Social media gives a new opportunity to be active and visible in society. The use of social media has grown rapidly and remains in a constant state of flux regarding its various platforms.[8] The way researchers interact in social media is dependent on their personality, career phase and circumstances. Social media activities present one of the ongoing ethical considerations regarding the use of time and priorities of all forms of engagement with the non-academic world. Typically, when a department, discipline or faculty decide to engage with social media, it is motivated by a desire to increase the profile of their work and market their expertise and abilities. Additionally, social media activity is often motivated by a desire to network with other researchers, groups and those benefiting from results. An evolving plan for the research community regarding social media use is likely to be a helpful guideline for individual researchers making decisions regarding their own involvement. On the other hand, being a very personal matter, there is always space for individual differences.

Presentations and comments in social media raise a further question on privacy. Often during the coffee breaks, people use quite direct and blunt language in commenting on recent events. A new recruit may receive a verdict: 'he cannot teach at all', 'how could they select such an idiot?', 'she will destroy the whole discipline'; a conference paper by a colleague might be evaluated as 'really poor', 'it was obvious she had not prepared at all' or 'he shared the same things he has done at least 100 times'. Social media invites sharing personal experiences, but it is quite another thing to use the above tone in social media discussions. Similar reasoning concerns other comments on colleagues' work and opinions. The community should ponder on the boundaries relating to the extent to which researchers should publicly discuss internal contradictions within the research community, or when, if ever, it is suitable to spread these disputes through social or printed media. The norms around what is socially acceptable to be shared are rapidly changing. As a result, we need to be aware of the need to possibly re-negotiate what is private and confidential and what can be openly shared when using social media. Understanding how this sharing can influence the community and how it is perceived is a starting point. When this is paired with a reflection on how the research community wishes to see itself and be seen by others, it has a greater ability to form guidelines and rules around social media activities.

PUBLIC SECTOR

The public sector is likely to use, or it at least should use, research-based evidence as part of its decision-making as a hallmark of evidence-based policy. Developing laws and regulations are the most concrete examples of the public decision-making process. Research evidence can and should influence how the laws are executed and how the less formal aspects of society carry out their functions. Public decision-making is informed by many factors and research evidence can provide impetus and reason for changing existing functions or ways of carrying out social responsibilities. In most cases research is present in the decision-making process through individuals, i.e. through researchers used as an expert in committees and in hearings or an author of a contract survey.

How does an individual researcher feature in this decision-making? When should a research be proactive and make sure the results are heard and incorporated in public discussion? Researchers may feel frustrated as they do not seem to be listened to in the public debate. They often speak a different language and lack understanding of the political decision-making process. Big business has their lobbyists – should research develop a lobbying system of their own?

In working with public administration and decision-makers, researchers inevitably face the 'scientific evidence is still lacking' problem. For example, an expert in psychology may be asked to give an unequivocal explanation for school shootings; a biologist may be expected to explain the reason for a sudden decrease in ants; or a media specialist is asked how many daily killings seen on TV a child can safely view without any disruption in their development. Maybe the most challenging field is nutrition, where strict regulations or recommendations are badly needed because of their huge impact on people's (and nations') health. Researchers may think that although many questions are still open, they are nevertheless the best people, due to their vast knowledge and understanding of the field, to make the 'educated guess' needed. On the other hand, researchers may also acutely feel they are out of their depth when faced with these questions. But if researchers are not the ones to answer them, who are?

As an example, let us look at what a consequentialist analysis could look like if a researcher was asked to be part of a committee when it is apparent that the output of the committee will not be utilised in any way as part of decision-making. In many countries the government and institutional archives are filled with detailed reports with no link to actual decision-making or change in behaviour, even when the committee's recommendations are based on solid evidence. Is the time invested in these committees balanced by any benefit? Could useful conversations and the possibility to meet interesting people be considered as a benefit to favourably balance the harm? On the other hand, it is often impossible to predict the consequences a dialogue has. Sometimes, participants of a committee use the knowledge they have obtained much later in diverse situations. This is a further element that makes the evaluation of benefits very difficult or even impossible. But one could ask, are only quantified activities valuable? How about applying principled ethical approach?

***

One of the strengths of the academic world is strict rules and strong cohesion in internal work. When researchers enter the world outside academia, they inevitably collide with another code of behaviour with quite a different understanding of what is allowed, desirable and functional. The strangeness of this environment underlines the need to discuss ethical issues related to these encounters as a collective exercise. Research communities are stronger if they have a shared understanding about the way to interact with different players in society. A good starting point for a guided dialogue could be respect towards counterparts outside the academic world as well as towards colleagues with another – local or global – orientation. This respectful foundation provides a collaborative environment to engage in guided dialogue on challenging questions regarding this important but complicated interaction. In this chapter we have raised multiple potential issues and questions worthy of being considered and discussed as individuals, small research groups and as a broader collective. How we respond to the issues depends on many contextual details, but the ongoing guided dialogue will provide structure and clarity for making good and reasoned choices.

Case study 1: plenty of invitations

1 You have been invited to the following committees:
   a National research career committee
   b University/department strategy group
   c University/faculty remuneration development working group
   d Departmental vision development group to identify future research foci
   e Faculty working group for developing postgraduate studies
   f National research council
   g University committee on public image
2 The media invites you to the following:
   a National magazine in your field for an interview on your recent research results
   b Science magazine to answer reader questions that are in your broad field of expertise, but not directly in your research area
   c TV interview/newspaper interview about an issue (a) directly linked with your research, (b) related to your research field, (c) loosely associated with your research field or (d) not related to your field but scientifically very interesting
   d TV current affairs programme discussing science policy in Theland
   e Magazine personal profile
   f Ladies magazine article about your life as a researcher, done at your home and sharing your favourite cooking recipes
   g A fashion article where you model different outfits for working life

Which of the above invitations would you accept? How would you make your decisions? Based on their perceived utility for you, your career, to the department/university, the audience? Or based on a sense of duty or responsibility as part of a research career? Do your current work pressures influence your decision and when would the invitation take priority over research or teaching activities? Would the presence of a more suitable expert influence your decision and how would you define expertise in the situation? If you did accept, would you openly share it with your colleagues? Why would you share or not?

Case study 2: which questions are scientifically significant enough?

The media asks for a short comment on a question loosely related to your field. The purpose is to give background to a story; you are not interviewed and your name is not going to be mentioned.

- Which month do bears start their hibernation?
- Is it possible to cure skin cancer?
- Why isn't a drop round?
- When is the next complete solar eclipse?
- Was Gogol a Ukrainian or Russian author?
- How many languages are spoken in the world?
- What is the chemical reaction resulting from mixing vinegar and baking powder?
- What is the difference between ethics and morals?
- Does a tin roof last longer than a triple-layer felt roof?
- How does a Muslim living near the Arctic Circle follow Ramadan during the winter months?
- Has anyone studied how Napoleon died?
- What is Higgs' particle?

Consider from the perspective of a researcher which questions would be meaningful to answer. Is it acceptable to tell the journalist to check the facts on Wikipedia? Should the question be answered to nurture relationships with the media so you have good lines of communication when you have something to share with the world? Is this type of utilitarian thinking appropriate to this type of question?

Case study 3: limits between scientific knowledge and people's own experience?

As described in this chapter, one of the challenges in interaction with the media is different foundations of knowledge. In science it is research; in everyday life it is personal experience or information accumulated from different sources. If we are studying genes, space or a language spoken in New Guinea, a collision between different angles of views does not take place, because people have no personal experience of these things. The situation is quite different if we are dealing with phenomena which belong to people's empirical world. Let us take an imaginary example.

Mosquitos are very harmful insects. Some of them spread diseases like malaria, yellow fever, Zika virus and dengue fever; some others are not dangerous but annoy people with their hum and biting. In Theland there are about 40 different species of mosquito which irritate people, both locals and tourists, in the countryside. Country people have their opinions about how to dress so that mosquitos are not interested in them. Jim, a nature scientist, decided to study this important question. He built a rather simple laboratory experiment: a cage with 50 local mosquitos. A test person entered the cage dressed in different colours. Jim counted the numbers of mosquitos biting the test person in one minute. Each time Jim changed the set of mosquitos in order to avoid the feeling of fullness effect. There were statistically significant differences between the colours, white being the best protection against the insects.

Jim revealed his findings to a newspaper and it was interested in writing a news story about it. Jim emphasised that these was only the first results and further research is needed. The newspaper was planning a heading like 'Wear white to avoid mosquitos'. In addition, they interviewed a local farmer who said the study was rubbish: 'Everyone here knows that red is the best colour to avoid mosquitos, the researcher has obviously never seen the countryside; it is awful that they use tax-payers money for studies that are totally useless.' It is impossible to say who is right, Jim or the farmer. As Jim mentioned, the results are preliminary and further research is needed. Indeed, there are a lot of possible sources of error in this study: different sorts of mosquitos may behave differently, lighting (sunshine vs twilight) may make a difference and the reactions of mosquitos may be caused by a combination of various factors rather than a single one.

The case raises important ethical questions. Was Jim's decision to contact the newspaper ethically justifiable from the consequentialist and principled approaches? Imagine similar situations with a possible collision between research and empirical knowledge. How should we handle the confusing fact that at a general level, scientific knowledge is more reliable than empirical knowledge, but occasionally the contrary may be true? Is it dangerous to admit that? After saying this, how can one demand more resources for research? And how should we deal with the practice the media has of making all opinions equal, whether they be based on research, personal experience or faith?

Case study 4: science blog

A research council in Theland has started a science blog. Researchers from different research fields are invited to contribute. The blog has six regular themes:

1   Can science ever be completely objective?
2   Are all research fields equally important?
3   Science policy and its pitfalls – what if something goes wrong?
4   Are women finally equal in research?
5   Dealing with ethical issues as a measure of scientific community.
6   What is exciting in my field at the moment?

Would you accept the invitation to contribute to the blog? What would influence your decision? Harm and benefit analysis: the impact of the blog, prestige associated with contributing to the blog, other pressing activities, who is asking? Or would you contribute as it is good to be 'visible'? What would your colleagues think of this? Do you feel it is your duty to accept as you have been invited? Which theme would you pick and why?

Case study 5: gaining public interest

The public discussion fluctuates and themes are often popular for a while before the main focus moves on to the next topic – alcohol-related health problems may have been important a few years ago, but now the focus is on the impact of obesity. Likewise, issues with the ozone layer have been preceded by discussions on carbon dioxide. If your research work does not overlap with the current public debate focus, but still has the potential to improve quality of life or economic viability, when would you have a responsibility to make the results known and important in the eyes of the public and decision-makers? What would evoke a clear duty to talk about observations and results outside the research world? Here are some fictional cases to consider:

1   Research suggests that water quality in a popular recreational lake in Theland is unsuitable for swimming. The most likely cause of the pollution is a sawmill located on the shore of the lake. These are the first results on the lake water quality, though locals have had their concerns. The sawmill is a significant employer in the area.

2   A correlation can be constructed using results from diverse research projects: (1) the more one watches TV entertainment the fewer books one reads; (2) the fewer books one reads the less able one is to understand communication by public authorities; (3) these people use more customer services and support functions in the community, creating an extra cost to society.

3   Industry is commonly using a chemical in its processes. Early animal tests suggest it could be carcinogenic.

4   Research suggests that poor sleep can influence driving ability at the level of 0.8 per mille of alcohol in the blood.

5   Follow-up research indicates that people from Theland work ineffectively in international collaborations and institutions. They trust the formal lines of communication too much and do not utilise social networks and unofficial channels of communication and decision-making.

6   New research reveals that a migratory bird breeding in Theland has breeding patterns that are currently incorrectly identified in textbooks. The new knowledge indicates that the nests are built on the ground rather than low tree branches.

7   As a by-product of a genetic study on asthma in a sub-population, the group finds out that the nominated father of the second child is often not the biological father.

8   Thorough analysis of Theland's presidents show that there is a negative correlation between success at school and success in politics.

If these were your results, how persistently would you work towards making them public knowledge? Would you seek the attention of the media or public decision-makers first? What if no one was interested in the new information? How would you discuss this with your colleagues in the department and in your research team? Consider whether the following would influence your decision-making:

1   How important is the issue for the individuals/society/economy?
2   How certain are the results?
3   How simplified is the information? Can it be described in a way that is easy to understand by anyone? Is there a risk that people will misinterpret the real essence of the news?

NOTES

1   The content of this chapter is related to the question of 'public engagement of science'. A good introduction to the topic is J. Stilgoe, S.J. Lock and J. Wilsdon

(2014), Why should we promote public engagement with science?, *Public Understanding of Science* 23:1, 4–15. The *Public Understanding of Science Journal* is one of the scientific fora where these matters are discussed.

2   Esa Väliverronen concretises the third mission of universities and researchers by changing the traditional saying 'publish or perish' into 'be seen in public or perish'. E. Väliverronen (1993), Science and the media: changing relations, *Science Studies* 6:2, 23–34.

3   On different expert roles of researchers, see: P. Weingart (1998), Science and the media, *Research Policy* 27, 869–879; E. Väliverronen (2001), Popularisers, interpreters, advocates, managers and critics: framing science and scientists in the media, *Nordic Review* 22:2, 39–48; H.P. Peters (2008), Scientists as public experts, *Handbook of Public Communication of Science and Technology*, eds M. Bucchi and B. Trench, London: Routledge, pp. 131–146; M. Bucchi. (2008), Of deficits, deviations and dialogues: theories of public communication of science, *Handbook of Public Communication of Science and Technology*, ed. M. Bucchi and B. Trench, London: Routledge 2008, pp. 57–76; E. Albæk (2011), The interaction between experts and journalists in news journalism, *Journalism* 12:3, 335–348; H. Collins (2015), Are We All Scientific Experts Now?, Cambridge: Polity Press.

4   Truth is not a simple concept, even in science. There are several theories for defining scientific truth, e.g. correspondence theory and coherence theory. A good introduction to the question can be found in the *Stanford Encyclopedia of Philosophy* (http://plato. stanford.edu/entries/truth). A practical approach to the question is founded on the collective opinion of researchers: truth is what the research community regards as truth. An interesting analysis of the differences of the notion of truth can be found in: J.A. Winsten (1985), Science and the media: the boundaries of truth, *Health Affairs* 4:1, 5–23.

5   On the deficit model and public understanding of science, a notion which has replaced the notion of 'science literacy', see: M.W. Bauer, N. Allum and S. Miller (2007), What can we learn from 25 years of PUS survey research? Liberating and expanding the agenda, *Public Understanding of Science* 16, 79–95.

6   On the history of 'selling science', see: D. Nelkin (1995), *Selling Science: How the Press Covers Science and Technology*, New York: W.H. Freeman. On the problems of active science promotion, see: F. Marcinkowski and M. Kohring (2014), The changing rationale of science communication: a challenge to scientific autonomy, *Journal of Science Communication* 13:3, 1–8.

7   The role of research and universities in a mediatised society and the complex relationship between researchers and the media are discussed, among others, in: T. Čonč and D. Kos (2015), Welcome to the jungle: science communication in the mediatized society. *Infuture* 38, 367–376; H.P. Peters (2013), Gap between science and media revisited: scientists as public communicators. *PNAS* 110, 3; S. Dunwoody (2008), Science journalism, *Handbook of Public Communication of Science and Technology*, ed. M. Bucchi and B. Trench, London: Routledge, pp. 15–26.

8   The involvement of researchers in social media is discussed in: X. Liang, L. Yi-Fan Su, S.K. Yeo, D.A. Scheufele, D. Brossard, M. Xenos, P. Nealey, and E.A. Corley (2014), Building buzz: (scientists) communicating science in new media environments, *Journalism & Mass Communication Quarterly* 91:4, 772–791; D. Brossard and D.A. Scheufele (2013), Science, new media, and the public, *Science* 339:6115, 40–41; H.M. Bik and M.C. Goldstein (2013), An introduction to social media for scientists, *PLOS Biology*, 11:4.

Chapter 9

Managing research careers

The main ethical considerations in managing a research career are:

1   Research is for many an exciting activity that takes a lot of time and attention, and is often not limited to official working hours.
2   Research is usually group work, which means individual decisions influence a large number of people who typically also influence these decisions.
3   Strong competition may cause researchers stress.

Ethics by the guided dialogue approach typically require researchers to consider the following key ethical questions in managing a research career:

•   Should the researcher consider other people when making decisions regarding their career? Who could these stakeholders be?
•   How does one balance activities that help to advance a career in research with obligations in one's personal life?
•   How does one determine future plans for a researcher – to stay in academia or to look for opportunities in other spheres in society?
•   How does one handle the possibility to study or work in a foreign university? Is it a positive goal or an obligatory burden in planning a career?
•   To which extend should a researcher be ready to widen her or his scope of interests and expertise during a career – to stay on familiar and well-known ground or to seek more adventurous and risky options?
•   How does one take care of personal health and form when there is pressure to use one's time in alternative ways?

The concept of a researcher is relatively new. Previously, universities employed teachers and their younger colleagues/assistants, who were very likely to become future university teachers. The university teachers of previous centuries and decades had secure careers with salaries that allowed for a comfortable existence in society. This often translated to help at home and an esteemed social position.

Today, researchers are in a different situation. Their careers are less secure, the pay not as competitive as in other careers in society, and the social position has changed. The large number of younger researchers means that university careers are not a certainty for anyone and even for those with secure positions, the employment requirements have dramatically shifted over the past decades.

Many consider research as a vocation, a passion to study and discover that which one feels called to. There are similarities to artists, with the need to show originality, passion, dedication and commitment in order to succeed in the chosen career. Research can similarly be a very comprehensive mental and cognitive experience that has existential meaning for the researcher. In addition, research often requires personal space and time to develop. Apart from comparison to artists, one can see in researchers' lives another seldom recognised component of wanting to do something good for society and humanity. In this respect, we may notice some likeness to professions such as nursing, policing or teaching. Researchers' mission may be to help people to better understand a phenomenon or for societies to be successful in economic competition.

The research world is also very competitive, as has been explored in previous chapters. Many research questions are the focus of multiple researchers in various teams and institutions. They all participate in the race to be the first to share results, and even those with small and unique research topics join the race to succeed in funding applications, and for career opportunities.

As a result, research careers typically require commitment in time and effort, which reduces researchers' ability to attend to other responsibilities in life. This is likely to have a negative impact on family life, for example. Obviously, everyone whose work is intensively engaging shares this problem.

How to balance different interests and meet responsibilities is highly dependent on personalities and context. Some people are more comfortable doing research with their laptop on a summer's day with children running around. For some, work is only carried out in the office and time at home is solely dedicated to other tasks.

Blending of work and personal time is a trend throughout academia and society in general. It is now almost expected for work to be included in what was previously personal time off. It is prudent to ask ethical questions around this trend. Has it become akin to a virtue that everyone should blend their lives in this manner? As a result, is it now unacceptable or considered poorly to refuse this blending and to strongly demarcate work and personal time? How will supervisors and departments balance different work–life balance preferences? What can be left for people to decide for themselves and what needs to be agreed together? All of these choices will inevitably reveal fundamental values and beliefs. These choices can be analysed and justified in relation to stakeholders and core values.

Identifying stakeholders

The primary stakeholder in these questions is naturally the **researcher**. In many ways, decisions regarding career direction and other life choices are typically considered to fall under basic concepts of autonomy. This proposes freedom to make personal choices based on personal values, desires and goals. In addition to autonomy, previous choices may have incorporated other people as stakeholders.

Family members are typically stakeholders in questions relating to one's career and use of time and energy. If researchers choose to work long hours and engage deeply with their work, family will inevitably feel the consequences. Children form a particular stakeholder group, as the impact on them is potentially significant while they hold only a partial ability to alter the consequences of their parents' choices.

Institutions and **society** are also stakeholders. Their employment decisions have a direct impact on the choices researchers can make regarding their use of time through the specific expectation of productivity. Similarly, the individual decisions researchers make have an impact on institutions. Working hard and producing results has the potential to influence society greatly. Simultaneously, the potential for overworking resulting in poor physical or mental health or broken families influences the research institution and society as well.

Within institutions the most direct stakeholders are immediate **colleagues**, **supervisors**, and **students**. This impact can be significant with one's closest colleagues and within smaller research groups, or relatively indirect in the case of larger groups and more distant colleagues. The way people collaborate at work creates the workplace culture together with its unwritten rules. This culture has a direct impact on everyone. An individual with a strong personality may have a huge influence on the whole collective, both positive and negative.

One of the key aspects in workplace culture is the balance between competition and collaboration. It is impossible, and most likely undesirable, to remove competition from a workplace. However, collaboration and interdependence are two sides of the same coin. The success of one in a department is likely to have a positive cumulative effect for others.

Challenging decision-making is often a result of defining stakeholders differently or disagreeing on how to weigh their interests. Are you going to focus on your own benefit/harm, the benefit/harm for your group, your department, your discipline or even your university and country?

Understanding rights and responsibilities

A right to make decisions for oneself is a fundamental right within most cultures. Even though this right is very strong, it is reasonable to pose the question of whether the researcher has responsibilities to consider other stakeholders as well when making decisions for their career and use of time and energy.

Multiple researchers and research groups often work on the same topic in a race to be the first to publish new discoveries. Careers and funding are also based on the same competitive structure, where the competition often takes place between colleagues and collaborators, as well as the more commonly recognised competitors. A researcher can easily find the competition a strong justification to work hard and long hours in order to succeed. Tough competition can be seen to reward those who have been most committed to their research endeavours. This justification can be particularly appealing for early-career researchers as the foundation of the research career is laid then, and catching up with others later may be difficult, if not impossible. From the rights perspective, does the undeniable competition translate into a right or even a responsibility to devote an exceptional amount of time to research activities?

Research questions follow the researchers when they close the door of their office or lab. Independent of time or space, the brain works on research problems. Researchers have to determine to what extent they should bring work home either concretely or in their words and thoughts. The two extremes are that no research-related conversations are held once the researcher opens the door at home, or that research is the dominant conversation topic at dinner, when socialising and even in the bedroom. New technology blurs the boundaries of work and other aspects of life. It is possible and easy to be physically present but completely absorbed by research activities. Could the situation in which the research work never ends be either a right of the researcher or even their responsibility?

In the case of family, responsibilities are highly dependent on the choices the family makes as a unit. Responsibilities will be easier to establish if at least the adults in the family share an opinion on the importance and nature of research work. In this situation, one partner may be willing to assume a greater responsibility at home and in family matters. Reasons for this may include appreciation of the importance and value of research work, or the options and possibilities research careers may open for the family in the long term. Individuals and families are different, and an outsider cannot establish decisions regarding personal rights and responsibilities.

The matters are complicated when the tasks the researcher is required to do for the family are not compatible with the responsibilities proposed by the research group/institution or perceived by the researcher as essential for the job.

Every research institution has its rules and regulations as an employer. These are typically coded in the employment contract, with corresponding rights and responsibilities for both the institution and researcher. No one can be forced to work in a particular position; the employment decisions are always a matter of an agreement. In this agreement, responsibilities and expectations towards the employee are typically exchanged with salary and career opportunities. While formal contracts define a particular set of rights and responsibilities, the reality in the workplace includes many other informal expectations that individuals typically identify as their rights or responsibilities.

These informal expectations form a grey area that should be discussed in the workplace. Guided dialogue would be initiated by asking how each researcher should distribute her or his time between different tasks. The big distribution is between research, teaching, administrative tasks and interaction with society. In each category there are many concrete responsibilities that can and should be identified. Usually a significant issue develops in various planning and developmental processes: do researchers feel it is a privilege or burden, a right or responsibility to participate in them? In some universities each employee, from doctoral students to professors, make a yearly working plan that reduces misunderstandings in expectations and goals of the work. However, as researchers' work is very creative and you have to react quickly to new situations and impulses, you can never plan your workload in detail.

From an individual perspective, it is possible to explore the sense of moral responsibility a little further. A researcher may experience moral responsibility to rescue the department from a difficult situation and agree to take on a position that is not in her or his personal interest. This thinking typically relies on two principles. One is a principle of reciprocity: if the department has supported me during my career, it is now my turn to support the department. This way of reasoning raises a further question: may I expect that after I have helped the department in a difficult situation, it should remember this when a permanent position for a researcher becomes available in the future? The other is a principle of solidarity: the department is our shared business and everyone should contribute to its well-being. The measure of solidarity is typically based on workplace culture. This sense of responsibility will naturally vary between individuals and their experiences at the department. Defining these unwritten experiences of rights and responsibilities is an important ethical challenge for both individuals and the research community.

The funding mechanisms and recruitment practices are set by the government or university board and sometimes by international organisations. Therefore the rights and opportunities presented to individual researchers and their supervisors are dependent on decisions made by those not directly involved in the research community itself. Who, then, carries a broader responsibility for research careers? Could we consider this responsibility to rest with political decision-makers and rectors, or does it reside firmly with individual researchers? If a ministry or rector directly funds doctorate programmes, could it then be considered to have responsibility for career prospects for doctoral students? Or could we think of two kinds of responsibilities: at the system level, the responsibility lies with those who have the power to build the system, but at the personal level researchers carry the responsibility for their actions within the given context?

Defining options

Options regarding the balance of research and life in general are vast and strongly contextual. In this section we will explore options on a more general level and focus on the different ways options can be evaluated, analysed and compared.

Research work is still to a large extent characterised by freedom to make choices. The working day is rarely based on fixed start/finish times, and the way work is done is highly dependent on the judgements made by the researchers themselves.

One of the challenges in comparing work–life balance options is the incompatible amount of information we have on different options. No amount of commitment or effort in research will guarantee a brilliant research career with top-class publications, funding or positions. From a consequentialist perspective the short-term harm is easy to identify – the loss of personal life, lack of ability to commit to a family, or exhaustion are all tangible and relatively certain. On the benefit side, one can find a sense of pride and accomplishment, the possibility for funding, positions or new research directions. The analysis is lopsided. There is certainty only on the side of harm, while the benefits are all based on assumptions and estimates. Individual values will determine how each person evaluates the value of potential benefits in comparison with certain harm.

The analysis is further complicated by the likely intrinsic benefit of actually enjoying the process of doing research. Research can be more akin to an exciting hobby than work, which in itself will provide immediate and certain benefits to be included in the analysis and for which researchers may be ready to sacrifice their personal time. Just as other people may spend their time doing craft, playing tennis or solving sudokus, the researcher may wish to engage with the research questions. Can we consider this option as equal among all other options? Or are there reasons why the option of research overtaking all other aspects of life is less beneficial or more harmful than other options? The way we spend our time is often a good way to reflect what we truly value in life, and thus the choices researchers make around time allow us to understand values further. This issue is especially significant for researchers with family duties.

If we take this thought experiment a little further, could we imagine a situation where we could justify that research is more important than anything else? From a consequentialist perspective the benefits of research can quickly multiply in a society, which could easily compensate for the harm experienced by an individual researcher. Following this line of thought has several flaws. First, it is difficult to prove that the efforts of one individual researcher have a significant effect on society, regardless of the field of study. Research is a group effort in most cases and application of results into something socially meaningful involves an even greater number of people. Second, and more fundamentally, this thinking suggests that we are entitled to consider sacrificing the happiness of one or a few in order to gain benefits for

many. The same logic would allow unwilling
participants in human experiments, for example.   [CONSEQUENTIALIST]

Let us look at some specific examples of choices researchers make and how
stakeholders, rights and responsibilities, as well as options, apply to them.

CAREER

There are no longer typical research careers. The career paths are competitive,
diverse, uncertain and require significant flexibility. Career choices force
particularly early-career researchers to make multiple decisions and weigh different
aspects from career prospects to family life in the process. Short contracts are now
common in the early-career years and becoming more common in the senior
positions as well. In some instances work is carried out under a number of
contracts running simultaneously to form full-time employment. The decisions
are often made using consequentialist approaches, and trying to weigh up
potential benefits with often very much acute harm. This analysis is often
supported by a virtue-based understanding of what would constitute a good
researcher and a good person.

Let us look at an example where an early career researcher is offered an
opportunity to cover a professorship for a short term in a different city, left vacant
by his former supervisor going on leave. From a career perspective this could be
advantageous as an experience. On the other hand, this would reduce research
output, which is key in all future job selections. The matter is possibly complicated
by family needs as the family may or may not be able to easily move to the other
city. The researcher may perceive the request as an opportunity and a positive sign
and reflection on his abilities, or see it is a responsibility towards the research
community and/or supervisor that has supported him up to this point. All ethical
principles can have a role in the decision-making, resulting in a complicated
exercise.

While university careers offer many opportunities to make decisions, a meta
decision is to decide whether to focus on university opportunities only, or to
broaden the focus to other employers as well. Interaction between the universities
and other research opportunities is formally encouraged. At top level it is not seen
as beneficial to have two separate patterns for research – one in academia and the
other in the private sector. Closer and more flexible relationships between these
two career paths can easily be seen as beneficial for all parties. Despite this logic
and top-level discourse, the early choices in particular are likely to determine the
direction of the career path. Whether to leave the university for 'real' employment
or to wait at the university for positions to open is a key question for many early-
career researchers.

A dedicated research career is likely to be attractive. To arrive at the point of a
doctorate is a result of years of dedication to the potential of doing research as a
career. But university positions are often precarious and everyone is forced to

weigh up the content of work against continuity and security. Depending on personalities and circumstances, the decisions may be simple or very complicated. Many will bring into the decision-making multiple considerations, including personal desires, career prospects, the possibility to have greater control of research questions, financial implications, family needs and expectations, the future of the department or importance of the research topic itself.

EMPLOYMENT

Research jobs have traditionally been considered highly flexible in the sense that individuals have been able to decide how and when they complete their research responsibilities. Many ethical questions arise with this notion of freedom. It may have been taken for granted previously, and in the new situation it must be redefined. One such situation is when the researcher lives a significant distance away from the university. This may be to facilitate family needs, but it may not be in the best interests of the department. The concern is unlikely to be about the actual content of the work as it is possible in many research contexts to work effectively away from the office. From a collegial perspective, presence at the department may have significant positive benefits. Would it be acceptable to require physical presence on certain days of the week? Being present would facilitate unofficial and social connections, which is likely to benefit the community, while less travel may be in the best interests of the researcher. The situation may hinge on the different benefits experienced by the community and the individual – whose needs take priority?

Another employment challenge is with short-term contracts, which have become a more common form of academic employment. Longer contracts or even tenured positions are a typical response to the current situation. In a situation where public funding is decreasing, offering permanent contracts can easily result in all positions being filled and a generation of early-career academics having no university research opportunities open up for years. This solution could strongly favour one generation over another. And how would that influence innovation and creativity? On the other hand, it appears simple to assume that if academic careers become a game of survival, the ability to develop or create something totally new will be reduced significantly as all efforts will be focused on securing the next employment opportunity.

***

The key terms in the ethical reasoning for a researcher's career are competiveness, flexibility and time management. Competiveness translates to a need to be active and effective if one wants to reach high goals. At the same time, working in groups requires the ability to work with people having the same or different goals. Flexibility is tested in planning the next steps in one's life. Options concern choices between an academic career and other working opportunities, possible changes of topics and areas of research and moving to other universities instead of staying in a safe and well-known environment. Regarding time management, there are a lot of choices to be made both at work and at home. At work a researcher has to distribute her or his time between research, teaching and other duties. Within all these activities there are a lot of further moments when a choice must be made. The main challenge, however, is balancing time between research and duties at home. For many researchers it is hard to get rid of developing research ideas and to engage with the small joys and problems of everyday life. A researcher may think of positive and negative consequences, duties and responsibilities and how an ideal researcher behaves in these situations.

As research is dominantly a people-driven activity and it is safe to assume that happy people work closer to the top of their game, employment decisions have a great collective impact. Guided dialogue can be used in research communities to assist in designing working patterns that will allow the achievement of research goals together with a happy and productive community of researchers. While the situation is not easy and is definitely rapidly changing, focusing on key values and creating an open process for designing employment has great ethical merit.

Case study 1: allocation of time

One of the key themes of this book has been exploring the ethical aspects relating to allocation of time. This is not a coincidence as time is the most valuable resource for all researchers and their employers. The allocation of time between different tasks is always a value decision, even though we often do not recognise it as such within our daily activities. We can explore the use of time from a consequentialist perspective by measuring the effectiveness of different time allocation patterns. Another approach is to consider time allocation as an extension of virtue – how would 'virtuoso' researchers allocate their time?

Using these two approaches, consider the following examples. You can allocate 4,600 hours per year. The figure is the total number of hours minus essential hours required for sleep, eating and commuting. What would your allocation look like? How would you allocate the time for the different individuals described below? What does the allocation say about your values, role expectations and assumptions on efficient research practices?

Different activities:

1   **Research:** reviewing existing literature, material acquisition, laboratory work, writing publications and directly collaborating with colleagues.
2   **Teaching:** contact hours, online teaching hours, preparing for teaching.
3   **Supervision:** supervising doctoral and Master's degree students.
4   **Self-development:** participating in courses and conferences, reading broadly.

5   **Engaging with the research community:** participation in scientific foundations, review activities, organising conferences.
6   **Administrative tasks:** departmental-, faculty- or university-level administrative roles, participation in working groups and planning.
7   **Engaging with society:** giving public lectures, writing popular science articles and books, member in non-scientific committees, board memberships, collaborations with businesses.
8   **Personal hobbies:** activities done for personal pleasure, e.g. reading, fishing, running or theatre.
9   **Family life:** spending time and handling responsibilities, e.g. looking after children, cleaning, maintenance, shopping or entertaining.

Different positions and individuals:

1   Neela, 25 years old; recently commenced postgraduate study; no teaching load; a two-year-old child; partner also working in research.
2   Bobbie, 30 years old; multiple short and overlapping contracts at the department mainly as a lecturer and research assistant; all contracts less than one year in duration; one-year-old child; partner works in the private sector.
3   Lee, 35 years old; university lecturer; 12-hour teaching load per week; married, three children (three, five and six years of age); partner works in the public sector.
4   Mathea, 45 years old; academy fund researcher; two hours of teaching per week; five doctoral students; divorced; 14 year-old child who lives with the other parent.
5   Andi, 55 years old; professor; four hours of teaching per week; 20 Master's students and five doctoral students; married, with three adult children and one grandchild; partner works in university administration.
6   Po, 65 years old; head of department; three hours of teaching per week; seven Master's students, seven doctoral students; married, adult children, five grandchildren; partner retired.

	Research	Teaching	Supervision	Self-development	Research community	Administration	Society	Hobbies	Family	Total
Neela										4600
Bobbie										4600
Lee										4600
Mathea										4600
Andi										4600
Po										4600

Figure 9.1 Time allocation exercise

Case study 2: allocation of tasks within a department

People are interested in different things. Some want to focus solely on research and others are genuinely interested in teaching and working in the research community (aka take part in administration). How we allocate tasks and thus time reflects many core ethical values and enforces certain normative standards.

1 Consider the allocation of tasks from the perspective of fairness and equality. How much of their time should individuals dedicate to research, teaching and/or administration? Is it ideal that everyone works in the same pattern, or should the allocation of tasks be based on interests/skills/position/experience? How would be allocate a task no one wants to do?
2 Consider a consequentialist argument: whose benefit would be served by equally dividing all tasks between the available staff? How would this decision appear from the perspective of responsibilities and rights?

Case study 3: big career decisions

You have recently completed your doctoral degree. You have been offered a one year contract to cover a maternity leave. There are a lot of factors which may influence your decision whether to take this opportunity. Consider what decisive things are to make you accept or not to accept the invitation. In addition to yourself, include other stakeholders in your decision-making, for example: your family, your employer, your current research community, your national research community, international research community.

1 The offered institutional position: professor – lecturer – researcher – administration.
2 The alignment with your doctoral research: almost exactly the same; overlapping; completely different. How would the differences here influence your workload and develop your expertise?
3 Geographical location: the same university where you recently graduated; different university in the same city; a university within your home country 100 km away; a university in your home country 500 km away; a university in another country.
4 Family situation: you live alone; with a partner who works standard working hours, no children; with a partner who is home with your two children.
5 Familiarity: you know the job/department well; you know them a little; they are completely new to you.

6   The reputation of the job offered: very prestigious; average reputation; unknown to anyone else.

7   The required workload: the compulsory tasks take up all the working hours; there is great flexibility to do your own research as well.

8   Alternatives to this offer: there are other offers to consider; you have applied for other jobs and you know you have been short-listed for at least one of them; there are very few jobs around at the moment to even apply for.

Chapter 10

Conclusion

Learning ethical skills in the framework of guided dialogue is quite an achievable task. However, each step in the process requires some effort in order to make ethically guided choices. In these concluding remarks we will touch on some obstacles that, according to our experience, may complicate or hinder the smooth course of ethical decision-making. To clearly explain the possible challenges we will use the four steps of ethical decision-making presented in Chapter 1. We will also remind you of some features of human thinking and reasoning because they cannot be ignored when considering this issue. At the end of the chapter we will answer some frequently asked questions in the context of research ethics by guided dialogue. They will, we hope, solve the last unclear questions in applying the guided dialogue approach.

The **first step** is recognising and accepting the existence of ethical questions. On the face of it this appears quite simple. However, there are natural differences in how people perceive questions as ethical. In addition, different research fields or research groups possess different levels of core ethical awareness. At one extreme the world is filled with ethical questions and issues, and every action/decision is a multi-layered ethical event. At the other end we find existence, where ethical issues do not feature at all. In this way of thinking all questions are factual and often quantitative in nature, and there is no need for ethical consideration. Strong routines are often present at this end of the spectrum, ethical issues are considered 'done' and there is no need for any further ethical consideration.

The major part of this book is dedicated to the **second step** of the process, when the question or issue that has been identified should be addressed. In other words, the situation requires us to make an ethical decision or choice. Throughout the previous chapters, the concrete skills of making ethically guided choices have been presented and discussed. These skills include the capability to identify stakeholders, recognition of rights and responsibilities, consideration of the available options and, finally, the ability to make actual choices by applying three ethical approaches, which are labelled in this book as 'consequentialist', 'principled' and 'virtue'. In identification of stakeholders it is usually quite easy to name the primary ones. In the case of supervision they are naturally the doctoral student and the supervisor. Secondary stakeholders are not always so obvious.

Here, the other doctoral students and colleagues of the supervisor are influenced by the supervision and are therefore secondary stakeholders as well. Institutional stakeholders such as the department and the university have to be considered as well. In some questions of supervision the whole research community can be seen as a further secondary stakeholder. Conducting doctoral studies and supervision are time-consuming activities and influence also families of the people involved. Considering the scope of stakeholders is sometimes not apparent and needs some training and sharing of the question with others.

Defining rights and responsibilities of the stakeholders is easier to tackle with the help of dialogue within the collective. Often, ethical issues are born out of different assumptions of rights and responsibilities held by different stakeholders. We also face a challenge in agreeing which of the ethical approaches are appropriate and how to define key concepts within them. Further, any application of the approaches is dependent on the ability to see options both broadly and clearly. When considering whether an overstrained supervisor should take on a new talented doctoral student, one can find, apart from the obvious options of yes or no, further solutions may resolve the ethical issue in this challenging situation, such as asking for a reduction in the other duties of supervision or trying to find another supervisor.

Guided dialogue is not linear, but guides the participants in asking questions and allowing the answers to influence understanding in multiple ways. The iterative process may feel frustrating as there are times when the matter does not seem to become any clearer and no real progress can be identified. This is quite typical and must be at times endured. When the dialogue continues, clarity does appear in values and the collective understanding develops. As the issues are often very complex and challenging, this may take time. But if guided dialogue is used regularly, stakeholders' ability to engage in it improves. This translates into a more efficient process and the significant issues rise more quickly to the surface to be addressed.

The guided dialogue is particularly effective when dealing with complex ethical issues like privacy in relation to big data or sharing raw data. When it is impossible to find a single ethical answer to a complex question, the next best thing is the ability to share the decision-making process. This increases understanding of the issue as well as our ability to find ways to respond to it appropriately, even when our best decisions can only attempt to manage a complex issue.

After we have tested the guided dialogue approach in questions of research ethics, the same methodology can be transferred to other complicated problems. Let us take distribution of workload as an example. While this task reflects values and has the potential to align/misalign with goals, it is often a rather practical question. Time is the most valuable thing we have. For ourselves and for our employers it is of great significance how we divide it between different tasks and activities. There are multiple stakeholders in this matter in addition to ourselves (students, colleagues, department, science, family, etc.). As time is always a limited resource, spending too much time to one thing means less attention given to others. That is a central notion in doing things 'sufficiently well', i.e. not too well. One can even argue that a teacher can prepare her or his lectures and seminars 'too' exhaustively if they understand the benefits of students in the wrong way. Sometimes less teaching and knowledge sharing results in more learning if we can activate the students to work individually or in groups. Therefore, asking broad questions, understanding stakeholders, defining benefit and harm in relation to all stakeholders, clarifying rights and responsibilities and key goals will help to make better choices regarding workload patterns.

The **third and fourth steps**, committing to an ethical choice and perseverance under pressure, deal with difficulties in implementing choices that have been reached through ethical reasoning. We often have desires that contradict the desire to do what has been recognised as the ethically best outcome. As described in Chapter 1, these competing desires may include a desire to be liked, financial gain, desire to help others, hedonistic desires or career opportunities. For example, desire to be liked may lead to inability to say 'no' to an applicant who wants to start doctoral studies. Sometimes the contradicting pressures come from outside. When a supervisor has weighed all options on the issue of taking a new doctoral student in a proper way from the perspective of all stakeholders and has decided not to take her or him, the supervisor may still refuse to put this decision into practice. The reason for this may be pressure from above (superior, head, dean), from below (other doctoral students) or laterally from colleagues. Sometimes there is no real pressure, only a perception of it.

People close to us typically influence our ethical thinking and behaviour. They can be the engine for making ethical decisions and simultaneously the reason why it may be difficult to follow through with ethical behaviour. We can call them *contextual factors* because each concrete case has its own specific features. In addition to social factors we also have many inherent personal characteristics that influence both our ethical decision-making and our ability to follow through with ethical behaviour. And we are here specifically talking about how our cognitive processes direct our ethical thinking. Our belief is that recognising these factors will allow us to avoid falling into these traps and to make better and more transparent ethical choices in theory and in practice. Therefore we will make a short survey of some pitfalls we meet in ethical reasoning.

Sometimes we are inclined to think that we live in an ideal world where people are always rational and capable of acting in a proper way. Unfortunately, this is not true. *Homo* is far from being *sapiens*. Our brains have their limitations and it is very hard for us to see the world through unbiased eyes. This is a very complex tangle of different human characteristics and we still lack understanding of many details on these matters. Nevertheless, we will highlight some of them from the perspective of making ethically grounded choices. Paying attention to these small practical things may seem pointless, because they are often quite obvious, but in fact the challenges in handling ethical questions depend on them greatly.[1]

Figure 10.1 reveals two major factors that influence human behaviour. There exists a tension between the circles. The core reflects the individual foundation

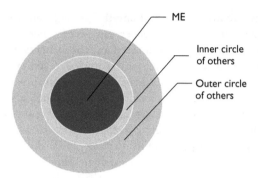

Figure 10.1 Individual within circles of others.

of human behaviour and the outer circles aspiration for social cohesion. A third strong factor is avoidance of cognitive effort. We give a short definition of these factors and then consider their role in various steps of ethical decision-making.

Avoidance of cognitive effort. Every change in our behaviour requires effort, and energy conservation gives a reason to avoid unnecessary cognitive effort. There is a certain logic behind this: human brains have limited resources and it is wise to save cognitive capacity when possible. So, on the one hand, doing things always the same way enables us to behave in an optimal way from the perspective of brain function, but, on the other hand, it creates a clear risk of blocking new and more innovative ideas from being considered and allowing alterations in behaviour.[2]

Individual centre. Every creature thinks of its own needs and survival. In human beings this appears in egoistic behaviour and in the way people see the world through their own eyes. Nothing is viewed from the perspective of neutrality, but through the filters we all have and create. Similarly, what is close to us appears more important than what is further away. There is a true story about the difficulty of realising what the world is like through eyes of others: a blind person was amazingly skilful in carpentry and he became so proficient that was able to repair a roof. What astonished the neighbours the most was that he was able to do that even in the dark of the night![3]

Aspiration for social cohesion. We do not live in isolation, but as a member of a collective; in fact, as a member of various collectives. Social membership is essential to our well-being in multiple different ways. To be able to be accepted by others we have to be cooperative and flexible with our own needs. To achieve this, we also adopt socially oriented ways of looking at the world and processing information. The need for social cohesion is in constant interaction with our egocentric world view, which adds to tension in ethical decision-making as well.

Now we will consider the influence of these factors on ethical reasoning. We focus on six risk factors, which typically complicate or hinder appropriate handling of ethical questions: egocentricity, personal experience, anchoring, otherness, routines and conformism (Figure 10.2). These risk factors typically enforce each

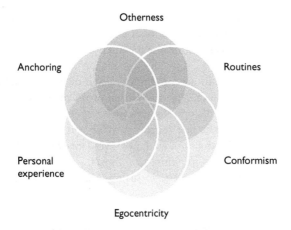

Figure 10.2 Risks in guided ethical dialogue.

other and influence our cognitive patterns in an interlinked way. Still, all of them bring their unique perspective; for the sake of clarity, we have presented them here separately.

EGOCENTRICITY

Egocentric cognitive and behavioural patterns are a broad notion influencing how we see and respond to the world. We see egocentric behaviour everywhere in society: in politics, in sports, in art, in business. Therefore, it would be strange if research was free of egocentric cognitive and behavioural patterns. Egocentric patterns can gain additional fuel from the current competitive forces within the research community. Researchers put a lot of time and energy into their research work and they are very eager to see returns from this endeavour.

Similar to athletes, researchers want to be better than other researchers. They want to publish in better journals, to get more citations and to win larger amounts of competitive funding. In such a situation there is a risk that some researchers succumb to temptation to engage in 'doping', which in research means falsification of results, plagiarism and other forms of violations of the responsible conduct of research. As we have discussed in this book, there are large grey areas where it is not always clear whether a certain act or measure is acceptable or not.

Egocentric patterns are always present in human behaviour. They develop into a problem when they override ethically grounded choices. Let us consider the same situation we already looked at in Chapter 2, where the reviewer of funding applications has in a most diligent manner reviewed the application and given it a score of four out of five. Then the reviewer remembers that a colleague has applied for the same grant and there are great prospects for collaboration with this colleague. To increase the chances of success for the colleague, the reviewer changes the score to three out of five, and to cover the change makes changes to the reasoning as well. The reviewer has taken appropriate steps one and two, but at step three other values and desires than doing the ethically right thing have been given priority. In this situation the inability to act ethically also negates his role as an expert.

Clear violations of generally accepted rules caused by egocentric behaviour are easy to see. It is often more difficult to manage problems in conducting guided ethical dialogue when the dialogue is fuelled by egocentric goals. Here, as in many other issues as well, the first thing in solving this problem is to recognise this feature in yourself. This does not guarantee avoidance of biased and egocentric patterns, but it enables us to minimise the impact and create positive space to develop other motivations to engage in dialogue and seek solutions to ethical issues.

THE POWER OF PERSONAL EXPERIENCE

Egocentric patterns can be partially explained by the power our personal experiences have in our decision-making processes. Recent research has shown what people have always assumed: we make our decisions often on the basis of a fast, intuitive conclusion rather than thorough rational thinking. Intuition develops all the time by collecting knowledge from our own life experiences and other people's opinions and stories. In that way we build stereotypes and presumptions, which then guide our behaviour. This has the benefit of saving cognitive effort and supporting our egocentric patterns.[4]

Personal experiences are raw material for efficient decision-making, but they also create a risk of biases in making choices. Consider supervision. Most probably supervisors adopt their routines from tacit knowledge gained by observing the behaviour of their own supervisors. This first experience is a strong element when they develop a model of a good or ideal supervisor. Commonly, they will then repeat both good and bad habits and practices of the previous generation in their own way.

Personal experience has a strong influence on how we perceive things to be and how we think they should be. The latter has great significance in ethical thinking. For example, the first assessments we, as early-career researchers, receive on our grant applications give us an idea of what assessments are about and how we perceive ourselves as applicants. Experiences, even when they are single, unique ones, can easily be interpreted as expressions of a trend, something we can assume to apply to all other similar situations. When we, after some years, act as referees ourselves, we will definitely remember our own experiences. Maybe we will imitate the statement and argumentation we received or, on the contrary, we have already years earlier decided to do this job better than that anonymous referee. Regardless of our response, the original experience shapes our response to new situations.

Our personal background, being my own research group, my own university or my own field, provides a specific reference point when we construct our understanding of a right and well-functioning research community. Also, possible negative experiences are an influential source of knowledge that we bring to each new situation. Cases we have personally experienced or observed can help us to raise and solve ethical questions that we encounter in new environments. Alternatively, personal experiences may cause biased decision-making when we too quickly extrapolate from those experiences to general truths and make assumptions. Our ability to use personal experiences as a way of clarifying our own values, goals and aims assists us in participating in guided dialogue with greater clarity. However, an assumption that personal experiences somehow represent a wider truth leads us to the next risk factor to guided dialogue, that of anchoring, which further narrows our perspective.

ANCHORING

Anchoring shows the strong power of our tendency to filter information.[5] Our brains are wired to seek information from our personal experiences and other sources that conform with what we already believe. This again allows us to conserve effort in changing our thinking. It also provides us with a sense of inner coherence. The sense of incoherence is typically unpleasant, if not intolerable. To avoid the unpleasant task of re-thinking, our consciousness has an ability to focus on and pick information to match what we already know and believe. This could translate into choosing to read articles that support our methodology and findings, re-telling stories that support our own behavioural choices or even seeing results partially to allow ourselves to prove our hypothesis.

A cognitive anchor provides the centre for our biased information filtering. The anchor is a piece of information to which all subsequent pieces of information are then compared. For example, imagine that a new person is about to join your research group. Further imagine that someone says out loud in a meeting that they have heard that the people who currently work with this new person have said she is rather lazy. Now this is the only thing you know about the new person. As she arrives in the group you will observe her behaviour – if she lingers in the coffee room, you are likely to see that as evidence of her previously suggested laziness; if she works really hard you may suspect that it is just a way to try to hide her laziness at other times, etc. Changing the anchor can require a significant amount of counter-evidence. In research work, we have many anchors. In research ethics, anchors can be beliefs about our research subjects (of course they wish to participate, I have never seen them object) or assumptions that using ideas is only sharing, that is what everyone does. And then we will find evidence to support our anchor within our experience and the literature.

Understanding that this is how our brain works allows us to take conscious steps to challenge this pattern of anchoring and information seeking: putting ourselves in the situation where we plan to allow ourselves to be influenced by new information and experiences; broadening our thinking by opening ourselves to dialogue with others to gain understanding. This will also help with our next risk, understanding otherness.

UNDERSTANDING OTHERNESS

People have direct access only to their own feelings and store of knowledge. However, in order to live in a society we have to learn somehow to understand others' thoughts, attitudes, goals and emotions.[6] Usually children develop this ability around the age of five.[7] Despite this ability, people often fail to perceive this otherness, or at least they fail to incorporate it in their approach to problems and issues. Here again the natural avoidance of cognitive effort offers an explanation. To put ourselves – consciously or unconsciously – in the position of other people requires significant cognitive effort. Egocentric patterns increase the difficulty by reducing the value of others' perspectives. These lay the foundation for frequent misunderstandings in communication. In concrete terms, this is due to insufficient thought about how to relay information to difference audiences, and a common-ground fallacy.[8]

Egocentrism, the power of personal experiences, together with the limited ability to accept otherness, has severe consequences for ethical reasoning. These complicate the ability to conceptualise situations where we find significant discrepancies in attitudes and values. For example, a person who is inclined to see things from the perspective of consequences will find it challenging to accept even the starting point of reasoning of a colleague who prefers ethics based on principles, and vice versa. As described in Chapter 2, the question of using experimental animals is a classic example of this kind of dilemma. Interdisciplinary cooperation of researchers typically offers tests for flexible thinking and an ability to see otherness as valuable. In interdisciplinary collaboration we often have to re-consider our understanding of what is good research and accepted scientific methodology. As these issues are at the very core of research, it is not easy to accept the validity of an alternative view.

Even when we are aware of our egocentric patterns, the power of personal experiences and our inability to see otherness, we are exposed to these in our decision-making. For example, in assessing applications one can fall into the trap of thinking 'other people are like me'. The conscious decision-maker may logically assume that if I am a little bit biased in my evaluation, probably the other referees are as well. And if I avoid being biased by being especially critical towards those applicants who are from my own field or university, I may safely assume others do the same. This can create a push for corrective behaviour of being extra lenient or strict in order to balance the assumed bias of others, which may be fuelled by either egoistic patterns or ideals of fairness and balance. And when everyone behaves this way, the assessment process suffers a loss of integrity, transparency and reliability.

Still, when our own experiences are reflected through an ability to understand otherness and we have a motivation to avoid egocentric patterns, we can better harness the positive power of our own contribution to collective ethical dialogue. When we realise that others have their own personal experiences, and how we all act from this space of personal stories, we are likely to increase our ability to cross both the boundary of otherness as well as reduce the power of our own stories and egocentric needs to blindly lead us in making decisions.

ROUTINES

We see every day how difficult it is for people to change their routines. There is a strong desire to keep everything as it has been. Yet again, routines allow us to conserve our cognitive effort as well as allow us to perform everyday actions and decision-making quickly and efficiently. This effort saving comes with a price tag – we can identify negative consequences of routine behaviour everywhere in researchers' lives.

Consider this example. Supervisors have, as a rule, a number of doctoral students. Therefore, it is understandable that they develop patterns of behaviour to deal with practicalities of supervision. These routines allow the supervisor to manage the supervision tasks without much thought for context, why things are done the way they are or how other stakeholders experience the supervision. Therefore, also ethical questions around supervision easily remain out of reach of explicit recognition and consideration. This creates a major hurdle for guided dialogue as only recognised ethical issues can be addressed, managed and, if necessary, resolved. In this respect, routines can become an enemy of ethical reasoning. Hence, it follows, especially when starting to pay more attention to ethical issues, that we have to be ready to face a multitude of ethical problems simultaneously. This is likely to be an unwelcome task that requires us to step away from our egocentric patterns, expand our personal experiences and allow us to see others' perspectives as valuable. After successfully engaging in guided ethical dialogue either with others or by ourselves, it will become easier to convince ourselves that it is rational to take ethics seriously. This allows us to develop the ability to observe the surrounding environment through an ethical lens. In a way, thinking ethically can become a positive routine.

While routines poorly support recognising ethical issues, standardised behaviour has a positive role as well. For example, the training of doctoral students and teaching research methodology are based on the research community traditions of transmission to the next generation. It is not reasonable to question a method or approach every time it is applied in research. But at the same time, for the progress of science, it is essential that we, from time to time, challenge the methodological foundation of research. The same applies to ethics. Routines relating to informed consent are helpful, but we must consider them truthfully at regular intervals.

We have recently seen new factors that force us to move away from traditional ways of thinking into new ones. Crowdsourcing is one example. According to a traditional view, it sounds rather unscientific to utilise ordinary people as research assistants and data collectors, but sometimes this is the only way to get information about everyday life phenomena. Developing new routines and methodologies also generates a variety of new ethical questions. In fact, another new way of doing research, use of big data, raises quite different and difficult ethical questions. The traditional way of thinking, based on the significance of factual evidence, pronounces: the larger collection of data we have, the more reliable the results are. This routine opinion no longer holds true in every particular case study as the huge amount of data does not follow the same statistical rules and it therefore requires us to explore what can be considered reliable evidence. The ethical challenges of big data also include complicated ethical questions relating to managing privacy and confidentiality.

When we develop an ability to question our routines, particularly our personal thought patterns, we have taken a significant step towards more aligned and transparent decision-making, and we have created a space for guided dialogue to assist us and our communities in the process. As explained above, we are more capable of taking part in the guided ethical dialogue when we accept that our own egocentric patterns often developed from a focus on personal experiences, which are strengthened by our inability to see otherness.

CONFORMISM

The last of the risks discussed here refers to our social nature. It is conformism.[9] This also is related to the avoidance of cognitive effort. If routines are more or less a personal thing, conformism and aspiration for cohesion among a collective are very social phenomena. Referring to Figure 10.1, we go out of the sphere of 'me' into the surrounding zones; the closer people are to us, the more important their opinions are. Desire to please others is a strong instinctive feature of humans. It makes our lives easier – and in that way spares cognitive resources. Depending on our attitude to situations in hand, we describe conformism as wise or cowardly behaviour.

Outside pressure may occur already at the very beginning of ethical reasoning, when we are either raising an ethical question or shutting our eyes to it. In these situations, conformism takes place without any visible pressure. Actually, what we see in such behaviour is a kind of self-censorship: we think it is not appropriate to raise the question we recognise and so pass over it in silence. Our personal experiences and need for self-preservation increases the challenges of speaking up against the dominant voice or raising something no one else has been willing to recognise.

The desire to be liked/respected/recognised often occurs in making choices. Let us take again the situation of a funding decision, the case of Maryam, discussed in Chapter 1. In assessing the application she may first come to a conclusion but then start thinking of possible consequences.

Maryam may have to respond to queries from the leading academics behind applications. This may appear daunting and Maryam may doubt her ability to justify her choice, particularly if the decision diverts away from academic evaluations. Maryam's experience, possible relationship with these academics, and her personality will influence how she perceives these tasks. She may also be subject to epistemic conformity within the research council or wishful thinking regarding the appropriateness and outcomes of her decision. The decision is also situated within an overall funding and research climate, which will provide a backdrop to Maryam's decision.

As everywhere, also in research communities we see hierarchies that inevitably include inequalities in the power structure. More recognised researchers and those having a formal leading administrative position are more influential in decision-making processes. In such an environment, conformism means a desire to please the bosses. This is a natural aspect in human communities, but it develops into a problem if research ethical problems remain untouched because of an atmosphere of fear.

***

We have considered some of the possible risks and obstacles in conducting ethical reasoning. These problems cannot be removed, but we can reduce their influence. According to our experience there are two aids to that: awareness and guided dialogue, which are intertwined (Figure 10.3). To be aware of ethical questions, we as individuals have to be interested in them. If so, we enter into dialogue on these issues – into real dialogue, which means the capability to express one's view in an understandable way and a willingness to listen to the opinions of others with respect and a desire to comprehend. This increases awareness of these matters and leads to a more fruitful dialogue.

What we have attempted to do in this book is to raise your personal awareness of research ethical questions and give you tools to conduct guided dialogue with other people regarding these questions.

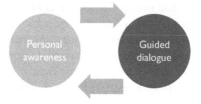

Figure 10.3 Guided dialogue feedback loop.

FREQUENTLY ASKED QUESTIONS

Finally, we will answer some questions we have encountered when using the material from this book in teaching. Probably, the readers have similar questions in mind.

Is an ethical choice always a conscious choice?
Yes. We continuously make decisions at home and at work. These become ethical when we recognise that we are dealing with an ethical issue and apply our values to the decision we are making.

Why should we consider our choices from an ethical perspective?
Ethical analysis and decision-making allow us to align our decisions with our core aims and values. This increases the well-being of both individuals and communities. Through ethical reasoning, our decisions become transparent, which in turn facilitates dialogue defining the criteria on what is ethically acceptable.

When are we forced to make ethical decisions?
Continuously – if only we recognise them. Many of us do not want to or cannot see the decisions from an ethical perspective. Others are more experienced and willing to see ethical decisions everywhere.

Does ethical reasoning always lead to the right and best outcome?
No. But ethical reasoning allows us to make more qualified choices. This does not necessarily mean they are better than choices made by other reasoning methods, but that they are a result of a transparent and conscious process. This can be considered to have value in itself and it will facilitate collaboration and continuous improvement of the decisions we make. One can see here a parallel with other activities in which skills are needed. The best football player in the world can fail in a crucial situation, but the probability for this is much less than in the case of an amateur player. A doctor with a university education may make a mistake in diagnosis while a layman may accidentally make the right diagnosis. However, this does not mean we should not rely on trained doctors. Something similar is true for ethical skills: they do not guarantee the right solution in every case, but in most cases they help us to make better choices than without these skills.

How do I know I am making an ethical decision?
Most likely you recognise that you are considering the decision from the perspective of multiple stakeholders. You will also seek to reason different choices based on their outcomes and how well they satisfy rules and guidelines. Most of the time you will also end up reflecting on how the decision aligns with your values and goals.

What is the difference between an ethical decision and morally right choice?
Moral choices require a measure of right and wrong, typically socially determined rules for behaviour in different situations. A morally right choice is the one that appropriately applies those rules. Ethical decisions are typical when we do not have set norms of behaviour and we have no clear understanding of the single right choice. Ethical analysis and reasoning is therefore necessary to arrive at a decision. However, in many instances most people use the terms 'ethical' and 'moral' interchangeably.

Is an ethical choice the same as prioritisation?
Prioritisation is closely related to ethical decisions. An ethical decision is, however, a more comprehensive concept than prioritisation, because ethical decision-making includes reasoning and clear alignment with values, while prioritisation can be made following multiple different reasons and scales.

How do ethical choices relate to the concept of an ethical dilemma?
Some of the problems we try to find solutions for through ethical reasoning are dilemmas. A problem becomes a dilemma when it is impossible to find a solution that satisfies the core needs of all stakeholders and we have to choose whose needs/values we are going to prioritise. However, we also apply ethical consideration to situations that are not dilemmas. One of the reasons for writing this book is to highlight the ethical choices we typically do not even recognise as ethical questions, but approach them automatically based on routine assumptions.

Can you learn to make ethical decisions?
Yes you can. This requires a conscious effort to learn and develop. These skills do not develop automatically alongside other research skills. It is also good to remember that no one ever reaches perfection in their ethical learning. Ethical skills invite life-long learning.

Is it possible to use ethical reasoning as a way to damage others?
Yes, there is always a risk that information is used for evil rather than good. This is not inherent in ethical reasoning however. Good ethical reasoning is poorly suited for harming others as transparency will reveal selfish and damaging intentions, which cannot be ethically justified.

Can you use ethical reasoning to justify selfish behaviour?
Yes, this is possible. Utility-based approaches create a theoretical space for this if one is able to reduce the number of stakeholders to just one and create a space to consider only the personal benefit and harm. A transparent process will, however, reveal the limited approach taken and open the space to voice counter-arguments to support a broader stakeholder consideration. It may become difficult to try to justify why only one stakeholder should be included.

This book has avoided presenting clear structured processes and guidelines. Would it be possible to give broadly applicable guidelines that could be applied in different ethical decisions?

The ethical choices faced by researchers are very diverse and thus it is impossible to give a single structured guideline on how to solve them. There are, however, general principles that will assist in approaching ethically challenging situations. One such principle is recognising and respecting all stakeholders. Another important principle is transparency. It is the precursor to making decisions through shared grounded dialogue.

NOTES

1   Petteri Niemi differentiates six major challenges in conducting ethics in research. We have adopted some of them; see: Petteri Niemi (2015), Six challenges for ethical conduct in science, *Science and Engineering Ethics* 22, 1–19.

2   On avoidance of cognitive efforts in people's behaviour, see: J. Bargh and Tanya L. Chartrand (1999), The unbearable automaticity of being, *American Psychologist* 54, 462–476; Ap Dijksterhuis (2004), Think different: the merits of unconscious thought in preference development and decision making, *Journal of Personality and Social Psychology* 87, 586–598.

3   The story is from Z. Torey (2004), *Out of Darkness: A Memoir*, Sydney: Pan MacMillan Australia; it is retold in: N. Epley (2008), Solving the (real) other minds problem, *Social and Personality Psychology Compass* 2:3, 1455–1474.

4   There are dozens of types of cognitive biases: Wikipedia lists more than 100 of them.

5   On anchoring, see: A. Furnham and Hua Chu Boo (2011), A literature review of the anchoring effect, *The Journal of Socio-Economics* 40:1, 35–42; G.B. Chapman and Eric J. Johnson (1999), Anchoring, activation, and the construction of values, *Organizational Behavior and Human Decision Processes* 79:2, 115–153.

6   On egocentrism in communication, see: D.J. Barr and Boaz Keysar (2005), Making sense of how we make sense: the paradox of egocentrism in language use, *Figurative Language Comprehension*, ed. Herbert L. Colston and Albert N. Kayz, Mahwah, NJ: Lawrence Erlbaum, pp. 21–43; B. Keysar (2007), Communication and miscommunication: the role of egocentric processes, *Intercultural Pragmatics* 4, 71–85.

7   T. Callaghan, P. Tochat, A. Lillard, *et al.* (2005), Synchrony in the onset of mental-state reasoning: evidence from five cultures, *Psychological Science* 16, 378–384.

8   On recipient design see, among others: Harvey Sacks, Emanuel A. Schegloff and Gail Jefferson (1974), A simplest systematics for the organization of turn-taking in conversation, *Language* 50:4, 696–735; Mark Blokpoel, Marlieke van Kesteren, Arjen Stolk, Pim Haselager, Ivan Toni and Iris van Rooij (2012), Recipient design in human communication: simple heuristics or perspective taking? *Frontiers in Human Neuroscience* 6; Arto Mustajoki (2013), Risks of miscommunication in various speech genres, In *Understanding by Communication*, ed. E. Borisova and O. Souleimanova, Cambridge: Cambridge Scholars Publishing, pp. 33–53. On 'ground fallacy' and 'false consensus effect', see: Herbert H. Clark (1996), *Using Language*, Cambridge: Cambridge University Press; Arto Mustajoki (2012), A speaker-oriented multidimensional approach to risks and causes of miscommunication, *Language and Dialogue* 2, 216; Kaisa S. Pietikäinen (2016), Misunderstandings and ensuring understanding in private ELF talk, *Applied Linguistics*, doi: 10.1093/applin/amw005.

9   On conformism, see: M.J. Hornsey, L. Majkut, D.J. Terry and B.M. McKimmie (2003), On being loud and proud: non-conformity and counter-conformity to group norms, *British Journal of Social Psychology* 42:3, 319–335; Jan-ErikLönnqvist, G. Walkowitz, P. Wichardt, M. Lindeman and M. Verkasalo (2009), The moderating effect of conformism values on the relations between other personal values, social norms, moral obligation, and single altruistic behaviours. *British Journal of Social Psychology* 48:3, 525–546.

Index

Locators in *italics* refer to figures and tables. Alphabetization is word-by-word.

academic community *see* research community

academic freedom 28, 37, 39–40, 114, 138

Academic Ranking of World Universities 165–6

academics *see* recruitment of academic staff; researchers; senior academics

accessibility of research 5; *see also* open access publishing

accountability: assessing research 175–6; doctoral training 4; open science 5; reviews 2–3

accuracy of publications: citations 71–2; wording 72–3

achievements, recognition of 28

acrobatics 142

active roles 182–3

added value 58

administrative functions: assessing research 157; assessment of 160; funding applications 141–2; role of researchers 5

advance reporting 190

aims: graduation 106; methodology 60; teaching students 104–5

altmetrics 161–2

anchoring 69, 219

animal use in research 44–6

animals, as stakeholders 182

anomalous results 33–4

anonymity, research subjects 49

applications: for funding 131, 137–8, 140–3; for research jobs 115, 116–17; stakeholders 115; *see also* recruitment

artefacts 182

assessing research 154–6, 171; case studies 171–6; consequentialist approach 158–9, 160, 164–5, 171, 175; financing formulas 163–5; methods 160–2; options 158–60; principled approach 159, 164, 175; rankings 165–6; researchers 157–8; rights 157–8; social impact 166–71; stakeholders 156; virtue approach 175; *see also* peer reviews

audience *see* target audience

authors, as stakeholders 65, 66

authorship: ethical questions 10; guidelines 79; order of names 79–80, 84; plagiarism 10, 70–2; publishing 67, 78–80, 84–5

autonomy, research subjects 48

background knowledge 40–1

balancing principle 147–8

behaviours *see* ethical behaviours; human behaviours

belief perseverance 69

benefit/harm approach 25–6; managing careers 206; natural environment 53–4; open access publishing 78; peer reviews 81; public interaction 187, 190–1; recruitment 117, 122

bias: anchoring 219; assessing research 164, 169, 171; choice supportive 69–70; conflict of interest guidelines 152–3; egocentrism 218; influences 215–17; personal experience 218, 219; recruitment 99, 124; understanding otherness 220

bibliometrics 3, 160, 161, 164–5

big data 55–6, 222

'black box' ideology 134
blogs 198
boundaries, topic selection 40
business sector 167

Capital University of Theland (fictional):
    assessing research 171–3; funding 148;
    recruitment 123, 126–7
careers 201–2, 208–9; case studies
    209–12; consequentialist approach
    206–7; employment 208; ethical choices
    207–8; ethical questions 201; options
    205–7; progression 4, 113–14;
    responsibilities 202, 203–5; rights
    203–5; stakeholders 203; types of
    position 118–19; work/life balance
    204–6, 209–10, 214–15; see also
    recruitment
carefulness 28
case studies: assessing research 171–6;
    careers 209–12; funding 149–53; public
    interaction 195–9; publishing 82–7;
    recruitment of academic staff 126–9;
    research process 57–61; teaching
    students 108–12
cell communication example 71–2
choice supportive bias 69–70
choices see ethical choices
citations: accuracy 71–2; bibliometrics
    161; changing practices 3; peer reviews
    82; previous research 70–1
citizens: interaction with research 191–3;
    social impact 168; as stakeholders 135
civil servants, as stakeholders 182
cognition: human behaviours 69, 216,
    221, 222–3; media 169
cognitive inertia 69, 216, 219, 220, 221
cognitive traps 69
collaboration, credibility of research 60–1
colleagues, as stakeholders 65, 91, 115,
    203
collective responsibility 116
collectives of researchers 156, 184
common ground, guided dialogue 8
communication: guided dialogue 8;
    multidisciplinary research 4; publishing
    66; recruitment process 99, 118; see also
    public interaction
compatibility, research topics 39–40
competency, peer reviews 81
competition: careers 202, 204, 208;
    intensification of 2; publishing 64

competitive funding 131, 136–8
completeness 74, 106
conferences 86–7
conflict of interest: funding 152–3; peer
    reviews 81; recruitment 116
conformism 69, 222–3
consent see informed consent
consequentialist ethics 22–7, 23; animal
    use 45; assessing research 158–9, 160,
    164–5, 171, 175; funding 137, 149–50;
    gene technology 47–8; human-made
    environments 52–3; managing careers
    206–7; public interaction 183, 187,
    190, 194; recruitment 100, 101, 117,
    122–3; stakeholders 36; teaching
    students 90, 92, 97
contacts, publishing 83
context of research 68–9
contract funding 131, 136, 151
contract research 135
contracts of employment 120, 204, 207,
    208
conventions, teaching students 103–5,
    221–2
coordinators, funding applications 141–2
council members, as stakeholders 134
credibility of research 60–1
crossdisciplinary research 3–4
crowdsourcing 5, 166, 221–2
cultural issues: global fairness 42;
    indigenous peoples 49–50; publishing
    64

Darwin's theory of evolution 180
data: big data 55–6, 222; crowdsourcing
    5, 166, 221–2; forms of publication
    73–4; misconduct 43; ownership 93;
    publicly available 34; researchers' own
    34
daytime test 30
deception 43; see also fabrication of results
decision-making: careers 205–7, 211–12;
    consequentialist approach 24–5;
    frequently asked questions 224–5;
    funding 134, 143–8, 147; guided
    dialogue 9, 12, 30–1, 213–15;
    managing careers 203–6; principled
    approach 27; public use of research
    193–4; purchasing decisions 54–5;
    recruitment of academic staff 120–3;
    recruitment of PhD students 98–103;
    social impact 168–70; virtue approach

29; *see also* options; risks in ethical
reasoning
decision-making cycles 30
departments *see* faculty
dialogue *see* guided dialogue
disciplinary differences: assessing research
157–8; multidisciplinary research 3–4,
141
discrimination *see* equality
dissertations *see* theses
divided publications 74–5
doctoral students *see* students; teaching
students
doctoral training: formalisation 4; funding
89, 102–3, 105; labour market 98;
quality of 90
donors 116, 148
doping 217
duplicated publications 74–5

ecosystems, as stakeholders 182
efficiency index 172–4
egocentrism 216, 217–18, 220
electronic databases 55
emeritus/emerita agreement 119
employment: doctoral training 98;
managing careers 208; work/life balance
204–6, 209–10, 214–15; *see also* careers;
recruitment
employment contracts 120, 204, 207,
208
enablers, as stakeholders 35
enterprises, as stakeholders 132
epigenetics 180
epistemic conformity 69
equality: balancing principle 147–8;
consequentialist approach 24; teaching
students 103–4
equipment: acquisition 54–5; funding 5;
technology 4–5; utilisation of 55
ethical, definition 8–9
ethical behaviours 11–14, 215–16, *216; see
also* human behaviours
ethical choices: assessing research 158–60;
careers 205–7, 207–8; consequentialist
approach 22–7; frequently asked
questions 224–6; guided dialogue
11–13, 17–18, *22*, 22–31, 213–15;
human behaviours 215–17; principled
approach 22–3, 27–9; public
interaction 186–7; publishing 67–8;
research process 38–9; teaching

students 96–8; virtue approach 22–3,
29–30; *see also* options; risks in ethical
reasoning
ethical decisions *see* decision-making
ethical fitness 11
ethical questions: assessing research 154;
careers 201; funding 130; guided
dialogue 7, 8–12, 14–22; public
interaction 178; publishing 63–4;
recognising 11, 12, 14–22, 213;
teaching students 10, 88
ethical sensitivity 12
ethics by guided dialogue *see* guided
dialogue
evaluation 155
evidence-based policy 193
evolutionary theory 180
existentialism 28–9
expected results, funding 151
experience *see* personal experience
experts, role of 179–80, 182, 185–6
external experts: responsibilities 157; as
stakeholders 115
external referees: assessing research 158,
170–1; funding 131, 138–9, 144;
recruitment 92, 117; as stakeholders 92

fabrication of results: anomalies 33–4;
egocentrism 217; misconduct 42–3
facilities, influence on topic selection 40;
see also equipment
faculty: assessing research 174–5;
responsibilities 95; as stakeholder 92,
132, 181–2; topic selection 101, 102
fairness: assessing research 157, 164;
funding 133, 139, 140, 143–4, 146;
global 42; media reporting 191; night/
daytime test 30; open access publishing
76–8, 80; publishing 66, 71, 81–2;
recruitment of academic staff 116,
120–1, 124–6; recruitment of PhD
students 10, 11, 18–19, 100–1; teaching
students 89, 92, 94
falsification of results: anomalies 33–4;
egocentrism 217; misconduct 42–3
family: managing careers 203, 204; as
stakeholders 65, 92–3, 203; work/life
balance 204–6, 209–10, 214–15
favouritism 83
feasibility 144
financers 134
financing formulas 155, 163–5

flagship research 139
flexibility of workforce 2, 208
food industry example 15, 16, 17–18
forums for publishing 67–8, 73–9
frequently asked questions 224
friends, as stakeholders 65
funding 130–1, 149; application writing
140–3; case studies 149–53;
competition for 2; consequentialist
approach 137, 149–50; decision-making
criteria 143–8, *147*; doctoral training
89, 102–3, 105; equipment 5; ethical
choices example 13; forms of *136*,
136–40, *139*; innovative project example
20–2; principled approach 138, 150;
responsibilities 133–6; rights 133–6;
social impact 170; stakeholders 131–3;
topic selection 41–2; virtue approach
150
funding bodies 65, 143–6
funding panels 143–6
future potential, as recruitment criteria
126, 128

gender issues 125, 147–8
gene technology 47–8
general public *see* citizens; public
interaction
geographical locations 72–3
global fairness 42
global researchers 181
globalisation 2
goals *see* aims
golden open access 77
graduate schools 95
graduation 105–8
grant-writers 132
green open access 77
guest authorship 78
guided dialogue 7–11, 213–15; assessing
research 154, 158–9; careers 201, 205;
ethical behaviours 11–14; ethical choices
22–31; ethical questions 7, 8, 11–12,
14–22; ethical skills 7–8, 11, 14, 213;
funding 130; personal awareness *223*;
public interaction 178, 194–5;
publishing 63; recruitment 121; research
process 32, 34, 38–9; routines 221;
values 7; *see also* consequentialist ethics;
principled approaches; virtue ethics
guidelines: authorship 79; balancing
principle 148; conflict of interest 152–3;

ethical choices 226; funding applications
133–4; research process 33

happiness maximisation approach 25–6
harm/benefit *see* benefit/harm approach
HEECT rankings 165
heterogeneity, researchers 1
Hirsch index 161
honesty: consequentialist approach 142,
183; funding 133, 140, 142, 150;
misconduct 42–3, 73; principled
approach 28, 166, 175; recruitment
117, 118; virtue approach 29, 166,
175
human behaviours 11–14, 215–16, *216*;
anchoring 69, 219; choice supportive
bias 69–70; cognitive inertia 69, 216,
219, 220, 221; conformism 69, 222–3;
egocentrism 216, 217–18, 220; personal
experience 218–19, 220; repetition,
power of 69; routines 221–2;
understanding otherness 220–1
human-made environments 52–3
hygiene principle 147

i10 index 161
impact of research: social impact 3, 145,
166–71; topic selection 40; *see also*
public interaction
indigenous peoples 49–50
individual responsibility 116
individuals *see* researchers; students;
supervisors
industry-sponsored research: food
example 15, 16, 17–18; topic selection
39–40
informed consent: materials and objects
50; research subjects 48–50; sufficiency
59
infrastructure 55
initiators, assessments 156
innovative research: funding applications
144; funding example 20–2; social
impact 167, 168, 169
institutions: employee expectations 204–5;
as stakeholders 132, 203
intended consequences 164
intentional deception 43
intentionality 73
interaction with public *see* public
interaction
interdisciplinary research 3–4

international audience 75–6
interpretations 34, 190
intervention research 50–1
interviews: media 186; recruitment 121, 123–4
'invisible hand' 24
IT-specialists 35

jobs *see* careers; employment; recruitment
journal editors 65
journalists 182
journals: peer reviews 80–2; publishing 68, 76; selection of 82–3

knowledge: media 187–8; probabilistic 180–1; scientific truth 180; social impact 167–71

laboratory assistants 35
labour market *see* careers; employment; recruitment
language: expert role 179–80; recruitment 121–3, 124–5; social media 193; *see also* wording
leadership, research team 140
lecturers, recruitment 118
legal issues, recruitment 102
Leiden rankings 165
libraries 55
listening skills 8
local researchers 181

managing careers *see* careers
material, quantity needed for publishing 58, 67
materials, produced by humans 50
maximum benefit principle 104
media: differences to science *189*; public interaction 183, 184, 186–91, 196; social impact 169; as stakeholders 156, 182
mentors, as stakeholders 65
merit: assessing research 160–2, 172–4; funding 144; publishing 64, 75, 78; recruitment of academic staff 114, 117, 121; recruitment of PhD students 19, 99–100, 102, 104; reviews 2–3
meta-analyses 76
methodologies: assessing research 160–2; research process 44–56; value of research 59–60
ministry, as stakeholders 182

misconduct: credibility of research 61; funding 135; plagiarism 10, 70–2; research process 42–3; trust 60–1
misinterpretation 190
mobility of workforce 2, 208
money: for public interaction 187; salaries 119
monographs 106
moral, distinction from ethical 8–9, 225; *see also headings under ethical*
mosquitos example 197
multidisciplinary research 3–4, 141

natural environment 53–4
needs of students 104
net benefits 25–6
networking 83, 144
night/daytime test 30

objectives *see* aims
objects, produced by humans 50, 182
open access 5
open access publishing 76–8, 80, 82
open data 5
open science 5
openness 78
opponents 92
optimism 142–3, 190
options (decisions): assessing research 158–60; careers 205–7; guided dialogue 17–18, 19, 21; public interaction 186–7; publishing 67–8; research process 38–9; teaching students 96–8; *see also* risks in ethical reasoning
otherness, understanding 220–1
outliers in results 33–4
over-optimism 142–3, 190

pallid dimension 69
panels *see* funding panels; review panels (recruitment)
parents 192
peer reviews: assessing research 159, 160, 162, 164–5, 170–1; changing practices 2–3; funding applications 146; publishing 80–2
perseverance 12–13
personal awareness *223*
personal experience: decision-making 218–19, 220; journals 83; peer reviews 81–2

PhD students *see* doctoral training; recruitment of PhD students; students; teaching students

plagiarism 10, 70–2

policy-makers 156

politicians 145

post-doctoral researchers 118–19

post-purchase reinforcement 69

post-review 3

potential, as recruitment criteria 126, 128

potential significant impact 68–9

power of repetition 69

power relations, supervisor-student 89, 105

presentations, social media 193

previous position holders 115–16

previous research: funding 150; referring to 70–1; sufficiency 58

principled approaches 22–3, *27*, 27–9; animal use 46; assessing research 159, 164, 175; funding 138, 150; gene technology 47; human-made environments 52; public interaction 187, 191; recruitment 100, 102, 118, 120, 121; stakeholders 36–7; teaching students 91, 97

prioritisation 15, 225

private foundations 148

private sector 167

probabilistic knowledge 180–1

professional secrecy 134

professors: recruitment 114, 118; role of 119–20

promotion *see* careers; recruitment

psychology *see* human behaviours

public, as stakeholders 65–6, 181–2, 192

public interaction 178–81, 194–5; case studies 195–9; citizens 191–3; consequentialist approach 183, 187, 190, 194; media 183, 184, 186–91, 196; options 186–7; principled approach 187, 191; public sector 193–4; researchers 179–80, 182–6; responsibilities 182–6; rights 182–6; virtue approach 187, 191

public organisations 182

public sector 168, 169, 184, 193–4

publication potential, topic selection 40

publicly available data 34

publishing 63–5, 82; assessing research 157–8; authorship 78–80; case studies 82–7; forms of 67–8, 73–9, 82–3;

frequency of 3, 160–1; options 67–8; peer reviews 80–2; responsibilities 66–7; rights 66–7; stakeholders 65–6; writing 68–73

purchasing decisions 54–5

QS (Academic Ranking of World Universities) 165–6

qualifications: quality of PhDs 90; recruitment 100, 124–6

qualitative studies, representative samples 51–2

quality of research: assessing research 161, 165; competitive funding 138; conferences 86; doctoral training 90; vs quantity 3

quantity of research: assessing research 160–1; conferences 86; amount needed for publishing 58, 67; vs quality 3

questionnaire studies 51–2

questions *see* ethical questions

quotes, accuracy 71–2

rankings (universities) 155, 165–6

rationality 24, 215

reactive roles 182–3

readership 182

reasoning *see* ethical choices; risks in ethical reasoning

reciprocity principle 205

recognition, ethical choices 11, 12, 13–22, 213

recruiters 115

recruitment committees 123–6

recruitment of academic staff 113–14; case studies 126–9; consequentialist approach 117, 122–3; language issues 121–3, 124–5; phases of 123–6; principled approach 118, 120, 121; responsibilities 116–18; rights 116–18; selection criteria 120–3; stakeholders 115–16; types of position 118–20; virtue approach 118

recruitment of PhD students: consequentialist approach 100, 101; examples 11–12, 18–20, 29–30, 108–9; organisation of 99; principled approach 100, 102; selection of 98–103; virtue approach 99, 102

references *see* citations; external referees

reliability of research 59

repetition, power of 69

representativeness: indigenous peoples
example 49–50; qualitative studies 51–2;
sufficiency 58–9
reputation 41, 82
research assessments 155; *see also* assessing
research
research collectives 156, 184
research community: assessing research
156, 170–1; funding 132, 135; public
committees 185; as stakeholders 35, 65,
66–7, 92, 132, 135, 181–2; target
audience 75; topic selection 101; trust
66–7; *see also* peer reviews
research context 68–9
research councils 145
research fields 181–2
research process 32–5, 56–7; case studies
57–61; methodology 44–56;
misconduct 42–3; options definition
38–9; quantity needed for publishing
67; responsibilities 37–8; rights 37–8;
stakeholders 35–7; topic selection
39–42
research subjects: anonymity 49;
indigenous peoples 49–50; informed
consent 48–9; as stakeholders 36
research team 35; *see also* colleagues
research topics *see* topic selection
research-based evidence 193
researchers: assessing research 157–8;
career progression 201–2; changes in
lives 5; data sources 34; expert role
179–80, 182, 185–6; funding
application writing 137–8, 140–3;
numbers of 1; public interaction
179–80, 182–6, 188–9, *188–9*, 195;
responsibilities and rights 37–8; social
impact 145, 166–71, *167–8*; as
stakeholders 35, 131–2, 181, 203; types
of position 118–19; *see also* recruitment;
senior academics
responsibilities 214; careers 202, 203–5;
ethical questions 16–17, 19, 21; funding
133–6, 149–50; public interaction
182–6; publishing 66–7; recruitment of
academic staff 116–18; research process
37–8; teaching students 93–5, 111
responsive roles 182–3
retirement 119
review articles 76
review panels (recruitment) 123–6
reviewers 65, 66

reviews: changing practices 2–3; ethical
choices 13; theses 106–7
rights 214; assessing research 157–8;
careers 203–5; ethical questions 16–17,
19, 21; funding 133–6; public
interaction 182–6; publishing 66–7;
recruitment of academic staff 116–18;
research process 37–8; teaching students
93–5, 111
risks in ethical reasoning 216–17, *217*;
anchoring 219; conformism 222–3;
egocentrism 216, 217–18, 220; personal
experience 218–19, 220; routines
221–2; understanding otherness 220–1
routines 221–2
rule utilitarians 28
rules *see* guidelines
rules-based decision-making 27–8

salaries 119
scale of material 58, 67
schedules, peer reviews 81
science blog example 198
scientific truth 180, 196–7
SCImago rankings 165
scope: assessing research 160; journals 83;
research quantity needed for publishing
58, 67
secrecy: anonymity of subjects 49; funding
134–5
selection *see* purchasing decisions; topic
selection
senior academics: career progression 114;
 peer reviews 2–3; recruitment 114, 118;
role of professor 119–20; *see also*
teaching students
short-term contracts 208
skills, ethics as 7–8, 11, 12, 14, 213
social cohesion 216
social impact: assessing research 166–71;
funding 145; and quality of research 3;
see also public interaction
social media 192–3
social responsibility 28
society, as stakeholder 93, 203; *see also*
public interaction
solidarity principle 205
stakeholders 214; assessing research 156;
careers 203; consequentialist approach
24; funding 131–3; identification
15–16, 18–19, 21; public interaction
181–2, 192; publishing 65–6, 74–6;

recruitment of academic staff 115–16; research process 35–7; teaching students 90–3
State Research Council (SRC) 138–9, 143–8
statistics: big data 56; misconduct 43
steering committees 156
stem cell research 47
students: ethical questions 10; graduation 105–8; recruitment example 11–12, 18–20, 29–30; as stakeholders 90–1, 115, 203; topic selection 42, 101; *see also* doctoral training; recruitment of PhD students; teaching students
subjects *see* research subjects
sufficiency 58
superiors 91, 94
supervisors: choice of 110–11; disagreement example 112; PhD candidates example 18–20, 29–30; responsibilities 93–5; as stakeholders 65, 90–1, 203; *see also* teaching students
supporting personnel 35, 65
surveys, university rankings 166
sustainable methodologies 28

target audience: expert role 179–80; international 75–6; publishing 74–5; as stakeholders 182
target collectives of assessment 160
tax-payers, as stakeholders 116, 132–3
teaching students 88–9; assessment of 160; case studies 108–12; consequentialist approach 90, 92, 97; conventions 103–5, 221–2; ethical questions 10, 88; graduation 105–8; options 96–8; principled approach 91, 97; responsibilities 93–5, 111; rights 93–5, 111; routines 221; stakeholders 90–3; virtue approach 92–3, 97; *see also* recruitment of PhD students
technical assistants 65
technology 4–5
tenure track positions 118–19, 128–9
textbooks 192
THE (Times Higher Education rankings) 165–6
Theland (fictional country): doctoral training 89, 108–11; funding example 136, 138–9, 143–8; geographical location example 72–3; graduation 105; language 75, 121, 124–5; recruitment

108–11, 124–5, 127–8; retirement 119; universal facts example 71
Theland's Technology Agency (TTA) 138
theses: publishing 105–6; quality of 90; reviews 106–7; stakeholders 92–3; topic selection 101–2
3R principles 45
time management: public interaction 187, 192–3; teaching students 103–4; work/life balance 204–6, 209–10, 214–15
Times Higher Education rankings 165–6
timescales: social impact of research 169; wording 73
topic selection: allocation of tasks 211; conferences 86–7; example 57; funding applications 140–2; research process 39–42; theses 101
traditions 58–9, 60
training *see* careers; doctoral training
transdisciplinary research 3–4
transparency: assessing research 164; authorship 79; open access publishing 78; plagiarism 71; principled approach 28; recruitment 99, 100–2
trap selection process 9
trendy topics 41–2
trust: collaboration 60–1; funding system 134–5, 150; research community 66–7
truth, scientific 180, 196–7

unintended consequences 164
universal facts, plagiarism 71
universities: funding 137; organisation of 95; public interaction 178–81; social impact 166–71; as stakeholders 132, 181–2
university rankings 155, 165–6
users of research 36, 133
utilitarian approaches 23, 28; *see also* consequentialist ethics

vague expressions 83
valid dimension 69
values: guided dialogue 7, 13–14; open access publishing 78
Vancouver Guidelines 79
virtue ethics 22–3, 29–30; assessing research 175; funding 150; public interaction 187, 191; recruitment 99, 102, 118; teaching students 92–3, 97

welfare *168*
'wicked problems' 4
willingness to communicate 8
wishful thinking 69
wording: accuracy 72–3; expert role
    179–80; funding applications 142; for

publishing 72–3, 75, 83; vague
    expressions 83
work/life balance 204–6, 209–10, 214–15
writing: funding applications 137–8,
    140–3; publishing 68–73; target
    audience 179–80; textbooks 192

CPSIA information can be obtained
at www.ICGtesting.com
Printed in the USA
BVHW051658160323
660609BV00009B/217